3D Animation for the Raw Beginner Using Autodesk Maya

Second Edition

3D Animation for the Raw Beginner Using Autodesk Maya

Second Edition

Roger King

CRC Press
Taylor & Francis Group
Boca Raton London New York

CRC Press is an imprint of the
Taylor & Francis Group, an **informa** business

CRC Press
Taylor & Francis Group
6000 Broken Sound Parkway NW, Suite 300
Boca Raton, FL 33487-2742

International Standard Book Number-13: 978-0-8153-8878-4 (Paperback)
978-0-8153-8879-1 (Hardback)

Library of Congress Cataloging-in-Publication Data

Names: King, Roger (Roger Alan), author.
Title: 3D animation for the raw beginner using Autodesk Maya 2nd edition /
Roger King.
Description: Second edition. | Boca Raton, FL : CRC Press/Taylor & Francis
Group, 2019.
Identifiers: LCCN 2018044705| ISBN 9780815388784 (pbk. : acid-free paper) |
ISBN 9780815388791 (hardback : acid-free paper)
Subjects: LCSH: Computer animation--Amateurs' manuals. | Three-dimensional
display systems--Amateurs' manuals. | Maya (Computer file)--Amateurs'
manuals.
Classification: LCC TR897.72.M39 K56 2019 | DDC 777/.7--dc23
LC record available at https://lccn.loc.gov/2018044705

Visit the Taylor & Francis Web site at
http://www.taylorandfrancis.com

and the CRC Press Web site at
http://www.crcpress.com

*To my family – Wendy, Martina, Isabelle, and Julien –
and to Alan Apt, technical book publisher and avid
outdoorsman, who set me on the path of writing this book.*

Contents

Preface: Anyone can do this

THIS BOOK IS INTENDED for people with very little or no background in 3D modeling, materials, lighting, animation, and rendering. Every example in this book is doable by a raw beginner. The chapters are organized around the various aspects of a small-scale 3D workflow, with first (1) an introduction to the entire 3D workflow and the Autodesk Maya interface, then (2) an introduction to polygon and NURBS modeling, (3) a focus on core modeling tools, (4) a focus on sculpting, (5) the application of materials to wireframe models, (6) various low-level and high-level design issues, (7) animating a scene, and finally, (8) rendering, with a focus on lights and cameras.

In order to be concrete and to provide numerous structured lessons, this book focuses on one specific 3D app, Autodesk Maya, but there are examples mixed in that use a handful of other 3D applications, along with a number of renderers and a few other utility applications.

This book is not a dump of the Autodesk Maya documentation. I assume that the reader will make aggressive use of that documentation, which is available via the Maya interface by going to Help → Autodesk Maya Help. But you cannot learn to do 3D modeling, animating, and rendering by reading the (excellent) Autodesk documentation out of context. Nor can you learn to do 3D work by studying it only in an abstract fashion. The focus of this book is to introduce basic concepts via step-by-step examples that the reader should be able to easily follow. This tutorial-oriented approach starts in Chapter 2. I strongly advise that you have Maya open and that you step through these lessons as you read. Only by performing the manual tasks associated with doing 3D work will the concepts sink in and the proper way to use a 3D application stick with you.

Any book that tried to cover Maya exhaustively would either be very, very long or very, very shallow. The goal of this book is to direct you to the parts of Maya you need to master in order to create complete 3D projects. With a sound intuitive understanding of these basics, you should be able to broaden and deepen your knowledge of 3D principles and of Maya.

The website for this book contains links to video tutorials; they parallel the structure of this book and they closely follow the examples used in this book: https://buzzking.com/AnimationTextbook/AnimationTextbook.html.

The images for this book can be found in color at: https://buzzking.smugmug.com/3D-Animation-for-the-Raw-Beginner-Figures/.

To get a completely free copy of Autodesk Maya for either Windows or a Mac, the reader can go to https://www.autodesk.com/education/home and create a personal account. This version of Maya is not hobbled in any way; however, it may not be used for commercial purposes and all Maya scene files will be internally watermarked as having been created with the academic (free) version. It is incredible that Autodesk does this for people who want to learn Maya!

If you are an instructor, a student, or anyone using this book, I would love to hear from you. My email address is buzz@BuzzKing.com.

A final note: the Maya interface changes from year to year, with colors and icons changing, the menus being modestly rearranged, and new tools being introduced. Occasionally, tools are removed, but only infrequently are substantive changes made to Maya. It is a mature and fairly stable application. The lessons in this book should be readily understandable, even if you are using a version of Maya released at some point after the publication of this book.

Acknowledgments

I HAVE TAUGHT ANIMATION AT the University of Colorado for many years, and I have had the pleasure of teaching computing, engineering, film, and art students. I have learned a tremendous amount from them and I am still excited every time I enter the classroom.

A few of the models in this book were not made by me. The gold chair in Figures 1.18, 1.19 and 1.26 to 1.28 is adapted from a chair taken from a "country kitchen" scene sold by Daz3D.com, which offers a powerful human figure animation application that is popular among sophisticated hobbyists. The windows in Figures 6.60 to 6.62 are adapted from windows that are sold by suplugins.com, which markets a fabulous renderer and component content system for SketchUp. The human characters and some of the smaller items in the cabana images in Figures 6.85 to 6.87 are also from Daz3D.com. The Vue scene material in Figures 7.93 to 7.100 are from e-onsoftware.com. The flamingo in Chapter 8 is sold by the very popular online 3D model store turbosquid.com; it was created by hariBi. The gold car in Chapter 8 is from turbosquid.com. All of these models were purchased for use.

The car blueprint in Figure 3.47 was taken from drawingdatabase.com. The cactus image in Figure 6.1 is from bonanza.com, which sells plant seeds; and yes, you can buy cactus seeds from them! Figure 7-91 is based on a lesson from my daughter Isabelle King, who tutored me on a high school trigonometry visualization I never learned. The 360° image used in Figure 8.46 is from illuminatedtools.com; they have a nice library of for-sale EXR images that are very inexpensive.

My editor Sean Connelly created the concept for this second edition of 3D Animation for the Raw Beginner, and in particular, I deeply appreciate the visual improvement from the first edition. My project editor,

Robert Sims, along with Paul Beaney and his team at Nova Techset, have been a pleasure to work with. The production of this book has been a rapid and extremely well-coordinated process.

Finally, my wife Wendy spent hundreds of hours editing this book, over and over. I want to thank her for her tremendous support.

Author

Roger "Buzz" King is a Professor Emeritus at the University of Colorado at Boulder and teaches 3D Animation for the Computer Science Department and the Alliance for Technology, Learning, and Society (ATLAS), an institute dedicated to the application of technology to the arts. He has trained over a thousand animation students and has no intention of stopping.

Buzz has done research in the management of 3D modeling and animation data, and the integration of large volumes of data. He has authored over 60 scientific papers, has been an editor with several major journals, and has served as the program chair for several international conferences. His research has been supported by DARPA, NSF, the Smithsonian, ONR, the US Navy, the DOE, the US Army, Martin Marrietta, IBM, and AT&T.

Buzz has a B.A. in Mathematics from Occidental College, and an M.S. and Ph.D. in Computer Science from the University of Southern California. He also has a Masters of Divinity from the Iliff School of Theology. He currently serves as a pastor and as a hospital chaplain.

Buzz has created a webpage for this book: https://buzzking.com/AnimationTextbook/AnimationTextbook.html. On this webpage are videos that cover many of the lessons in this book, *as well as video tutorials that present bonus material not included in this book.*

CHAPTER 1

An Introduction to 3D Modeling, Animation, and Rendering with a Focus on Autodesk Maya

With a survey of the Autodesk Maya interface.

IN THIS CHAPTER, WE look at the overall workflow of using Autodesk Maya, and the various windows in the Maya interface, along with the purposes of the tools the interface presents to the user. We also consider the basics of working with the media and applications used in basic 3D projects. An overriding goal is to begin focusing on the aspects of the highly complex Maya interface that will enable a beginner to build complete 3D projects.

THREE-DIMENSIONAL WORKFLOW OVERVIEW

Autodesk Maya is arguably the most popular 3D modeling, animation, and rendering application. Its interface is extremely large and complex, but only a small subset of it is needed to create complete 3D single-frame renderings and videos. The central task of this book is to convey that critical core of

Maya, that is, to take a deep vertical slice of Maya and present it to the reader. With this slice of Maya, complete projects can be built. This slice also serves as a knowledge platform to which beginners can incrementally add as they master more and more of Maya.

The basic unit of work in this book will be a "scene" file, which includes all the information needed to create a 3D rendering or a 3D video (although Maya itself does not render video). In this book, we will look at the entire 3D workflow, including the creation of vector-based "wireframe" models that make up a 3D scene, the application of materials to the surfaces of these models, the insertion of lights into a 3D scene, the animating of the 3D models in a scene, and the rendering of a scene.

WIREFRAME MODELS AND PIXEL-BASED RENDERING

When designing applications, we typically make a sharp distinction between the internal logic of the application, that is, what data it uses and what computations it performs on that data, and the interface of the application, that is, how the user accesses the data and the computational capabilities of the program. In 3D modeling and animation, this distinction is particularly critical to keep in mind: the internal data structures used to represent 3D models inside an application like Maya are very different from the way in which we display these 3D models. The models are stored and manipulated internally as 3D vector data structures, but they must be displayed, that is, rendered, on 2D pixel-based displays. This distinction gets to the heart of what 3D modeling and animation is all about: Autodesk Maya allows the user to create scenes with wireframe models in them, prepare them for rendering by adding materials and lights, and then render them as pixel-based images. Thus, the Maya interface supports the process of creating a scene with wireframe models in it and then translating this scene into an extremely different format, namely a series of digital images that can then be turned into videos by a video editor.

WIREFRAME MODELS

Consider Figure 1.1. This image, taken from the "Viewport" of the main Maya window, is of a polygon sphere. (We'll worry about what this means soon.) The important point is that this is a 3D structure formed of lines. This is what we call 3D vector graphics. A line is, by

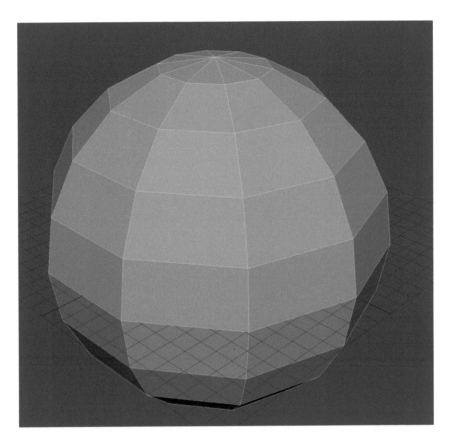

FIGURE 1.1 A polygon sphere.

mathematical definition, something that exists in 2-space, but a "mesh" (or wireframe) of lines in 3-space forms the "wireframe" of a 3D object.

Yet, consider how we view this sphere on a computer screen; our 3D wireframe must be displayed as a 2D grid of pixels. This is true in the Viewport as well as when we "render" the sphere for final display, as in Figure 1.2. Again, this is what rendering is all about: taking a 3D vector geometry model and displaying it as a pixel-based image. Maya must give the user a quick-and-dirty pixel-based rendering in the Viewport so users can see what they are doing as they develop their scene.

FIGURE 1.2 A material on the sphere.

A QUICK OVERVIEW OF THE MODELING
AND ANIMATION WORKFLOW

Here's an overview of a typical 3D workflow within an application like Maya. First comes the modeling phase where the wireframe is created. In our case, the model consists of a wireframe sphere, as in Figure 1.3.

Second, a "material" is placed on the outer surface of the wireframe. This is a good place to make a critical distinction. This book is about "surface" modeling, that is, the creation, animation, and rendering of 3D models that consist only of wireframes with what can be thought of as infinitely thin outer surfaces. In other words, there is nothing there except the surface; the model has no interior. This is not the kind of modeling we would use if we were designing, say, a nuclear bomb or a computer

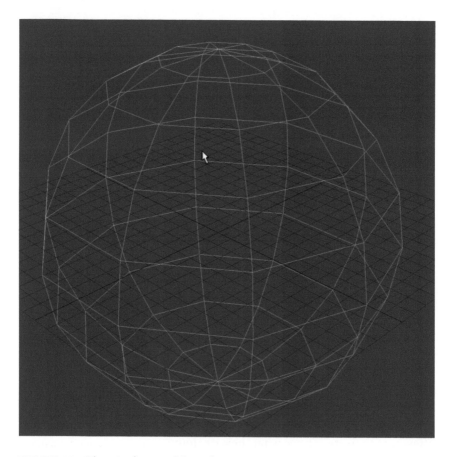

FIGURE 1.3 The wireframe of the sphere.

motherboard. We could design the outward appearance of our nuclear bomb or make a marketing model for our motherboard with Maya, but to actually design either of these, we need to know what is on the *inside* of our model. Surface modelers like Maya are generally used to create models used for entertainment or visualization (such as in architecture) purposes, not for engineering or product development. Let's get back to our second stage; this is where we place an infinitely thin material on the outside of our wireframe. The material is a mathematical definition of the way light bounces off and/or refracts through the surface of the model. If we were to render what we see in Figure 1.3, the render would be blank because there is no material on the surface of the model. If we look at Figure 1.2, the wire mesh sphere has had a material placed on it. The material tells the renderer that light will both pass through it and bounce off of it; the material is thus glasslike. It has no color, so the render consists of shades of gray. There is something hidden here in our second phase: lights. The material on the sphere will not render if there isn't light bouncing off the surface of the object. It is the combination of a material and lights that allows the surface of the object to be seen in the render.

The third phase consists of animating the sphere. We might have it bounce up and down. Or we might change the outer surface of the sphere over time, perhaps by having the surface of the sphere compress inward and then flex back outward. Or, we could do both: the ball could flatten on the bottom when it hits the ground and then go back into a spherical shape when it goes back upward.

Our fourth phase consists of rendering the ball as it bounces up and down. This consists of turning the animation of the ball into a series of pixel-based images that we can display as a video clip. This gets us to our second topic of this chapter: images and video.

This is a good time to introduce some critical pieces of terminology. An "object" is something that is stored inside the underlying Maya database. An object could be something that is directly rendered, like a sphere. It could also be something that affects the appearance of a rendered object; a material is an object. Objects have "attributes," which are often other objects; a material can serve as an attribute of a sphere object. A "tool" is something that is used to craft Maya models; tools have "settings." Three important tools are Translate, Rotate, and Scale, and basic settings of these three tools are the orientations of the three axes around which we translate, rotate, or scale objects like a sphere. (The word "translate" is

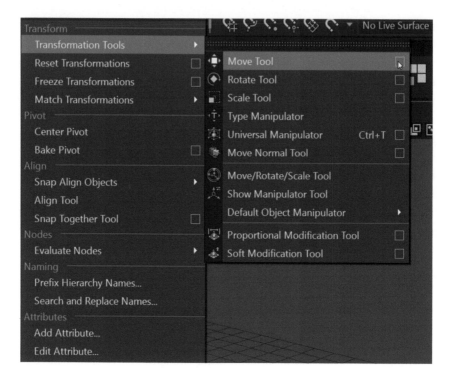

FIGURE 1.4   Accessing the settings of the Move tool.

more commonly used in mathematics and in other 3D applications, but Maya calls this tool "Move.") The sphere itself is not considered a setting of the tool. The settings of a tool can be accessed by clicking on the square box that appears to the right of a tool menu selection; in Figure 1.4, we are accessing the settings of the Move tool.

A QUICK OVERVIEW OF IMAGES, AUDIO, AND VIDEO

Video is a series of pixel-based images. The idea is to change the image quickly enough so that there is the illusion of continuous movement. Here are some basic terms. An image is created in some "format," like JPG or TIFF. (Note that Maya uses the very high-quality EXR standard as its default format; but since these are extremely large images and generating a full minute's worth of EXR images for a brief video short can easily overwhelm the storage of a student's machine, we will use JPG as our default format in this book.) An image is also specified in some "resolution," which has to do with the number of pixels in it, such as 1024 by 1024. There is another use of the word resolution, and it refers to the number of pixels per inch. A common number—the default in Maya—is 72. This is actually fairly low, and later, when we use images to create "textures" for materials (to do things such as give them color or patterns), we will discover that some texture images have a much larger number of pixels per inch.

Sound is also encoded in "formats," such as MP3, WAV, and AIFF. A series of images, along with sound, are bound together into a video "container" or "container format." Video is created using some number of images per second; this is known as the "frame rate." Somewhere in the ballpark of 18 frames per second, we are fooled into thinking we are looking at continuous motion. In Maya, we usually generate at least 24 frames for every second of animation.

Maya exports images, not video. A video editor must be used to turn the images, along with a sound file, into video. If we generated 24 frames for every second of animation in Maya, we would generate video that uses 24 frames per second. The sound file is not output by Maya, but a sound file that is created with some other program, typically an audio editor, can be input into Maya so that it can be used to time the animation in Maya. For example, we might have a sound file of a ball bouncing; we would input this file into Maya so that we can time the movement of the ball upward and downward to coincide with the timing of the thump, thump of the ball bouncing. It is important to remember that this sound file must later be input separately into a video editor in order to blend it together with the series of Maya-rendered images to create a piece of video. Also, when sound is pulled into Maya, it must be in either the WAV or AIFF format, but most video editors can handle other formats, as well, such as the compact MP3 format.

In sum, Maya renders images. It is not a video editor. It is also not an audio editor. Typical programs that are used in the same workflow with Maya are the video editors Adobe Premiere Pro (adobe.com), Apple Final Cut Pro (apple.com), and Vegas Pro (magix.com), and the sound editors Adobe Audition (adobe.com) and Steinberg WaveLab (Steinberg.net). Maya artists use programs like Adobe Photoshop (adobe.com) to process texture image files. A Maya material might be associated with one or more texture image files to make a material look like brick or wall plaster or some other human-made or natural pattern. Texture images are often made from photographs, but they can also be created from scratch with Photoshop or a drawing/painting application like Corel Painter (corel.

com). Not all textures are defined by using a texture image; there are also textures that are procedural; that is, their appearance on the surface of an object is computed by software and not derived from texture images. We will make use of a procedural texture when we look at a special Arnold renderer material called "Mix" in Chapter 5. (Arnold is the renderer that ships with Maya.)

AN OVERVIEW OF THE MAYA INTERFACE: THE MAIN WINDOW

Let's look at some important 3D modeling, animation, and rendering concepts in the context of Autodesk Maya's interface. Figure 1.5 shows the main Maya window, where the user spends much of their time. Importantly, when the user performs a "Save" operation using the File dropdown at the very upper left of the window, the file is usually saved as either an .mb or .ma file. "mb" means Maya binary and is a binary (1s and 0s) representation

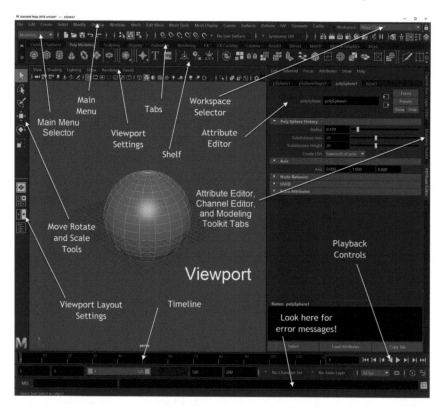

FIGURE 1.5   The main Maya window.

of the scene under development. Our model, the pink sphere, sits at (0,0,0) in the 3D scene. "ma" refers to Maya ASCII and consists mostly of Maya MEL code, where MEL stands for Maya Embedded Language, the Maya scripting language. (As it turns out, you can create entire scenes by writing them in code instead of using the Maya interactive interface.)

About two-thirds of Figure 1.5 consists of a lighter gray area with the pink sphere at the center. This is the modeling area, where Maya provides a nonstop real-time render of the model under development. At the top of this area is a series of dropdown menus beginning with one labeled "View." These menus, along with the row of icons below them, are where the user can adjust settings that affect the appearance and other localized properties of the design area (as opposed to the actual underlying properties of the scene under development). To the left of the gray work area are four buttons that form the Viewport Layout Settings. In this case, the top button has been selected (it is selected by default); it causes the viewport to consist of a single "perspective," where the scene is viewed at an angle and not directly along any of the three dimensional axes. Above the Viewport Layout Settings are buttons for a handful of very commonly used tools; the bottom three of which are Move, Rotate, and Scale.

There are two high-level menus that affect the overall layout of the Maya interface. The far upper-right menu, called the Workspace Selector, has been set to "Maya Classic"; this controls the layout of the window as a whole, and the Classic setting makes the interface look the way it appeared in releases of Maya previous to 2017. This Classic setting is very popular, but later in this book, we will work with other settings. At the almost far upper left of the window is something called the Main Menu Selector (MMS). This adjusts the makeup of the Main Menu; the MMS affects the makeup of menu items to the right of the "Windows" dropdown. The Mesh, Edit Mesh, and Mesh Tools menus are used heavily in polygon modeling (and thus we will use them heavily in this book). A bit below the Main Menu is a series of tabs; these are used to populate the "Shelf," which provides iconic button shortcuts to tools that appear in the individual dropdown menus that make up the Main Menu. In Figure 1.5, tools that are frequently used in polygon modeling populate the Shelf; these include tools that are used to create standard polygon "primitives" like Sphere, Cube, Cylinder, Cone, and Torus, which appear in the left side of the Shelf; clicking on one of these icons (which are actually buttons) will place the appropriate primitive in the Viewport and center it at (0,0,0).

To the right of the gray work area is the Attribute Editor. This allows us to adjust the attributes of whatever object is currently selected. In Figure 1.5, the Sphere is selected; we see that its radius is 8.479. Objects typically have many attributes, so they are arranged in tabs; the third tab from the left is currently selected. To the right of the Attribute Editor are three tabs that let us display either the Attribute Editor, the Channel Editor, or the Modeling Toolkit. The Channel Editor displays attributes of an object that can be used to animate it; these include Move, Rotate, and Scale. The Toolkit is another way (besides the Main Menu and the Shelf tabs) to access commonly used tools.

At the bottom of the main window is the Timeline, which provides access to the frame settings that are used to animate the objects in a scene. Currently, this is set to 120 frames. At the bottom right are the Playback Controls, which allow the user to run through the frames to view the animation. (We see here that, as in video editing, frames are in essence used as units of time.)

A final, very important area of the main window is at the very bottom right. This is where, among other things, error messages are displayed. It's a very good idea to make sure that this area is not blocked by some other window or application on your computer display. Keep an eye out for anything appearing in red.

THE HYPERSHADE

The prefix "hyper" in English is usually interpreted as referring to too much of something or an excessive number of something. Before we get to the relevance of this prefix in the name of the Hypershade window, let's consider a couple of terms. The first is "material," and we have already discussed this. Another word is "shader." This term is used heavily in 3D modeling and is a very general term. It refers to many aspects of a scene that have to do with how objects in the scene render. In the Hypershade, the user can create shader networks, which include such things as materials, textures, and lights. As for the prefix "hyper," I assume that it means that this is where *all* the shader networks are created and maintained (as opposed to too many of them).

In Figure 1.6, there are roughly four areas. In the upper left are a series of tabs that allow the Maya user to manage various items in the Hypershade. These include Materials, Textures, Lights, and Cameras. This is a good point to pause for a moment and make note of the overriding paradigm of the Maya interface, something that is common to many 3D modeling and animation applications. Maya uses a live action metaphor. In particular, we always view a scene (in the Viewport) from the perspective of a camera. And we always render a scene from the perspective of a camera. This notion is so core that a default camera is created when a new Maya scene is created; in other words, we can't see anything in the scene except through a camera, so Maya creates a default one for us to get us started. In Figure 1.5, we are viewing the pink sphere from the perspective of this default camera. Without this camera, we would not be able to see anything in the Viewport or render anything.

It is crucial to keep in mind that when we move about the scene, we are moving the camera we are looking through, rather than moving the scene so that we can see all aspects of it. Maya uses three terms that are borrowed from the use of physical movie cameras. To move the camera forward and backward, we "dolly" the camera by using the scroll button on our mouse. To "pan" the camera, that is, move it left–right and right–left, we hold down the Command/Alt key or the Option/Windows key, along with the middle mouse button, and move the mouse from side to side. To "tumble" the camera, that is, to move around the objects in the scene, we hold down the Command/Alt key or the Option/Windows key, along with the left mouse button, and move the mouse. Many people find Maya much easier to use if you have a mouse with a middle button/scroll wheel. The middle mouse button can also be used to move objects between windows in Maya.

Continuing with the live action metaphor, we must remember that we cannot see anything in the Viewport or render anything without lights. Unless there is light bouncing off the materials on our objects, nothing is visible. And yes, there is a default light and we are using it in Figure 1.5. (But Arnold will not render light created by the default light; a new light must be created before rendering with Arnold.) We see now why shader networks must contain things like materials, lights, and cameras: they are critical to rendering, whether we are talking about a final render or the quick-and-dirty render that Maya provides for us in the Viewport.

We see in the upper-left area of the Hypershade (in Figure 1.6) a material called "aiStandardSurface1." This is a material that comes with Arnold, the default renderer in Maya. Arnold is sold by Solid Angle (solidangle. com). Previous to Maya 2017, Maya shipped with a renderer called mental ray (the name is spelled with a small m and small r). Mental ray is owned

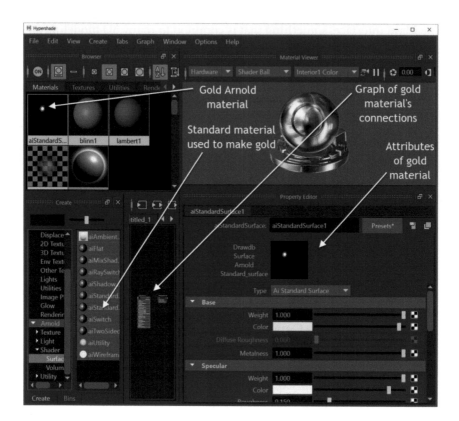

FIGURE 1.6   The Hypershade window.

by NVIDIA (nvidia.com, the graphics card company) and, until recently, could still be bought from NVIDIA and used as a plug-in to Maya—but much to the chagrin of many professional users of mental ray, it has been taken off the market, presumably so that NVIDIA can promote their other renderer called Iray, which we will look at later in this book. Autodesk bought Solid Angle and began shipping Arnold with Maya in 2017; at the same time, it stopped shipping mental ray with Maya. The Arnold material that we see in the upper left of the Hypershade comes with a number of attribute "presets"; I have chosen the one that gives it a gold look. Note that it is the material of an object that makes it look like it is made of gold; it is not the wireframe or "geometry" of an object that does this. In the lower-left area of the Hypershade we see some menus that can be used to create such things as materials, textures, and lights. In the lower-right area of the Hypershade are the attributes of the gold Arnold material. (These same

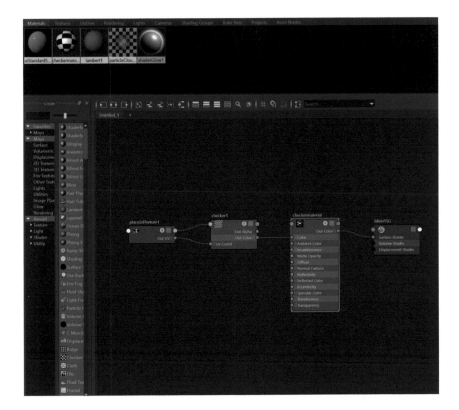

FIGURE 1.7   A shader network.

attributes can be seen in the attribute editor of the main Maya window.) Finally, in the center bottom of the Hypershade is a two-node network that represents the gold shader. Since this is a bit hard to see in Figure 1.6, Figure 1.7 is a close-up of another network, one that shows a material called checkermaterial that is using a texture called checker1 to give it a black-and-white checkered look. This shader includes a placement node that is used to adjust the way the checker texture is laid down on an object. Using this node, we can, for example, make the individual checker boxes bigger or smaller.

PUTTING OBJECTS IN HIERARCHIES

At this point, we introduce an extremely important concept in Maya. By going to the Window dropdown in the main Maya window, we can access a window called the Outliner; see Figure 1.8. (The Window menu item

FIGURE 1.8   Outliner window.

in the Main Menu can be used to pull up all of the windows we cover in this chapter.) This window is used to place objects in hierarchies. It underscores one concept that is easy to grasp and a concept that is somewhat subtler. First, the more obvious one. In this window, we see that there is a hierarchy with three objects in it. One is a car body; another is the right door; the third is the right door window. The door is a child of the car and the window is a child of the door. Why? There are multiple reasons for this, but perhaps the most important one has to do with animating objects. An object inherits the movement of its parent but can have its own independent motion. Thus, if the car moves forward, the door and the window will move along with the car. But, the door can be opened while the car is moving. And regardless of the movement of the door and the car, the window can be moved up and down. Putting objects in proper hierarchies is critical when it comes to animating these objects, and in particular, this facilitates the relative motion of one object with respect to another.

The subtle concept has to do with the notion of a "model." Although the word "modeling" appears in several places in the Maya interface, there is no notion of a model itself in Maya. We create objects and we put objects in hierarchies. Usually, the roots of these hierarchies indicate just what we consider to be the models in our scenes. In other words, an object is a concrete thing in Maya, but a model is in the eye of the user, and the user's intentions can usually be inferred by looking at the various object hierarchies in the Outliner window.

THE RENDER WINDOW AND RENDER SETTINGS

Figure 1.9 shows us a render of a sphere that has been assigned the material discussed above. We see that a checkerboard texture has been used to give the material the checkerboard appearance. It's worth noting that the reflectivity and other critical aspects of the material are defined by other attributes of the material; this particular material is very reflective, which

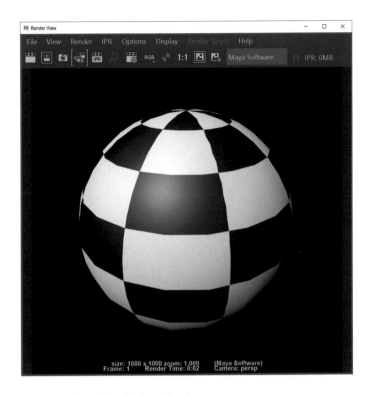

FIGURE 1.9   Render of checkerboard sphere.

is indicated by the bright spot near the center of the sphere, where light is sharply reflected. See Figure 1.10. The Render window is used to control the process of rendering the final series of images that are output after the models have been constructed and animated in the scene. It can be opened by going to Options → Render Settings in the Render View (as seen in Figure 1.9). Some particularly critical settings are indicated in the figure.

At the top of Figure 1.10 is a selector that can be used to choose the renderer; in this case, Arnold has been chosen. There are tabs below this selector; they organize the many settings involved in the render process. The Common tab (shown) is common to all renderers. The other tabs pertain to the specific renderer chosen. Printed below these tabs is some information supplied by the renderer. In particular, it tells us how the rendered frames will be named and where they will be stored after they are generated.

This is a good time to point out that Maya uses a very specific folder hierarchy. In the documents directory of the user (this is true for Windows and Macs), the Maya installer creates a folder called maya. Within this is a

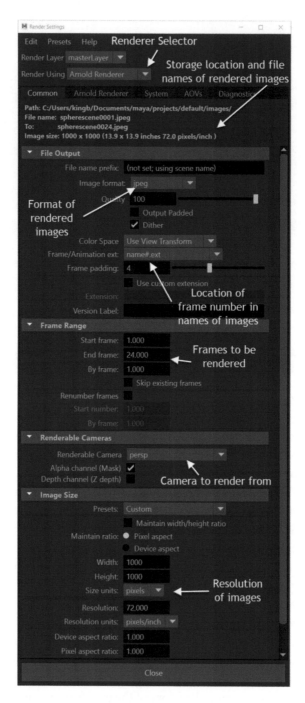

FIGURE 1.10 Render Settings window.

projects folder. Within this, the user creates a folder for the given project; each project consists of a number of scenes (each scene stored as an .mb or .ma file). Instead of creating a specific project folder, I used the default project folder created by Maya. Thus, my project is called "default." The folder called "images" is where the renderer places its rendered images. A new project folder can be created by going to File on the main window and choosing Set Project. This same menu selection can be used to return to an existing project to continue working on it. Importantly, when moving a project between two computers, it is critical that the entire project folder be moved, as scene files (which are in the scenes folder within the project folder) reference files that appear in other folders within the project folder; a common consequence of not moving the entire project folder is to lose the textures assigned to various materials.

Below the tabs is a menu that can be used to choose the format of the rendered images. In the figure, JPEG has been chosen. Further down is a setting that must be set if (and only if) more than one frame is going to be rendered. Specifically, the pound sign (or hash mark) is inserted somewhere in the name of the rendered image. It represents an integer that starts with 1 and is incremented by one for each subsequent frame. Below this, we see that the render will start with frame 1 and stop at frame 24, and the final 1.000 entry means that every single frame will be rendered. If this last setting were, for example, set to 10, only every 10th frame would be rendered. As a note, 24 is a common frame rate chosen in Maya, so these settings likely indicate that one second's worth of animation will be rendered. Further down is the name of the camera to be used for rendering. The default camera is chosen; its name is persp, which means "perspective" because it points at an angle across the scene and not directly down any of the three axes. We see some resolution settings. The frames will be 1000 by 1000 pixels, with 72 pixels per inch.

Figure 1.11 shows the Render View again. In this case, we note the location of the Options dropdown that can be used to pull up the Render Settings window. It also shows us the Renderer Selector; thus, the renderer can be selected in both the Render View and Render Settings. Finally, the button at the far left is used to render a single frame. It's important to note that this window and this button are used *only* to perform single-frame renders—which are usually test renders and not final renders. If the user has chosen to render multiple frames (by using the Render Settings to set the frame number property of each rendered

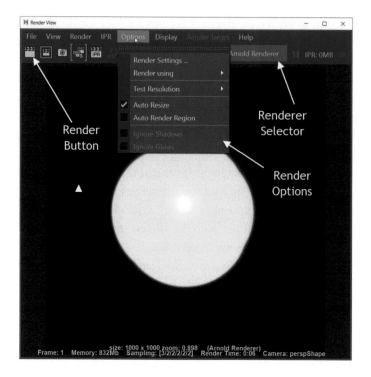

FIGURE 1.11   Render View window.

frame), the render must be performed in the main window by setting the Main Menu Selector to Rendering, then choosing Render → Batch Render. *But* if you are using the free version of Arnold that ships with Maya and you do *not* have a separate standalone Arnold license, you cannot do a true batch background render as just described. Instead, you must do a foreground render by choosing Render → Render Sequence. For the student or someone working on a small-scale project, the difference is insignificant. When you do a batch render, the frames are silently written to the Images folder inside the Maya Project folder. But if you do a foreground render, the images all appear one by one in the Render View window, the same place where a single-frame render appears. The disadvantage is that if you have a powerful computer that would allow you to work on another Maya scene while you are rendering, only a batch render allows this, not a foreground render. The point is that if you want to be able to continue working while you are rendering, you need to pay for a separate Arnold license.

SCRIPTS

Here is something very intriguing. The user has an alternative for most of the things done with the user interface; almost all tasks can be carried out in code. Maya has associated with it a native scripting language called MEL. It is a non-object-oriented language and dates back to a time when many 3D applications came with their own home-grown scripting languages. In recent years, many applications have been switched to Python, and newer applications are being built with Python as their native scripting language. By going to Windows → General Editors → Script Editor, the user can pull up the window seen in Figure 1.12. This is where the user can enter MEL commands. In the figure, I have written a single-line script that creates a polygon sphere with a radius of 5, and it is named MySphere. Every MEL line ends with a semicolon. Finally, it is important to note that over the last several years, the Maya developers have been creating a Python alternative to the MEL syntax; at the time of this writing, it is in its second (very) major refinement and is incomplete. We will not learn the MEL language in this book, although in Chapter 7 we will take a quick look at writing a simple script to rotate the wheel of a car.

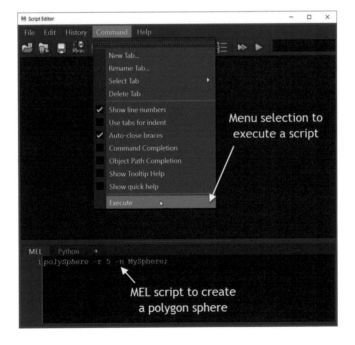

FIGURE 1.12   Script Editor window.

THE GRAPH EDITOR

By going to Windows → Animation Editors → Graph Editor, the user can pull up the window seen in Figure 1.13. We won't talk much about this now, but this window is frequently used to fine-tune animation that is designed in the main window. Importantly, we note that three primary channel attributes are Translate, Rotate, and Scale, and since this is a 3D application, there are actually nine separate attributes. (We note that there are tools that translate, rotate, and scale, and objects can have attributes whose values tell us how they have been translated, rotated, or scaled.) The graphs to the right of the figure track the translation, rotation, and scaling of a given object (the one that is selected in the main window) along the three dimensions over a series of frames. This particular figure shows us what MySphere is doing over the course of 78 frames.

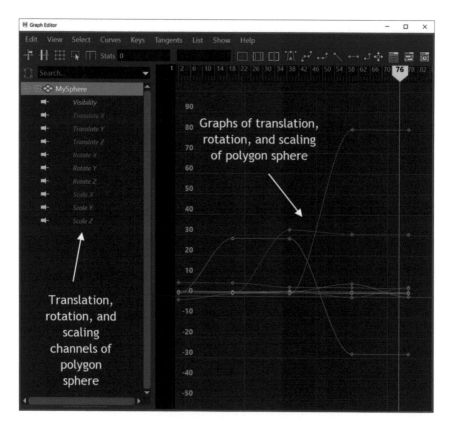

FIGURE 1.13   Graph Editor window.

THE UV EDITOR AND THE 2-SPACE OF MATERIAL PLACEMENT

Objects in Maya exist in 3-space. Each object inherits the position of its immediate parent in the Outliner window. But there is another set of dimensions in Maya, and it consists of 2 axes. So that these dimensions are not confused with the dimensions of 3-space, they are called u and v. They define the left–right and up–down axes, respectively, of the surface of a given object, and these two dimensions control how a material is placed on the surface of an object. If the user goes to Windows → Modeling Editors → UV Editor in the main window, the UV Editor window can be opened. We see it in Figure 1.14. We will discuss this later, but for now, we note one important thing. The content of this window corresponds to the rendered sphere of Figure 1.9. By using the tools provided in the menus of the UV Editor, we can adjust just how the checkerboard appears in the rendering

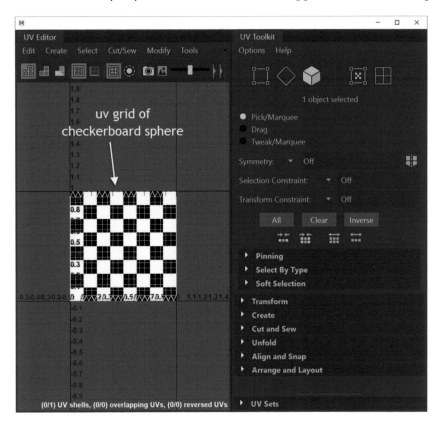

FIGURE 1.14   UV Editor window.

by adjusting the way the material of the object is laid down on the object. The checkerboard square in Figure 1.14 corresponds to the (u,v) space that wraps around the sphere.

A NOTE ON THE MAYA INTERFACE

By going to Windows → Settings/Preferences → Plug-in Manager (as in Figure 1.15), we can pull up the Plug-in Manager window (shown in Figure 1.16). We point this out for one critical reason. The Maya interface, along with its large and complex set of tools, is engineered as a set of plug-ins. By default, not all of the plug-ins that make up the Maya application are loaded when Maya is opened. A "plug-in" in Maya is not at all necessarily a third-party piece of software; most of them are native pieces of the Maya application. But third-party plug-ins also appear in this window; these consist of two sorts of plug-ins, ones that the Autodesk people have used in building Maya and ones that the user must pay for and install separately—often, these are renderers. (At the top of Figure 1.16 is a third-party renderer called Redshift that I use and have installed separately, and which we will look at in Chapter 8.) The reason we are taking note of all of this is that this plug-in architecture is important to keep in mind. If Maya misbehaves or some functionality doesn't seem to be present in the Maya interface, there might be a plug-in that needs to be loaded.

FIGURE 1.15   Accessing the Plug-in Manager.

FIGURE 1.16 The Plug-in Manager.

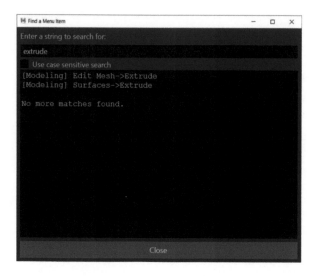

FIGURE 1.17   The Help Menu.

A NOTE ON NAVIGATING THE MAYA INTERFACE

Here is an extremely useful piece of advice. By going to Help → Find Menu, one can type in a term. Maya will then give you the path to any locations in the main window's set of menus where that term appears. In Figure 1.17, I have typed in "extrude," a very important modeling tool. Note that it appears twice in the interface, once for polygon extruding and once for nonuniform rational basis spline (NURBS) extruding (the "surface" entry). This Help Menu option is a fantastic way of overcoming the dizzying massiveness of the Maya interface. It takes a long time to remember where everything is, and this feature can help the beginner become oriented quickly within the interface.

It's also useful to note that if you go to Help → Maya Autodesk Help, your browser will be opened. The Maya documentation will appear. It is excellent, tightly written, largely comprehensive, and full of clean examples.

A FOCUS ON POLYGON VERSUS CURVED LINE MODELING

Before moving on to Chapter 2, where we will focus on basic modeling, let's take a quick look at the two—very different—kinds of modeling supported in Maya. The first kind of modeling, polygon modeling, is by far the most common form of 3D modeling used in 3D applications.

FIGURE 1.18   A seemingly organic chair.

In polygon modeling, all surfaces are made up of a mesh of polygons, that is, two dimensional, straight-line shapes. Generally, these polygons are either triangles or four-sided quadrilaterals, or "quads" for short. Consider Figure 1.18. It is a rendering of a chair. This is a surface model, the outside of which consists of a mesh of polygons. The renderer has taken the wireframe, along with the information that the surface should be a reflective gold, and created the image. The pad on the chair looks fairly organic, by which we mean that it has smoothly curved surfaces—apparently. But if we look at Figure 1.19, we see that the chair, including the pad, consists entirely of 2D surfaces. The only reason it appears organic is because the pad, and in particular the edges of the pad,

FIGURE 1.19 The polygon chair.

consist of many polygons. This is how a polygon model is smoothed, by increasing the number of polygons until the desired level of smoothing has been achieved.

Now, consider Figure 1.20. This is a rendering of a model that again seems very organic. But in Figure 1.21, we see that it has not been made organic by having a large number of polygons on the surface of the model. In this case, the model was made with curved lines. This model was

FIGURE 1.20　**A seemingly organic chalice.**

made with the second kind of modeling that Maya supports—NURBS modeling. We will delve deeper into this in Chapter 2, but for now, we note that curved-line models are created in a very different manner than polygon models; there are specialized polygon modeling tools, and there are specialized NURBS modeling tools, and these two sets of tools only overlap in part.

FIGURE 1.21   **A truly organic chalice.**

TRANSLATE, ROTATE, AND SCALE

Looking at modeling from the perspective of a polygon model, we say that a wireframe or mesh consists of a number of *vertices* in 3-space, with some of these vertices connected by *edges*. These edges break the surface of the model into some number of polygons or *faces*. (In NURBS modeling, as we will see later, different terms are used to refer to "edges" in particular.)

One of the backbones of 3D surface modeling, whether we are using polygon or NURBS modeling, are the three key tools: Translate (again, Maya calls this Move), Rotate, and Scale (see Figures 1.22 through 1.24).

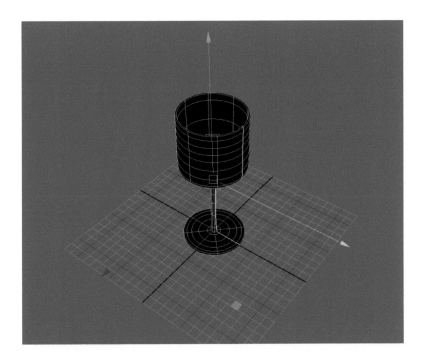

FIGURE 1.22 **Translate.**

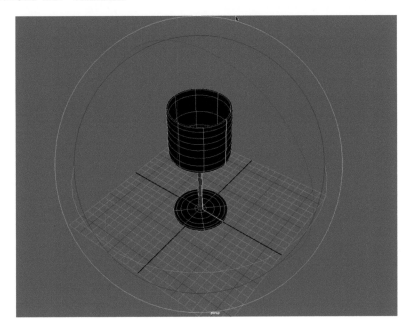

FIGURE 1.23 **Rotate.**

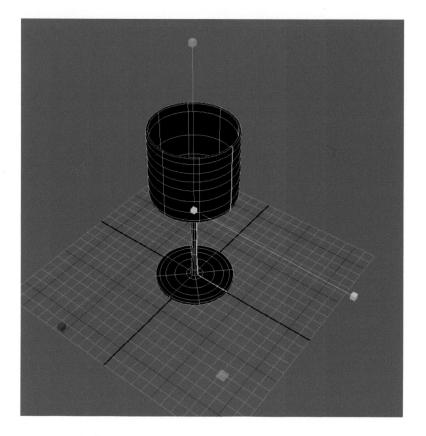

FIGURE 1.24 **Scale.**

These tools, which are available on the left-hand side of the Maya interface, are core, underlying primitives used in all 3D modeling and animation applications. Many of the modeling and animation tools that we will discuss in this book in a sense compile down (to use a programming term) to translation, rotation, and scaling. Another way of looking at it is that often, in the Maya interface, it is not obvious that a tool we are using is essentially implemented by using some combination of translate, rotate, and scale operations. We can translate (in 3-space) vertices, edges, and faces as we shape a model. We can also rotate edges and faces to craft a model. And, we can scale edges and faces—and objects themselves—as we craft a model (which is made up of one or more objects). Similarly, we can animate an object by translating, rotating, and scaling a model differently as a series of frames go by. Thus, translate, rotate, and scale are key to animating models, as well. We will see this in Chapter 7. This might seem repetitive, but it is a very critical fact: the Maya tools Move (translate), Rotate, and Scale are fundamental tools that underlie much of what goes on inside Maya, and this is true for all 3D applications. We use these tools heavily as we model and as we animate—but often they are being applied for us by the application as we use some higher-level tool.

LOW-POLY MODELS

Sometimes, though, we don't have the option of adding enough polygons to make a surface smoothly organic. This happens in particular in video games, when rendering must be done in real time so that the game can respond to user input. As it turns out, the more polygons, the longer the render takes. This is because the renderer must process the effects of light bouncing off and/or refracting through every single polygon in a scene. Consider Figure 1.25. We see that there is a tool that will reduce

FIGURE 1.25   The Reduce Poly tool.

FIGURE 1.26 Fifty percent poly reduction.

the number of faces on a polygon model. We might do this in order to take a detailed model and create a low-polygon version of the model that will render quickly in a video game. This alternative version will usually appear less organic than the original. We see in Figures 1.26 through 1.28 what happens when we sharply reduce the number of polygons on the surface of our gold chair. It becomes angular—but it will render faster.

In this book, we will focus on creating models for single-frame renders or for batch rendering in order to make the frames needed for a video, and we will not focus on modeling to create game content. But in either case, the more faces, the more render time. The problem is that having a large number of polygon faces in a scene can lead to long render times because the renderer has to calculate the movement of light

FIGURE 1.27   After a few passes of 50% poly reduction.

as it hits all of those polygon faces; we will look at this in Chapter 8. A good compromise is to carefully craft a model so that there are large numbers of polygons only on parts of the surface where detail is actually needed: we will use this as an ongoing heuristic in the modeling in this book.

One of the complications of using NURBS modeling is that renderers want polygon models as input to them. (In Chapter 8, we will take a more sophisticated look at this issue.) In order to keep a NURBS model smooth during the render process, it must be translated into a large number of polygon faces. Thus, NURBS modeling, while it has the advantage of allowing certain kinds of organic models to be more naturally made, tends to lead to models that are costly to render.

FIGURE 1.28   The not-so-organic chair.

THE THREE-DIMENSIONAL WORKFLOW

To end this chapter, here is a review of a typical 3D workflow. In this book, we will focus on modeling, materials, lighting, animation, and rendering basics for the beginner—the raw beginner. For this reason, our models will be for the most part basic, with a special emphasis on interior architectural modeling. This is because modeling human-made things, with their flat surfaces and right angles, is in general less challenging than modeling complex, organic surfaces like natural terrain or human faces. We will assume that the unit of work is a Maya scene, with some number of objects placed in hierarchies, and with materials, lights, and cameras in the scene. The workflow that we will use is the following:

1. Find something in the real world that you either want to mimic or use as inspiration. It is very important for the beginner to get "reference images" (usually photographs) that will help get proportions correct. It is equally important to use reference images because they contain realistic detail that is necessary for producing what we call "photorealism," that is, final renderings that could be mistaken for high-definition photographs of the real world. A common mistake by the beginner is to simplify the modeling process by removing detail—but this leads to superficial, unrealistic models and thus nonphotorealistic renderings.

2. Create wireframe models using polygon and/or NURBS modeling. The objects that make up models must be carefully named and placed in hierarchies to ease the application of materials, to facilitate the animation of objects with multiple moving parts (like a car whose windows can be opened while the car is moving, that is, windows that inherit the movement of the car body under which they are children in the hierarchy), and to make it easier to reuse components in future models.

3. Put materials on the models and place lights in the scene. The modeler might use the default light in Maya while creating wireframe models, but it is important to test materials under the lights that will actually appear in the scene. You might also use default materials like Maya lamberts (all objects are created initially with a lambert material on them; this is a nonreflective material), but lights must be tested with the materials that will be on the models in the scene. We see that lights and materials are highly interdependent.

4. Animate the objects in the scene. Models might move with respect to each other. Parts of one model might move with respect to other parts of the objects that make up this model. Models might also be rescaled (or in general, reshaped) in three dimensions or rotated in three dimensions as part of the animation. Models might also collide. Particle effects can be added as a further source of motion. Some 3D artists like to do some or all of their animation before finishing the application of materials.

5. Render the animation as a series of individual frames. In this book, we will assume that Maya will render 24 frames per second. During

phases 2–4, you are likely to do many single-frame test renders to judge the quality of your work and to evaluate the materials and lights. All renderings are done through the perspective of some camera. These test renders might be done through the default camera, but that is not the camera that will be used for the final render. Often, new cameras are introduced early in order to more carefully evaluate a developing scene from various angles in 3-space. These cameras may or may not be used for the final rendering.

6. A sound track, if desired, can be created in an audio program, as Maya is not a sound editor. The audio track can be imported into Maya in order to coordinate the animation and the sound.

7. The rendered frames are imported into a video editor, along with the sound track, and the video editor is used to export a final video. Since rendering is done from the perspective of a camera, and multiple cameras might be used to capture the animation, there might be multiple rendering batches that need to be turned into separate video clips that are then edited again in the video editor to create a single, final video.

Finally, many experienced modelers and animators prefer to create their wireframe models completely or almost completely before moving on to materials and lights and animation—as suggested by our seven-stage workflow. But the beginner needs to test wireframe models early on in order to spot modeling errors. This is best done by applying materials that approximate the materials that will be used for the final render; it is also necessary to create a realistic lighting situation by approximating the final lighting for the scene. Thus, the beginner mixes in modeling, applying materials, creating lights, creating cameras, and rendering early on, and therefore does not proceed through phases 1–7 in a strictly linear fashion. The bottom line is that only the experienced 3D artist knows what a wireframe model will eventually look like in a final rendering—a beginner must therefore apply materials and create lights early in the workflow process.

SOME ADVICE

Since the number of polygons (or "faces") in a scene is very important when it comes to the time needed for rendering, it is useful to turn on an option for the Heads Up display within the Viewport; it will keep you apprised of the size of your scene in terms of number of polygon faces. In Figure 1.29, we see where to find the setting for turning on this option; we must click Poly Count. In Figure 1.30, we see a scene that we will work with later in this book. There is only one object in the scene, a flattened cube. So, as you can see from the Heads Up display, there are only six polygons in the scene. One reason to keep this display in your Viewport is that it is very easy for a modeler to unintentionally create a scene with a very large number of polygons. Suppose, for example, you are modeling a theatre. You create a seat for the theatre, and to make it look nice, you smooth it out by adding a lot of polygon faces. Then you realize that the theatre needs 2000 seats …

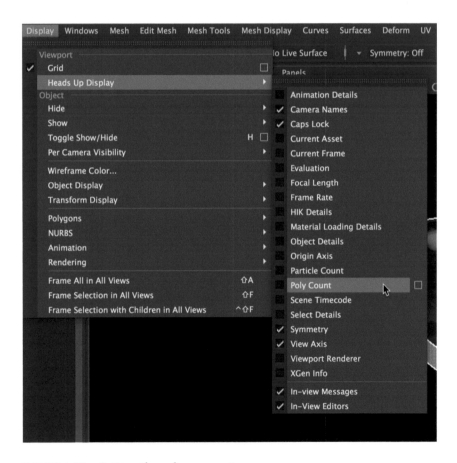

FIGURE 1.29 Getting the polygon count.

FIGURE 1.30 The polygon count.

A developing scene can become cluttered. To toggle the visibility of a set of objects, click on the blue stacks-of-squares icon in the left half of Figure 1.31. Then shift-select the objects and turn them into a visibility layer. Then, as in the right half of Figure 1.31, click the visibility "V" box.

Finally, control-Z is an undo. Set its depth at Windows → Settings/ Preferences → Preferences → Undo → Queue size.

FIGURE 1.31 Creating a visibility layer.

CHAPTER 2

The Gold Standard of Polygon Modeling and the NURBS Alternative

With examples: *A polygon glass table, a T-shirt made out of cloth, a chalice, and a NURBS glass table.*

I N THIS CHAPTER, WE focus on the basics of polygon modeling and NURBS modeling. An important issue is the extreme differences between these two techniques. The way that one creates a model with polygon tools is very different from the way one would build a similar model with NURBS tools—and the differences in these two approaches reflect a deep contrast between the way a polygon model and a NURBS model are represented mathematically. Often, the key difference is one of a top-down vs. a bottom-up approach, but this is an oversimplification. In the end, modelers are free to use their creativity to use polygon and NURBS tools to turn what they have in their imagination into a stunning 3D scene.

THE SIMPLICITY OF POLYGON MODELING

Consider Figure 2.1. In it we see the components of a simple polygon model, a table. It consists of 11 different meshes; each mesh is made of polygons,

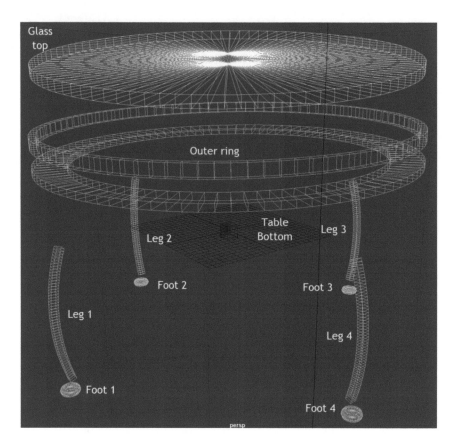

FIGURE 2.1   Components of a polygon table.

in this case quads (four-sided polygons) and triangles. In Figure 2.2, we
see a rendering of that table. Figure 2.3 shows one piece of the table. The
vertices of the polygons appear in a pinkish color and the edges of the
polygons are blue.

Each vertex is defined by a coordinate in 3-space: (x_i, y_i, z_i), and the
entire set of vertices in the component can be expressed as a set of vertices
in 3-space: $\{(x_i, y_i, z_i)\}$. The only other thing we need to know to completely
specify this component mathematically is what vertices are connected
by edges. This can be expressed as a set of vertex pairs, where each pair
represents the beginning and end vertices of a line: $\{(x_{i1}, y_{i1}, z_{i1}), (x_{i2}, y_{i2}, z_{i2})\}$.
We can generalize this to the entire glass table, with its components moved
into place, as in Figure 2.4. The entire table can be completely defined as
a set of components, where each component consists of a set of vertices

FIGURE 2.2   Polygon table rendered.

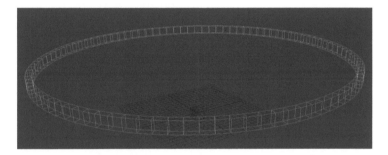

FIGURE 2.3   A component of the table.

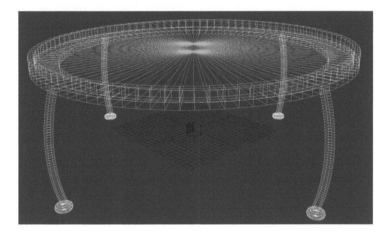

FIGURE 2.4   The wireframe of the table.

in 3-space and a set of lines that connect some of these vertices. In other words, the information needed to specify a polygon model is extremely simple from a mathematical perspective.

COMPONENT DESIGN

One more piece of information is generally desired in order to completely specify the model, and that is the hierarchy of the components, as discussed in Chapter 1. A reasonable hierarchy appears in Figure 2.5. We are probably not worried about animating the table, but one reason for creating the hierarchy is so that we can move the entire table by grabbing the bottom of the table.

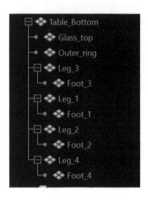

The mathematical simplicity of polygon modeling makes it easy to represent a model inside a 3D application like Maya. Further, graphics cards typically render triangle-based meshes, and quads can be turned into triangles simply by bisecting them with diagonals. These two facts make it more efficient internally to model with polygons than to model with curves, but there is a more important reason to use polygon modeling.

FIGURE 2.5 Table hierarchy.

The simplicity of modeling with polygons carries over to the user's experience: conceptually, it is easy for a modeler to visualize the process of crafting a model out of polygons.

There is something else that is useful to note. Why did we break the table down into these 11 components? We could have constructed it as a single mesh. After all, we are indeed not trying to animate the table by having the legs walk it across a room, right? True. But by breaking it into components, we can easily replace a component if we decide we don't like the way it was modeled. More importantly, when it comes time to put materials on the model, the job is a lot easier if the components of the model correspond to the separate pieces that we are likely to manufacture the table from in the real world. This way, it's very easy to make the top out of glass, but the rest out of metal. And although in Figure 2.2, the rest of the table is made out of one material, it's quite conceivable that we would reuse our model and perhaps make the feet out of a different-colored metal than the rest of the table. And maybe in another version of the table, the outer ring would be made out of a different material than the bottom of the table. In other words, by carefully crafting the table out of components, we facilitate the later reuse of our model in a different 3D project.

POLYGON MODELING IN MAYA

Figure 2.6 shows the Create dropdown menu. (The File, Edit, Create, Select, Modify, Display, and Windows dropdowns are identical for every setting of the Main Menu Selector.) Polygon modeling usually begins by starting with a "primitive," which consists of a base mesh; then this mesh is crafted into either an entire model or an object that makes up part of the model. This is why polygon modeling is generally viewed as a top-down process; we begin with a primitive and then reshape it. In the figure, we see that there are a number of polygon primitives available in Maya; the ones that are used most commonly are Sphere, Cube, Cylinder, Cone, Torus, and Plane. Although it was added to Maya fairly recently, I find the Pipe primitive to be very useful.

Once we create a Cylinder, we adjust its attributes in the Attribute Editor, as seen in Figure 2.7. In particular, the radius is 29, the height is 1.5, and the subdivisions are set to 100, 1, and 1. Now we have made the glass top. In Figure 2.8, we have gone to the first tab in the Attribute Editor and

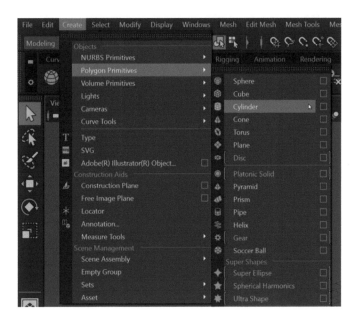

FIGURE 2.6   **The Create Menu.**

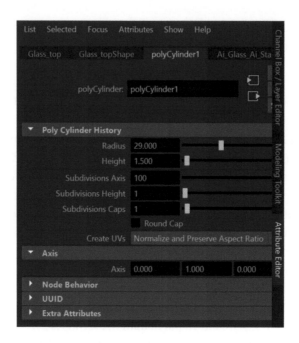

FIGURE 2.7   Attribute settings for the glass top.

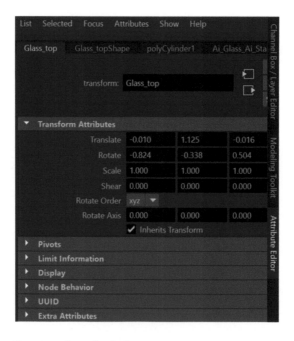

FIGURE 2.8   Changing the cylinder's name.

renamed the cylinder Glass_top. Renaming objects makes it dramatically easier to locate components in the Outliner. Since a scene can quickly become packed with large numbers of polygon primitives, we often go the Outliner and click on a component so that it will be highlighted in the Viewport; this is how we can select an object that might be difficult to click on in a complex scene.

The part of the table that encases the glass top is made out of two components, the Outer Ring and the Table Bottom. Both of them are Pipe primitives from the Create dropdown. Assuming that the reader is following along and building each example in this book, I leave it up to the reader to set the attributes (Radius, Height, Thickness, and three Subdivision attributes) of the two pipes. Note that the number of subdivisions chosen for all of the components of the table is based on how smooth the components need to be.

The feet are created by selecting Create → Polygon Primitives → Torus. The Radius, Section Radius, and two Subdivision attributes must be set.

It's important to move an object only along one axis at a time. This means that you should grab one of the three arrows on the Move tool rather than clicking on the center of the Move tool, which will cause the affected object to be dragged through 3-space rather than along a specific axis. If an object is moved randomly through 3-space, it will make it difficult to line it up with other components. Likewise, it is important to avoid rotating objects; if we were to rotate the glass top, say, so that it was no longer flat against the x-z plane, it would be difficult to later line it up properly with the outer ring and the table bottom.

The legs are the only components that cannot be created by simply rescaling a polygon primitive. To create a leg, we begin with a polygon Cube. We then adjust its height and subdivisions. But with the leg, we are not choosing the subdivision attributes to facilitate smoothing, at least not directly. We need to set the Subdivisions Height attribute large enough so that we can apply something called a Bend deformer. We need a number of subdivisions so that once the leg is bent, it is smooth; this is because vertices are used as the bend points of the object being deformed. The Bend deformer will not bend the leg properly without the subdivisions being set first. Here are the steps we follow. First, we create a polygon Cube and increase its height; then we add a number of subdivisions along this height. Second, we apply a Bend deformer. Figure 2.9 shows the selection of the Bend deformer tool; this must be done with the polygon cube selected in

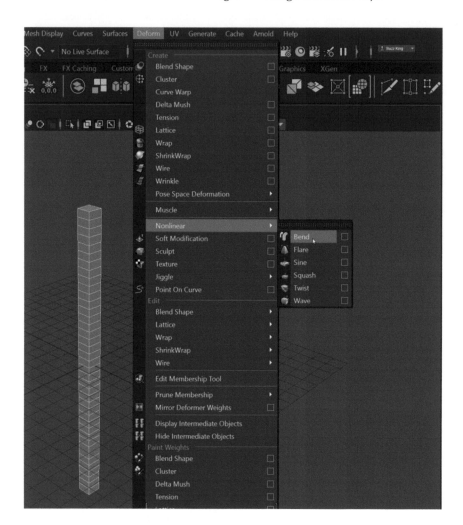

FIGURE 2.9   Creating a Bend deformer.

the Viewport. The Bend deformer is very heavily used in Maya polygon modeling. We can use it to roll up garden hoses, bend rain gutters, and create curved subway tunnels. In Figure 2.10, we move the Curvature slider of the Bend deformer tool to cause the chair leg to bend. We need to make a copy of the bent leg (by selecting the leg and going to Edit → Duplicate). We then use the duplicate of the leg to make three more copies; the original leg, which is attached to the Bend deformer, is not used, because if it is moved, the Bend deformer will re-bend the leg. In general, when any of the nonlinear deformers shown in Figure 2.9 are used, the deformed object is

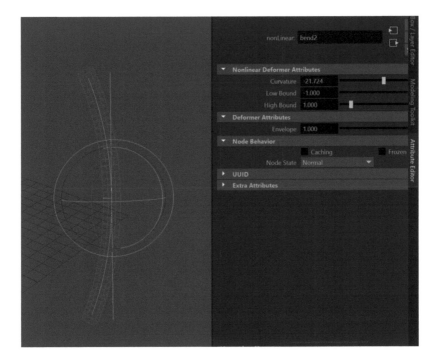

FIGURE 2.10   A Bend deformer.

copied, and the original is not used in the final model. An alternative to duplicating the object that has been changed by a deformer is to select the object and go to Edit → Delete by Type → History.

THE POLYGON MODELING PROCESS IN MAYA

We see in the example above a common way to carry out the polygon modeling process: by building a model out of components where each component begins with a polygon primitive. Each of these primitives is an object within the Maya database. These objects are then arranged into a hierarchy in the Outliner.

Another approach is to craft a model out of a single primitive. When making this sort of model, a common workflow is to create a primitive, such as a Cube, but with very few vertices and edges, then to incrementally add vertices and edges and use this added detail to "push/pull" our model out of the primitive. We will create a T-shirt. In this example, we'll look at two very important polygon modeling tools, Extrude and Smooth, and we will also take a preliminary look at particle dynamics.

ADDING DETAIL ONLY WHEN NEEDED

In Figure 2.11, we make a polygon Cube, and in Figure 2.12, we adjust its attributes to make it 15 by 15 by 5, and then set the subdivisions to 3, 4, 1.

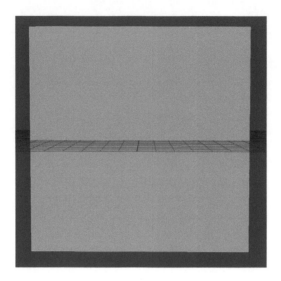

FIGURE 2.11   A poly cube.

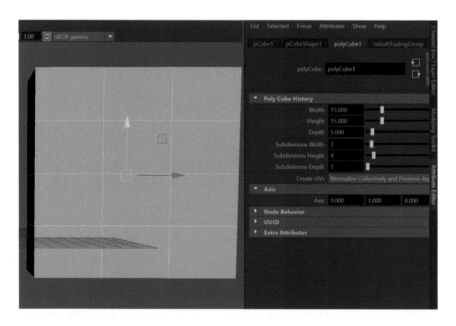

FIGURE 2.12   Cube subdivisions.

What we're doing is approximating the overall dimensions of the T-shirt and then creating the divisions we will need to cut out a neck hole and create two sleeves. There is an important modeling strategy to keep in mind when performing polygon modeling: add detail, in the form of new edges and vertices, only as needed. In Figure 2.13, we have right-clicked and this

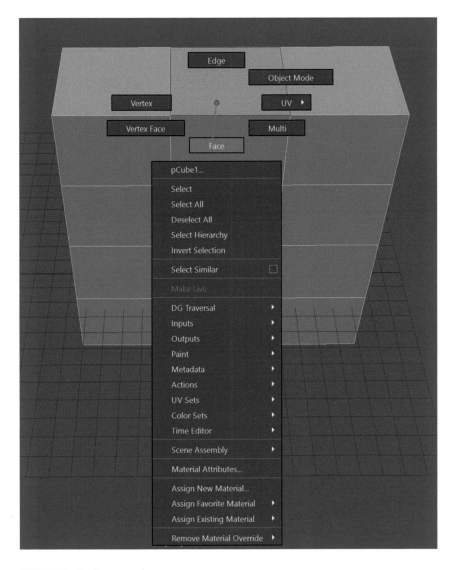

FIGURE 2.13   **Face mode.**

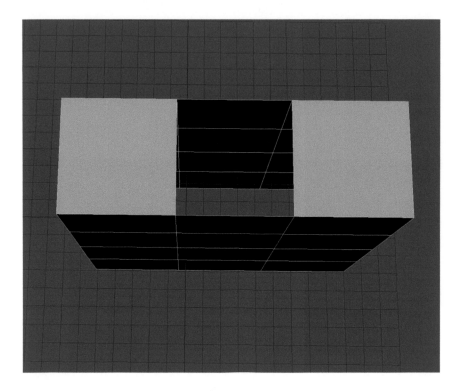

FIGURE 2.14   Four faces deleted.

has pulled up a context-sensitive menu called a "marking menu"; we then choose Face mode. This menu is very important; for now, we note that it is used to move between four common contexts in which we perform polygon modeling: Object, Face, Edge, and Vertex. (A face is a single polygon.) Once we are in Face mode, we select the top middle face and hit the Delete key. We have made a neck hole, and we see this in Figure 2.14. We also delete the three faces at the bottom of the T-shirt so that eventually, someone can slip it over his or her head.

We are still in Face mode. Next, we shift-select the ends of the two arm faces at the top of the cube. Then we choose the Extrude tool, as shown in Figure 2.15; we can extrude in multiple modes, and here we are extruding faces. We pull out the two arms by moving the yellow arrow, as seen in Figure 2.16. Extrusion is a heavily used polygon modeling tool, especially in push/pull modeling. In Figure 2.17, we right-click and go into Object mode. Now, we use the Smooth tool, and in fact, we use it four times, as

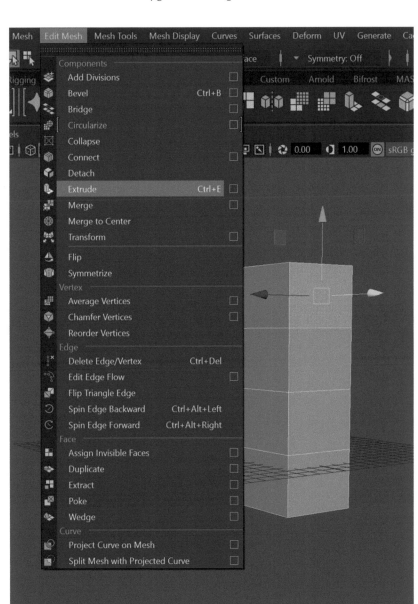

FIGURE 2.15   The Extrusion tool.

seen in Figures 2.18 through 2.20. (We can accomplish the same thing by setting the Divisions setting of the Smooth tool to 3 and then using the tool only once.)

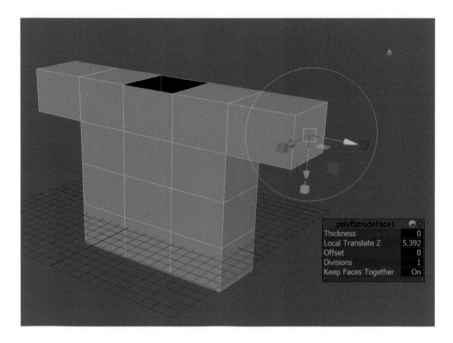

FIGURE 2.16   **Extruding a sleeve.**

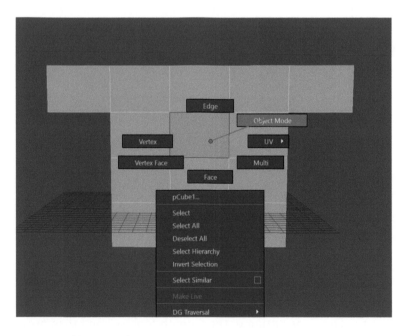

FIGURE 2.17   **Object mode.**

SMOOTHING ONLY WHEN NEEDED

There are two very important things to point out here. First, we see again the principle of only adding detail as needed. Smoothing, since it creates new faces, is a form of adding detail. We have waited until now to smooth the T-shirt, which the tool does by adding vertices and edges (and thus faces); if we had done the smoothing before pulling out the sleeves, it would have been very hard to make the sleeves. Second, the Smooth tool is very powerful, and often the result is an extremely different overall shape. In this case, a key reason why the Smooth tool does what we want can be seen in Figure 2.19. If we look at the underarms of the T-shirt, we see that it adds faces that are not parallel to either

FIGURE 2.18   The Smooth tool.

the sleeves or the body of the shirt. In particular, the Smooth tool wants to intelligently bridge any two faces that are at right angles to each other.

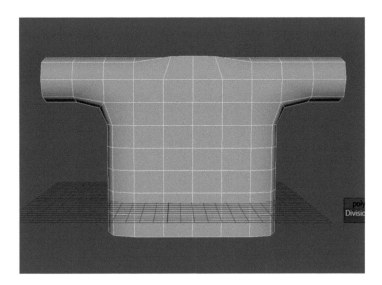

FIGURE 2.19   One level of smooth.

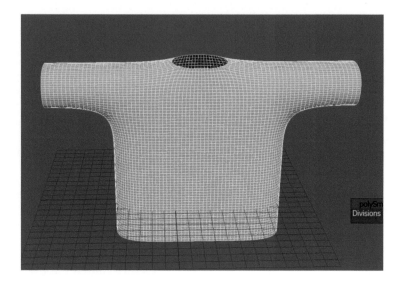

FIGURE 2.20   Four levels of smooth.

This is very critical to understand when using the Smooth tool. Notice in Figure 2.21 what happens if we take a cube with no subdivisions and smooth it by 3 levels. It almost makes a sphere! Later, in Chapter 6, we will look at a similar tool in an application called Modo, and we will gain some more insight into why smoothing an object that has very few vertices and edges can dramatically alter its geometry.

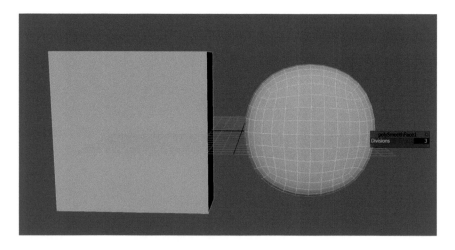

FIGURE 2.21   Smoothing a cube.

DYNAMICS AND CLOTH

To round out our T-shirt example, we're going to take a quick look at particle dynamics. What we are going to see is a powerful relationship between polygon geometry and particle dynamics—namely that one can be used to generate the other. We'll only discuss dynamics at a very high level for now; we return to the topic in Chapter 7 on animation. In Figure 2.22, we have placed a polygon plane below the shirt and turned it into a "Passive Collider," that is, a plane that will not move but will be collided with by the shirt. In Figure 2.23, we adjust the Main Menu Selector to "FX." Then, in Figure 2.24, we are in Object mode (by selecting Object after right-clicking on the T-shirt) and we turn the shirt into "nCloth." What this does is turn every vertex of the shirt model into a particle that can move in a semi-independent fashion; each vertex is bound to the ones that are close to it, but they can move independently to some degree.

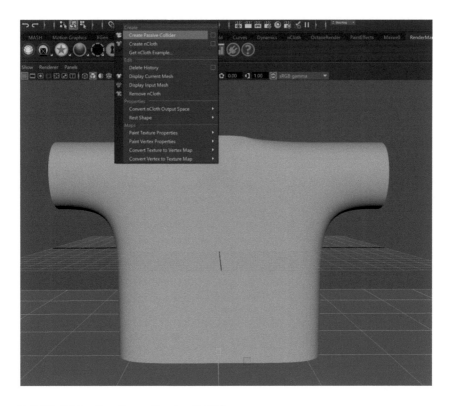

FIGURE 2.22 Creating a Passive Collider.

FIGURE 2.23   The FX Main Menu Selection.

Next, with the shirt still selected, we create a Gravity Field that will then affect the motion of the shirt. See Figure 2.25. In Figure 2.26, we have hit the Run button (the forward-pointing triangle icon) in the Playback controls; this runs the simulation consisting of the shirt being pulled downward by gravity. Turning the polygon shirt into a system of particles has created a clothlike effect that makes the shirt crumple as it hits the Passive Collider.

So, why is polygon modeling still the gold standard? In part, it is the ease with which it can be understood and used in a top-down incremental fashion. And, of course, polygon modeling also naturally fits with the functioning of graphics cards, as they historically have been built to render meshes made of triangles. (We will look at graphics cards in Chapter 8 on rendering.) But the real reason, perhaps, is that polygon modeling has been around a long time and has become the most developed modeling capability in many or most major 3D modeling applications. Interestingly,

FIGURE 2.24   Creating nCloth.

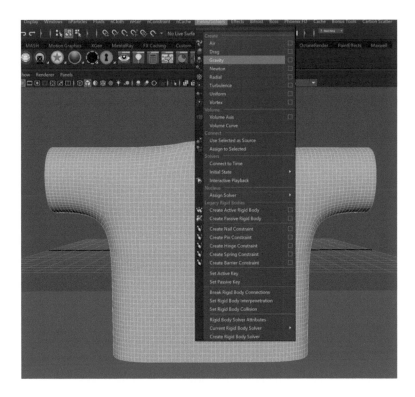

FIGURE 2.25　Placing a Gravity Field on the shirt.

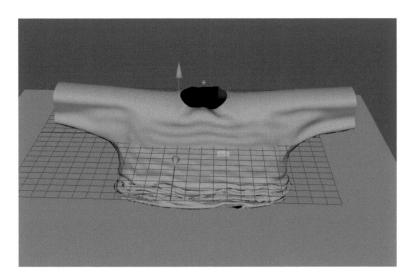

FIGURE 2.26　Running the scene.

you cannot turn a NURBS object into cloth in Maya the way you can turn a polygon object into cloth, and in general, polygon modeling is much more deeply and broadly embedded in the Maya application than is NURBS modeling. That's why we discussed nCloth in this introduction to polygon modeling: because within Maya, it is intimately tied to polygon modeling. Only polygon meshes (wireframes) can be turned into a connected graph of particles and thus form nCloth.

NONUNIFORM RATIONAL BASIS SPLINE MODELING WITH NONUNIFORM RATIONAL BASIS SPLINE CURVES

With polygon modeling, we typically begin the modeling process with some sort of complete surface form, like a Sphere, a Cube, or a Torus; again, these are called "primitives" in Maya. There is also a set of NURBS primitives that can be found on the Create dropdown. However, we often do *not* begin the NURBS modeling process by starting with a complete primitive. We often start with lines.

NURBS modeling—it stands for nonuniform rational basis spline—is a curved-line modeling technique that is similar mathematically to Bezier modeling, which is an extremely common technique and is available in many drawing and painting applications, as well as in text editing and document preparation applications that allow the user to create line drawings. In these two techniques, NURBS and Bezier, rather than representing a model as a set of connected, straight lines, as in polygon modeling, it is defined by a set of curved lines. These curved lines are themselves defined by "control vertices" (to use Maya terminology). These CVs, as they are called, are fed into polynomials that then define the shape of the curve by creating (x, y, z) vertices on the curve. Interestingly, often the only CVs that lie directly on the curve are the beginning and end vertices. Thus, the CVs control the shape of the curve, rather than necessarily lying on the curve. The one exception is a straight line (which, if you think about it, is a kind of curved line), where all the CVs lie on the line. Also, we often create a continuous series of curves that mathematically are separate NURBS or Bezier curves, where the final end point of one curve is the beginning endpoint of another curve.

To put things more precisely, a NURBS curve is defined by some polynomial mathematics, along with a set of CVs in 3-space. In Figure 2.27, the NURBS CV Curve tool is selected. In Figure 2.28, consider the lower-left quadrant of the image. This is the front orthographic view,

FIGURE 2.27 The CV Curve tool.

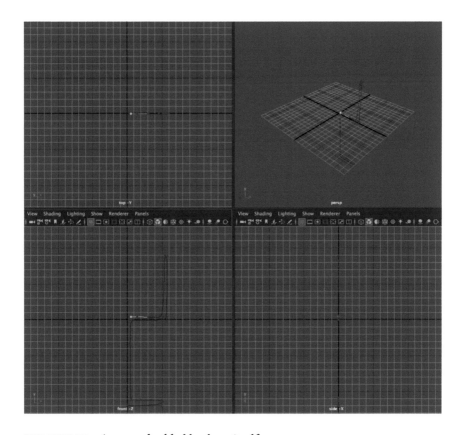

FIGURE 2.28 A curve doubled back on itself.

and it is in this quadrant where we are using the CV Curve tool. (The top-right view is a perspective view, while the other three, top, front, and side, are orthographic views, in that each of them is flattened along some axis.) In the front view, that is, in the lower left-hand part of the main window, we have started at the bottom of the grid, very close to the z axis, and we have used the CV Curve tool to lay down a series of control vertices. They are in red, with the last one in yellow. Note that we start at the bottom, work our way up, and then backtrack a bit by going back toward the z axis. The result is a line with several sharp curves in it. Now, whenever the line makes a sharp curve, it appears that the CVs are on the line. But it only looks this way because whenever the line in Figure 2.28 makes a sharp turn, we have deliberately put two or more CVs close together. We thus see that we can surgically control the shape of a curve by placing CVs close together, as this causes the curve to be very close to the CVs.

CREATING NONUNIFORM RATIONAL BASIS SPLINE SURFACES

Now, in Figure 2.29, we are using a NURBS tool called Revolve. Many of the key NURBS tools are under the Surfaces dropdown. The reason for

the name of this dropdown is that when we define NURBS models, we often start with lines and then move them through 3-space to create surfaces, which then define the shell of our model. Thus, we tend to say that NURBS modeling is focused on surfaces rather than complete primitives, like Spheres. Consider the result of the Revolve tool, as seen in Figure 2.30: we have made a chalice or wine glass. Note that the reason we doubled back at the top of the curve is so that the cup would have a lip, instead of ending with a sharp edge. In other words, since no real-world object is infinitely thin, we needed to make a lip for our cup.

FIGURE 2.29 The Revolve tool.

Importantly, when we revolved this curve, Maya created more lines to flesh out the surface of our cup. This is what NURBS modeling is all about—building surfaces, including adding new curves, that are defined

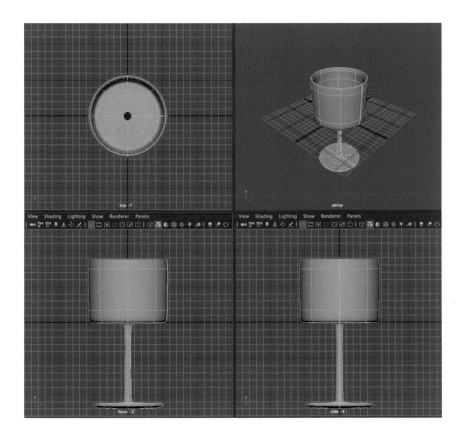

FIGURE 2.30 The revolved curve.

by the positions of one or more initial curves in 3-space, and how these initial curves have been moved with respect to each other and with respect to the three dimensional axes.

A FOCUS ON CONTROL VERTICES

To consider CVs more closely, look at Figure 2.31. The endpoints, cv1 and cv5, are on the curve. But cv2, cv3, and cv4 are outside the curve. We can see how the control vertices dictate the shape of the curve without the line going through every CV. If we were to move cv2, cv3, and/or cv4 upward in the positive y direction, the curve would be made steeper. If we were to move cv2 in the negative direction along the x axis, we would be widening the curve. Note that, unlike the curves that make up the cup in Figures 2.28 through 2.30, the CVs in Figure 2.31 are far apart, and thus, the CVs

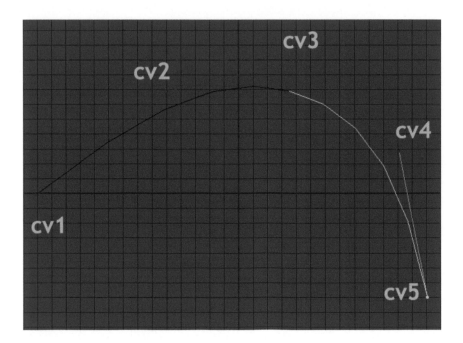

FIGURE 2.31   A CV Curve.

(except for the two endpoints) are not very close to the curve. If we wanted to make a very tight curve, we would put our vertices close together, as we did on the curves in Figure 2.28. In Figure 2.31, the CVs actually do, in a very precise way, control the shape of the curve just as they do for the curve in Figure 2.28, but the curve in Figure 2.31 shows us why it can take a little time to develop an intuitive feeling for exactly what curve will be formed from a given series of CVs.

There is something very exciting about NURBS curve mathematics: it scales cleanly. Given a set of CVs, along with the polynomials that define the points of the curve as a function of the location of the CVs, we are given the exact shape of a curve—not its physical length.

FIGURE 2.32   The Loft tool.

LOFTING

We will now use the Loft tool to turn two curves into a surface. This tool is shown in Figure 2.32. The three steps of making the

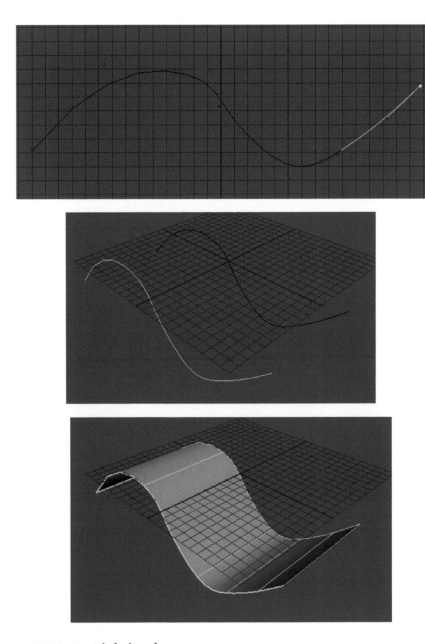

FIGURE 2.33   A lofted surface.

surface are shown in Figure 2.33. First, we select the curve we made in Figure 2.31, as in the top of the figure. Then we select Edit → Duplicate, which creates a second curve. Then, the two are moved apart but left parallel in 3-space, along the x/y plane, as in the middle image of the figure. Then, with the two curves shift-selected, we choose the Loft tool, and this creates the surface at the bottom of the figure. Again, we make a surface by manipulating curves—not by beginning with a 3D primitive.

EXTRUSION

Consider Figure 2.34. Note that one of the NURBS primitives is a Circle—an option we do not have with polygon modeling, because we usually don't create polygon models by beginning with two-dimensional objects. (This is also why the polygon Create dropdown has many more primitives to choose from: we probably want more variety in

FIGURE 2.34   A NURBS circle curve.

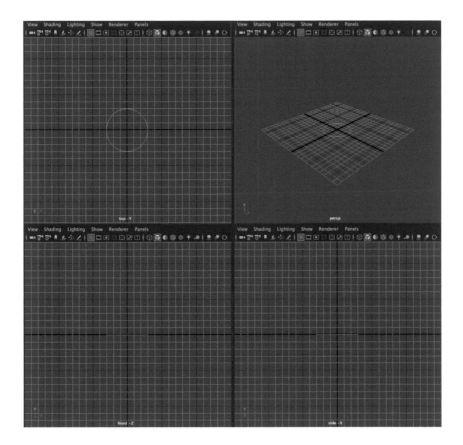

FIGURE 2.35   The circle.

our primitives if we are, most of the time, going to create a model by beginning with a three-dimensional primitive.) We see the circle we have created in Figure 2.35.

In Figure 2.36, we have used the CV Curve tool to create a curve. (It is actually two connected curves; look closely at the bottom of the line—it bends backward a bit.) As with the lofting example above, we are carefully leaving our curves on specific planes so that we can work with lines that we know are either parallel or (in this case) at 90 degrees to each other. We then shift-select the first curve (the circle), then the second curve, and choose Surfaces → Extrude. We get the surface found in Figure 2.37, which could be a pipe or ducting in a house.

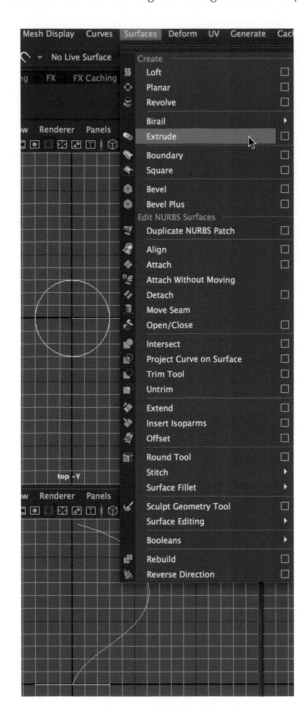

FIGURE 2.36   The Extrude NURBS curve tool.

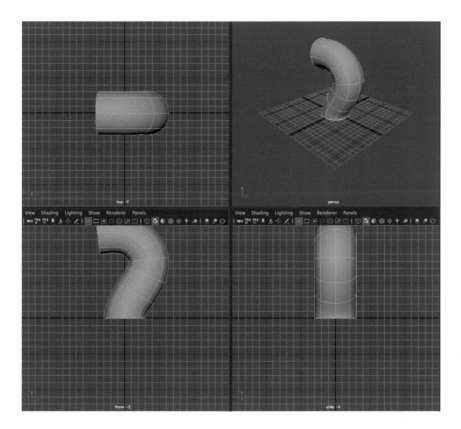

FIGURE 2.37   The extruded pipe.

A CLOSER LOOK AT CURVED LINE MATHEMATICS

We return to this issue of the CVs of a curve controlling the shape of that curve, but only in an indirect fashion. We noted earlier that NURBS modeling is similar mathematically to Bezier modeling. Since Bezier mathematics is used heavily in many modeling applications and it is easier to explain, and since Maya also supports Bezier curves (but in a much more limited way than with NURBS curves), we will look at Bezier mathematics. Legend has it that Bezier, an engineer with the French car manufacturer Renault, in the late 1950s, needed to design the curves in cars in a way that was precise and scalable. Rather than drawing a curve on a piece of paper that was 15 feet long (perhaps), he only had to give the builders of the car a couple of polynomials and some control vertices. They could then construct the precise curve he had in mind and scale it up to the size of the car. It is also said that another French car engineer, Paul de Casteljau, who worked for Citroen, developed a very similar technique simultaneously. And, in fact, it is believed that the technique we call Bezier modeling is actually the version of this technique that was developed by Casteljau.

Consider Figure 2.38. There are four CVs on the bottom of the figure. Those four control points, along with two polynomials of degree 3, which are at the top of the figure, define the curve at the bottom of Figure 2.38. In general, if there are n control points, we need two polynomials of degree n − 1 to create a curve. To generate a point along the final curve, we feed in the values for the four CVs (which are in 2-space), along with a value for t, into the two polynomials, and the polynomials produce an x value and a y value for the curve. Notice that t lies between 0 and 1. What this means is that we can create as many points as we want on the curve by supplying numbers between 0 and 1. In other words, we can provide whatever level

$$x[t] = x_0 + 3t(x_1 - x_0) + 3t^2(x_0 + x_2 - 2x_1) + t^3(x_3 - x_0 + 3x_1 - 3x_2)$$

$$y[t] = y_0 + 3t(y_1 - y_0) + 3t^2(y_0 + y_2 - 2y_1) + t^3(y_3 - y_0 + 3y_1 - 3y_2)$$

$$0 \le t \le 1$$

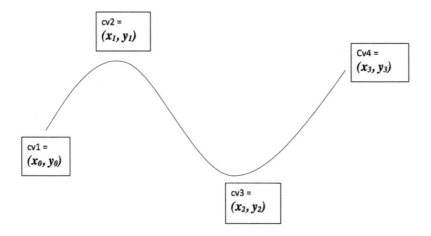

FIGURE 2.38 Bezier polynomials and a curve.

of precision we need: we lay down a Bezier curve by calculating as many points on the curve as are required to make it smooth. This allows us to scale a curve up to an arbitrarily large image without any loss of precision: perhaps the car designer only needs the curve to be viewable on a piece of paper, while the builders of the car need the curve to physically be much larger. But either way, all the designer and the builders need are the two polynomials and the four control points. The only difference is that the builders of the car would probably generate far more values of t in order to make sure the manufactured curve on the body of the car is perfectly smooth. So, Bezier mathematics—as well as NURBS mathematics—allows us to build unambiguously specified curves and draw them out at any scale with just a handful of CVs and some mathematics. And, if we want to fine-tune a curve that we are using on the body of a car, we simply move one or more of the CVs around in 2-space until we like the shape of the curve. There is no need to start from scratch.

Here's another way to look at the importance of both Bezier and NURBS mathematics. Consider Figure 2.39. On the left is a polygon Sphere. On the right is a NURBS Sphere, consisting of a modest number of curved lines. Note how many more straight lines it took to define the polygon sphere—and it is not even smooth! The left side of Figure 2.40 shows us just how many straight lines are in the polygon sphere: it is subdivided

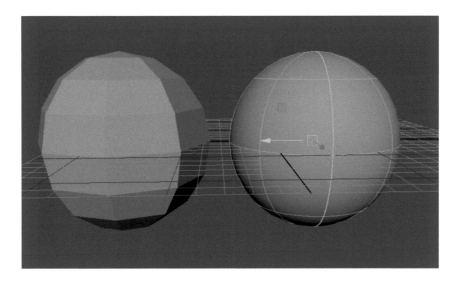

FIGURE 2.39 A polygon and a NURBS sphere.

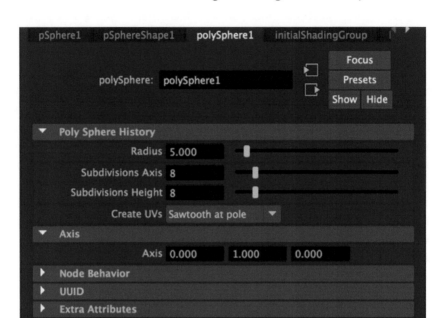

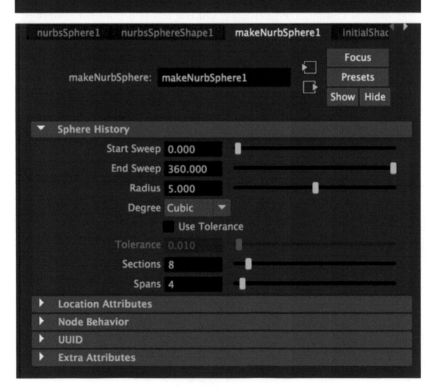

FIGURE 2.40   The definitions of a polygon sphere and a NURBS sphere.

8 times horizontally and 8 times vertically. On the right side of Figure 2.41, we see the attributes of the NURBS sphere. It is sectioned in a similar way, but it is smooth because it is made out of curved lines. Instead of having to create a smooth sphere by using a very large number of polygon sections, a NURBS sphere can be created with a small number of CVs, along with some mathematics that, again, is similar to Bezier math.

A SWEEP

Consider the attribute of the NURBS Sphere called "sweep." In Figure 2.41, we have moved the slider that controls the sweep, opening up the sphere. We cannot do this in polygon modeling. This reinforces the fact that the NURBS Sphere is created by sweeping a curve through 3-space. If the number of subdivisions were increased, it would not impact the shape or size of the sphere! The only line that controls the shape and size of the sphere is the single curve that is being moved when we open up the sweep.

Look at Figure 2.42. A NURBS torus, unlike a polygon torus, has a sweep. It is made by moving a circle in 3-space. Contrast this with a polygon torus, which is a mesh of 2D polygons. How can we define a NURBS torus? We can supply a set of CVs that, along with some mathematics, define a circle, and then we can rotate that circle through 3-space. Some repetition is warranted, as this is a very important distinction. How could we define a polygon torus? We could supply a set of points in 3-space, along with

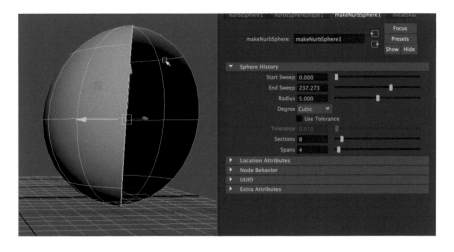

FIGURE 2.41   The sweep of the NURBS surface.

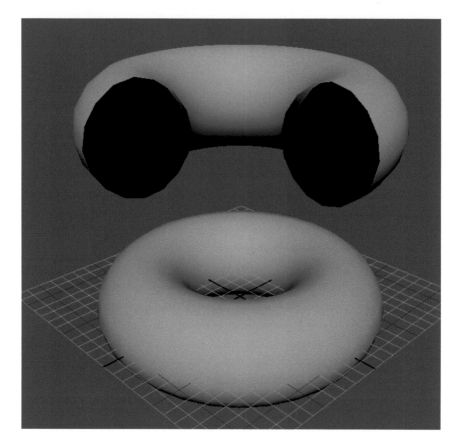

FIGURE 2.42   The sweep of a torus.

a set of pairs, with each pair defining a straight line; these pairs tell us
which vertices in 3-space form edges of polygons. We see that polygon
modeling is all about forming meshes out of polygons, while NURBS
modeling is all about defining (indirectly) curves and then moving them
through 3-space.

CONNECTING NONUNIFORM RATIONAL
BASIS SPLINE SURFACES

When creating NURBS models, since we are often working in a bottom-up
fashion by turning curves into surfaces, rather than working top down
by molding a single polygon primitive, we often find ourselves having to
connect multiple surfaces to create a single object.

In Figure 2.43, we have two wavy surfaces. In Figure 2.44, we right-click, obtain a context-sensitive menu, and go into Isoparm (Edge) mode on both of the surfaces. Then we shift-select the leading edge of each surface, as in Figure 2.45. In Figure 2.46, we then choose the Stitch tool from the Surfaces dropdown. The immediate result is in Figure 2.47. After we hit enter to end the Stitch tool, we get the continuous surface in Figure 2.48.

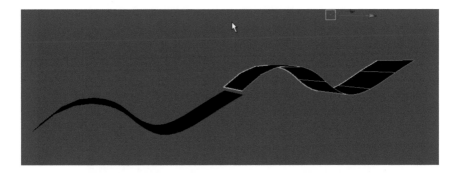

FIGURE 2.43   **Two NURBS surfaces.**

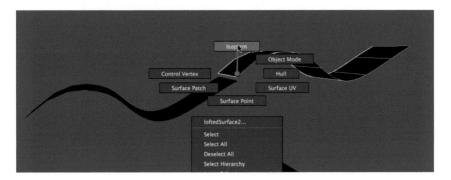

FIGURE 2.44   **Isoparm mode.**

FIGURE 2.45   **Neighboring isoparms.**

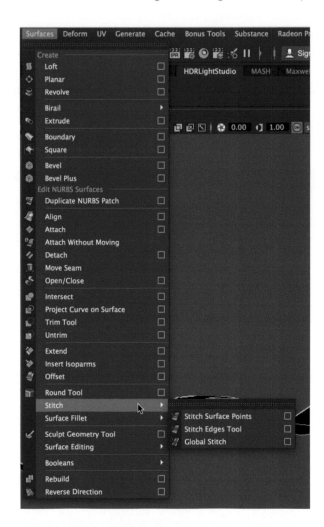

FIGURE 2.46 Stitching two edges together.

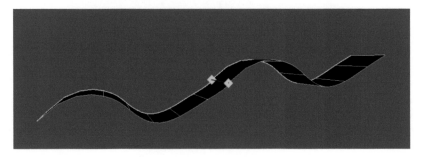

FIGURE 2.47 The result of the stitch.

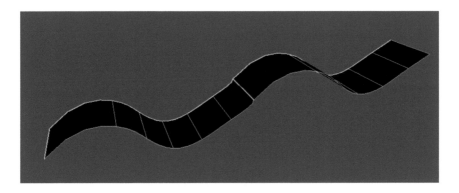

FIGURE 2.48   A new single NURBS surface.

ISOPARMS

When one right-clicks on a polygon object, the context-sensitive menu that pops up is very different than the one that pops up when one right-clicks on a NURBS surface. Lines in NURBS models are not called lines or curves: they are called isoparms. An isoparm is a curve that lies on a single plane. In Figure 2.49, all of the curves are actually isoparms—but,

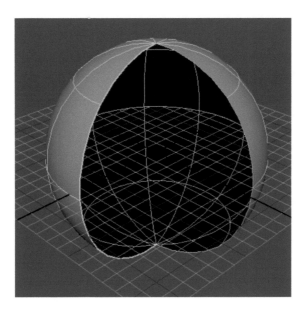

FIGURE 2.49   Two isoparms on a sphere.

importantly, the horizontal isoparms go all around the sphere, while the vertical ones only cover half of the sphere. Also, an isoparm lies along the sweep.

ANOTHER EXTRUSION

In this example, we will first create a two-dimensional template out of curves, and then we will extrude this template around a circle to create our desired 3D shape. In Figure 2.50, we create a series of curves with the CV Curve tool and place the CVs so close to each other at the curve points that we are making almost straight lines. But rather than creating actual straight lines, this will later result in a surface that has smoothed edges. The series of curves made with the CV Curve tool is in Figures 2.51 and 2.52. In Figures 2.53 through 2.55, we create a circle that will be used as an extrusion path for the template shape we made with the CV Curve tool; part of this process involves rotating the template 90 degrees across two planes. An important point is that since the shape in Figures 2.51 and 2.52 was made out of lines and is not a 3D primitive, it does not have a center pivot automatically assigned

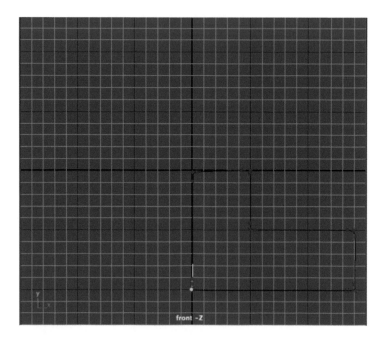

FIGURE 2.50 The template for extrusion.

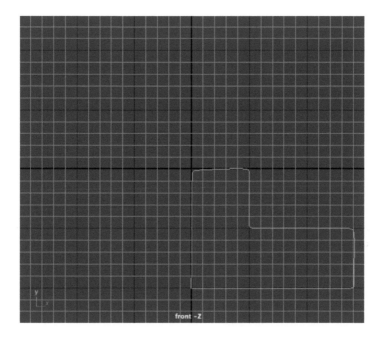

FIGURE 2.51   After terminating the curve tool.

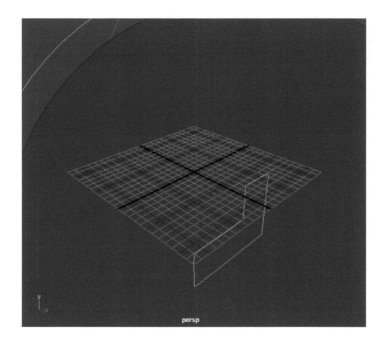

FIGURE 2.52   The template in 3-space.

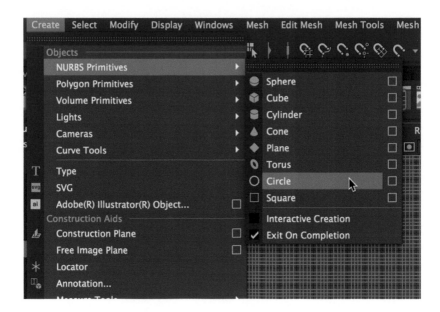

FIGURE 2.53   The extrusion path.

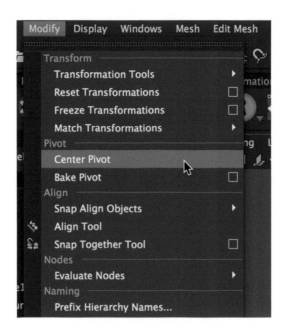

FIGURE 2.54   Setting the center pivot on the template.

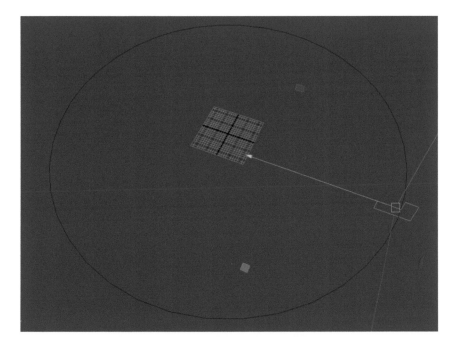

FIGURE 2.55 After rotating the template.

to it; this is why we must set the pivot in Figure 2.54. In Figure 2.56, we select the tool that will extrude the template around the circle; note that we click on the box on the menu item in order to access the tool's settings. Then, in Figure 2.57, we set the Extrude tool to make Polygons—not NURBS, so the resulting geometry is actually a polygon shape. The final result is in

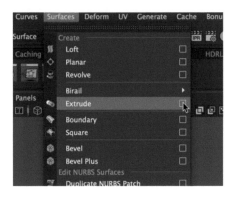

FIGURE 2.56 Opening the extrude tool with settings.

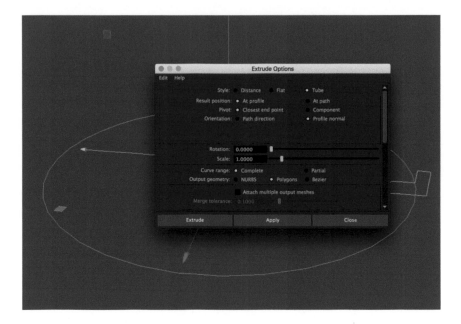

FIGURE 2.57   Creating polygon geometry.

Figure 2.58. We've just discovered another way to make the table top that we made earlier in the chapter! Only this time, it is made out of one piece, not two.

In Figure 2.59, we click on the box next to the NURBS Cylinder tool to pull up its settings. We adjust its height and width in Figure 2.60; we also give it a top and a bottom because NURBS Cylinders do not come with integrated tops and bottoms by default, as polygon Cylinders do. The resulting table top is in Figure 2.61. In Figure 2.62, we extrude a circle through a curved line (made with the NURBS CV Curve tool) to make a leg. The final table is in Figure 2.63. The only step that has been left out is creating the four feet for the legs. Now, we have completed our glass-top table and have made it by a largely different method.

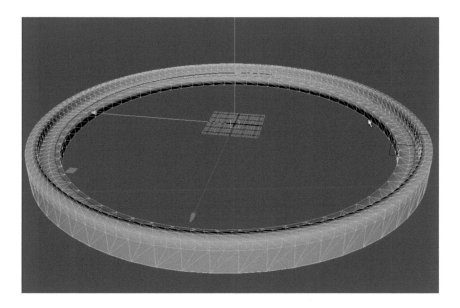

FIGURE 2.58 The resulting extrusion.

FIGURE 2.59 Opening the NURBS cylinder tool.

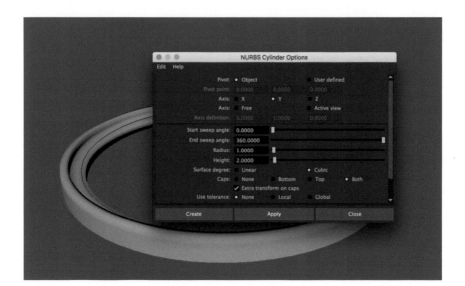

FIGURE 2.60   Giving the glass a top and a bottom.

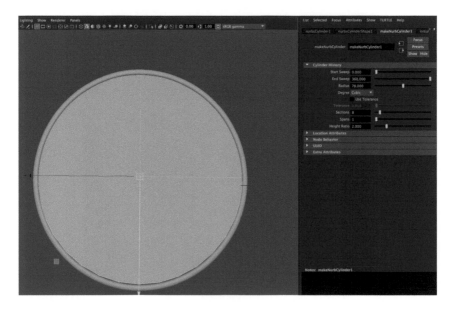

FIGURE 2.61   The rim and glass.

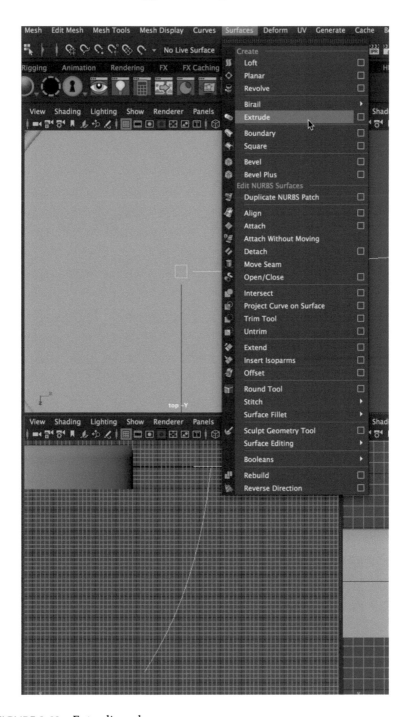

FIGURE 2.62 **Extruding a leg.**

FIGURE 2.63   The made-with-NURBS table.

CHAPTER 3

A Focus on Simplicity

A Core Set of Modeling Tools in an Overwhelming App

> **With examples:** *Adding detail to the T-shirt and making a Moai, an arch, a table, and a wall.*

W E NOW GET DOWN to the nuts and bolts of determining what aspects of Maya the beginner should focus on. The interface of a sophisticated application like Maya cannot convey how it should be used; in this chapter, we look at a handful of concrete examples so that the reader can begin to develop an intuitive sense of how to build models with Maya.

THE IMPORTANT POLYGON MODELING MAIN MENU DROPDOWNS

Our job in this book is to attack the Autodesk Maya interface and reduce its massive size and complexity. Our goal is to allow the beginner 3D animator to create complete 3D projects while only having to master a relatively small subset of Maya. The important thing to note about Maya is that it provides many, many ways of getting a given job done, and it also supplies numerous specialized tools. Thus, beginners can get the satisfaction of building full, sophisticated projects early on, and then gradually expand their knowledge of Maya over time. A complete understanding of Maya typically takes years. In this chapter, we take an initial look at the key tools used by modelers who are crafting meshes with polygon geometry.

At this point, it's important to point out that Autodesk tweaks Maya every year, and one of the most common changes is to relocate tools in the Main Menu dropdowns. Another is to replace tools with similar ones, delete a redundant tool, or merge two or more tools into one. But the basic organization and nature of the tools is only very rarely changed. So, if your version of Maya doesn't look exactly like the images in this book, try using the Help → Find Menu tool, or, if you are looking for a polygon modeling tool, just carefully examine the Mesh, Edit Mesh, and Mesh Tools menus discussed in this book. If you are looking for NURBS tools, examine the Surfaces dropdown. Also, each year, when a new version of Maya is released, a menu item will appear in green if it is new or changed; this is another way of orienting yourself when Maya seems to look a little different. You can turn off this "green is new" feature by going to Windows → Settings/Preferences → Preferences → Interface → Highlight what's new in this release-and unchecking the box.

We start with Figure 3.1. The Create menu is where we find the polygon and NURBS modeling primitives. Each primitive is an "object" in Maya terminology and has a number of attributes. For polygon meshes, there are a lot of choices. This list has been expanded in recent releases of Maya, and in this book, we will mostly use Sphere, Cube, Cylinder, Cone, Torus, Plane, and Pipe. When you create a primitive, you can adjust its attributes in two different ways: (1) by selecting the box icon in the dropdown menu when creating the primitive and then changing the tool's settings before creating the primitive, or (2) by adjusting the primitive's attributes after creating the primitive. If you want to move, rotate, or scale the primitive, you can first create it and then use the appropriate tool by finding it at the left side of the Maya Viewport. But I discourage the use of the Scale tool to change the scale of an object. It's better to adjust the attributes in the Attribute Editor and to insert precise numbers; freeform scaling can produce objects that are difficult to use later on in the modeling process, as their size will be somewhat arbitrary. (Note that if, after scaling, rotating, or moving an object in 3-space, you want to zero out its attributes so that the current values for its size, location, and rotation become base values, select Modify → Freeze Transforms.)

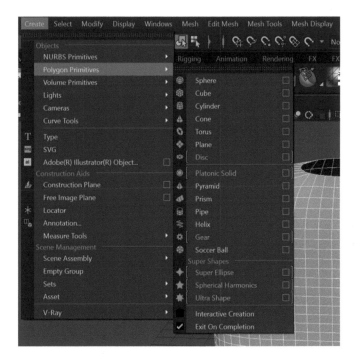

FIGURE 3.1 The polygon primitives.

Consider Figure 3.2. It shows the Mesh, Edit Mesh, and Mesh Tools menus in the center of the Main Menu. ("Mesh" is used to refer to a wireframe of a polygon object.) These menus are where polygon modelers spend much of their time. (Remember that the Main Menu Selector has been set to "Modeling.")

In Figure 3.3, which shows the Mesh tools dropdown, there are two items that we will make heavy use of: Boolean and Smooth. The Boolean menu item actually provides three tools, Union, Intersection, and Difference. They are a quick way of creating a new shape out of two different polygon meshes. But the result of using a Boolean tool can be an object that behaves oddly later in the modeling process. And, using a Boolean tool on two primitives that have already been significantly modified

FIGURE 3.2 Important polygon menus.

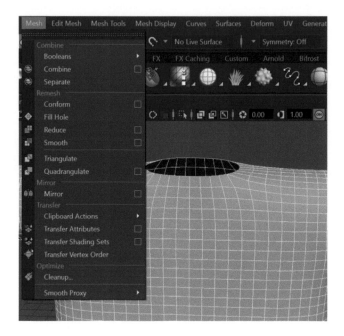

FIGURE 3.3   The Mesh tools.

since their initial creation can create a bizarrely shaped new object. The issue is that the Boolean operations in Maya are a bit unpredictable and unstable—*to put it mildly.* It's best to use them very early in the modeling process before the two objects in question have been modified much, then keep in mind that other tools might behave oddly. The Boolean tools will behave in a somewhat more stable fashion if the two objects being manipulated have roughly the same level of edge/vertex detail. Smooth is a tool that can be used to add detail and simultaneously smooth either selected faces or an entire object. The beginner might find the result of the Smooth tool to be unexpected, as it will create new faces that are at an angle to existing faces, as we saw with the T-shirt; it takes time to develop an intuitive understanding of exactly what it does to a mesh.

In Figure 3.4, we see the Edit Mesh dropdown. It contains a somewhat eclectic set of tools. Add Divisions is a good way of adding detail to a selected face. Bevel can be used to smooth a single edge, as it turns an edge into a plane. Bridge can be used to create a number of different modeling effects; one of the most common uses is to create archways. Extrude is a tool that we will make very heavy use of in this book; it is a key tool in the

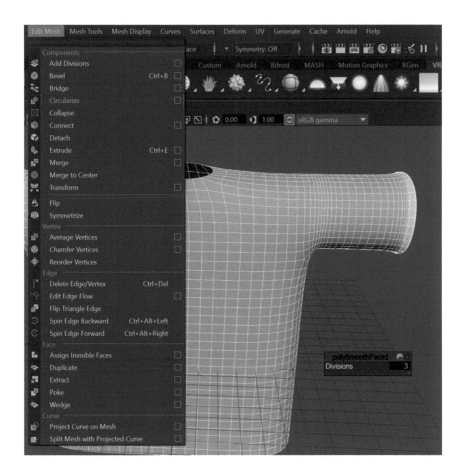

FIGURE 3.4   The Edit Mesh tools.

polygon modeling process. We will also make use of a few other tools in this dropdown.

In the Mesh Tools menu (see Figure 3.5), we use Insert Edge Loop and Multi-Cut as ways of adding edges (and therefore faces) to a polygon object, and thereby adding detail. Multi-Cut is a more localized and surgical tool, while Insert Edge Loop tends to add detail to large portions of a polygon object, as, much of the time, it adds a loop of edges that wraps entirely around an object.

The tools that appear under the Mesh Tools → Sculpting Tools menu selection are very useful when trying to make graceful, organic changes to a polygon mesh, and they are fairly new to Maya. There is another sculpting tool available under the Surfaces menu; it has been in Maya longer than the

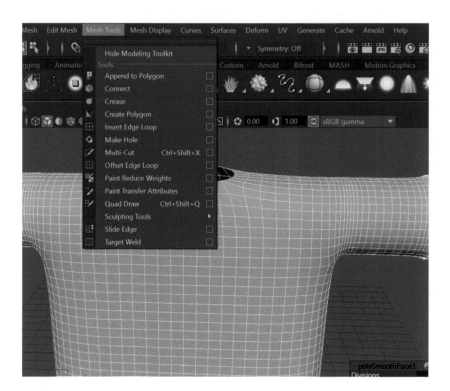

FIGURE 3.5   The Mesh Tools tools.

sculpting tools found under the Mesh Tools dropdown; we will use this tool below. (Note: The Surfaces menu will be of even greater interest when we discuss NURBS modeling.) These tools are a powerful alternative to using more traditional polygon tools to flesh out the details of a polygon object. One of the key reasons is that sculpting tools, as well as a handful of other tools in Maya, allow a polygon mesh to be manipulated in a way in which the impact of tool is strongest at the location of the cursor and gradually decreases as we move away from the cursor. Other tools that behave this way are the Soft Modification Tool (see Modify → Transformation Tools) and the Move tool (also found with the Transformation Tools) with the Soft Select box checked off in its settings.

In recent years, sculpting has become a very popular modeling technique. Two widely used 3D applications that are largely devoted to sculpting have emerged and gained large user bases. They are Pixologic's ZBrush (pixologic.com) and Autodesk's Mudbox (Autodesk.com), with ZBrush by far the more popular app among professional animators. (In fact, the tools that appear in Mesh Tools → Sculpting Tools appear to be inspired by the toolset available in Mudbox, so don't be surprised if Mudbox disappears from the marketplace. With the addition of these tools to Maya, I have pretty much stopped using Mudbox.) Most sculpting applications, including Maya, support touch screens and pressure-sensitive pens; I tend to do my sculpting with Maya on a Microsoft Surface, then move back to my more powerful desktop machine to continue working.

ADDING DETAIL TO A MODEL

For our first example in this chapter, let's take a look at using a polygon tool to add detail to a model. In Figure 3.6, we select the Insert Edge Loop tool. In Figure 3.7, we see the result of using the tool; loops of edges have been added around the ends of both sleeves of the T-shirt. Obviously, we are doing this before smoothing the shirt. To get a feel for the Insert Edge Loop tool, it's best to simply experiment with it. It creates a loop at 90° to an edge that you select. In Figure 3.8, the Extrude tool is being used. We have shift-selected the narrow faces that form a loop around the end of the sleeve, and then extruded all of them simultaneously. In Figure 3.9, we see the result of doing this on both sleeves. We now delete the ends of the sleeve; see Figure 3.10.

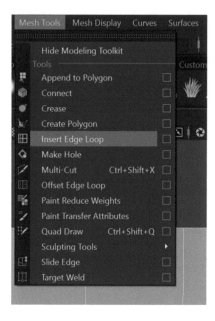

FIGURE 3.6 **Edge loop tool.**

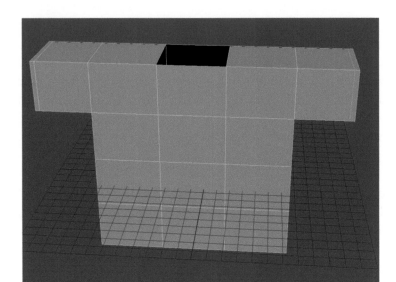

FIGURE 3.7   **Edge loops added.**

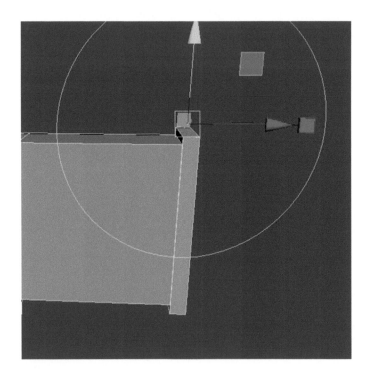

FIGURE 3.8   **Extruded faces.**

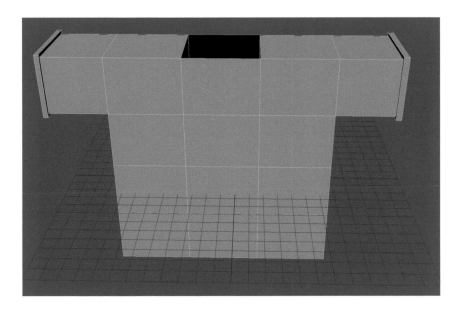

FIGURE 3.9   Seams on T-shirt sleeve.

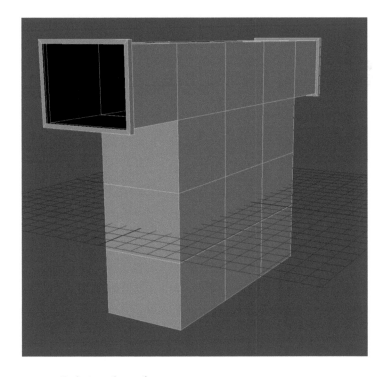

FIGURE 3.10   Deleting sleeve face.

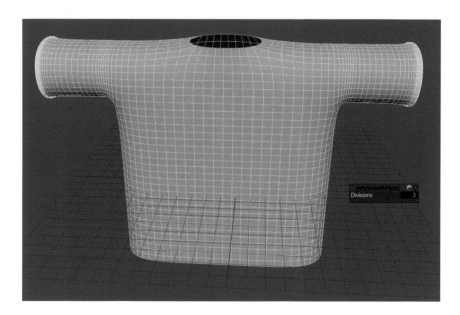

FIGURE 3.11   After three levels of smoothing.

In Figure 3.11, we now add our three levels of smoothing. (Note that Maya often pops up a small box that details the settings of a tool; it gives us a chance to change them within the Viewport. In this case, we see the Divisions setting of the Extrude tool.) Our example shows us how to add a seam to the end of a T-shirt sleeve.

THE IMPORTANCE OF HAVING A PLAN

This is a good time to discuss a critical aspect of modeling with an application like Maya: having a plan before you begin modeling. It's difficult to do this when you are first beginning, but a key sign of modeling maturity is when you can visualize how you will carry out a modeling project before you begin. If you don't plan things carefully, you can easily get to a point where you can go no further. As a simple example, consider what would have happened if we had smoothed our T-shirt before deleting the end faces of the sleeves and the bottom faces of the T-shirt: we would have been left with an extremely tedious job of deleting large numbers of faces. There are things a beginner can do to lessen the impact of finding themselves in a modeling catch-22. First, frequently make numbered versions of your .mb file, like teeshirt1.mb, teeshirt2.mb, and so on, so that you have something to go back to when you find yourself in a bind. Second, remember a few key heuristics: (1) add details, in the form of vertices, edges, and faces, only as you need them; (2) try sketching out on paper the steps you would imagine taking before making your first click in the Maya interface; (3) when you are first learning to model, begin with models that can be created with a handful of steps, such as the examples in this book; and (4) use reference photographs or real-world 3D objects as a guide when you model. By using reference images, you will be far more likely to get proportions right and add the relevant detail to your model. And yes, appropriate detail is critical to making a model look realistic!

USING REFERENCE IMAGES

Let's look at using a reference image and/or object. There's an island about 2000 miles off the coast of Chile called Rapa Nui. It is a Chilean territory, but its indigenous population is Polynesian. It is also known as Easter Island because a European adventurer "discovered" it on an Easter Sunday in the 1700s. On the island, there are several hundred statues, called Moai, that were constructed by inhabitants between 1200 and 1500. The statues represent the ancestors of the inhabitants. Some of them are close to 30 feet in height. Some of them consist only of heads; the Moai statues that have bodies have disproportionately large heads. Figure 3.12 is a photo of a small, carved Moai being held in my hand. The double cylinders on the top of the statue's head represent the topknots traditionally worn by male inhabitants of Rapa Nui; most of the statues do not have these cylinders. Figure 3.13 is a photograph I took of a row of Moai statues on an altar along the coast, facing inland; the Moai that is the second one in from the right has a topknot. Figure 3.14 is a render of the model we're going to make, but we won't worry about the materials on the Moai until Chapter 5.

We're going to make a statue that is a loose reproduction of a Moai. In this case, the main goal of using a reference image (or, in this case, a reference image and a reference miniature) is to make sure we capture the visual spirit of the iconic Moai. What are the

FIGURE 3.12   Wooden Moai miniature.

FIGURE 3.13   Row of Moai statues.

FIGURE 3.14   A render of a Moai.

relative proportions of the statue's facial and bodily features? What are the dominant facial features? These statues are aged. How does this affect the details of their geometry? If we pay attention to questions like this, when the viewer looks at our final model, they'll immediately think of the Moai statues, even if they can't remember where they've seen them.

SMOOTH SHADING IN THE VIEWPORT AND A BOOLEAN OPERATION

Before we jump into our example, it's worth noting that there are two very important radio buttons in the Viewport Settings. They are shown in Figures 3.15 and 3.16; Wireframe and Smooth Shade All on the Shading menu allow us to move back and forth between wireframe and a shaded mode of viewing our developing model.

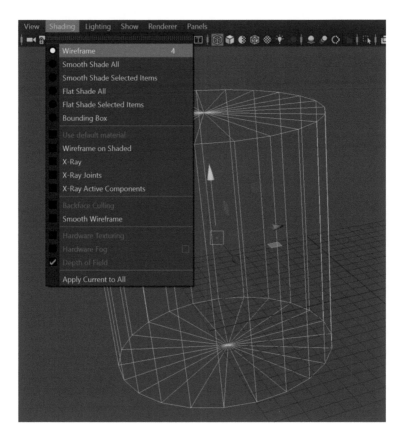

FIGURE 3.15 **Wireframe cylinder.**

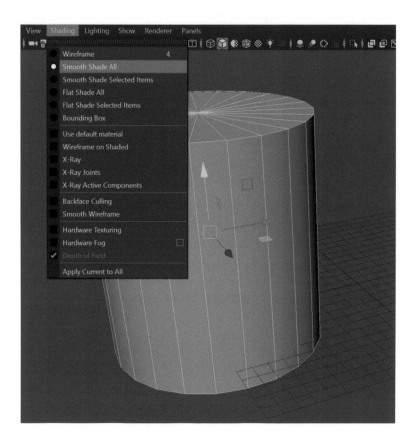

FIGURE 3.16 Smooth Shade mode in Viewport.

USING A BOOLEAN TOOL

Now, let's look at the cylinder in Figure 3.15; its horizontal divisions have been carefully chosen so that two of them will form the nose of the Moai. It's a compromise. We might have preferred to have had about half as many divisions and then we could have used exactly one subdivision for the nose; but we need the cylinder to ultimately be smooth, so we start out with more subdivisions to make it easier to smooth the entire cylinder later.

In Figures 3.17 and 3.18, we see a Boolean subtraction being performed. We line up the cube to encompass a little less than half of the cylinder, then we shift-select the cylinder followed by the cube. We then subtract the cube from the cylinder and get the result seen in Figure 3.18. The remaining half-cylinder does have a back on it. The Boolean subtraction is a very popular operation, and when performed early in the modeling process it

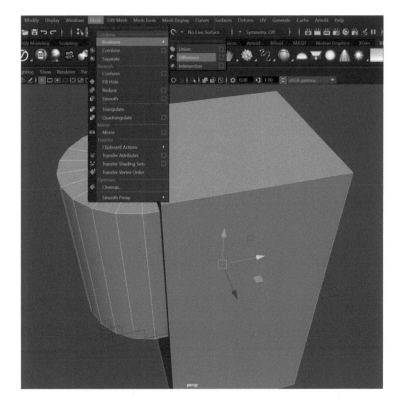

FIGURE 3.17   The Boolean Difference tool.

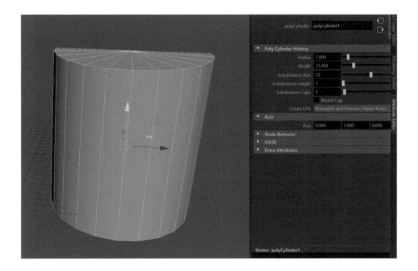

FIGURE 3.18   Result of Boolean Difference Tool.

usually has the desired results, but as stated earlier, it sometimes has a bizarre outcome, such as completely deleting both objects.

PUSHING AND PULLING IN POLYGON MODELING: MAKING THE MOAI'S (HUMAN) FACE

Figure 3.19 shows the Moai after some basic modeling steps have been taken. These include the insertion of some edge loops and some basic push/pull modeling. One distinction is worth noting. Consider the nose of the Moai. Now, look at Figures 3.20 and 3.21. In the first figure, we see a noselike shape being made by first going into Face mode (with a right-click to get the context-sensitive menu that allows us to choose between various modes), then extruding the face. After this, the extruded face was rotated with the rotation tool available at the left side of the Maya interface. In the second figure, we have gone into Vertex mode, shift-selected the two bottom vertices, and then pulled them with the Move tool. The two results are very similar. The difference is that in Figure 3.20, the resulting top of

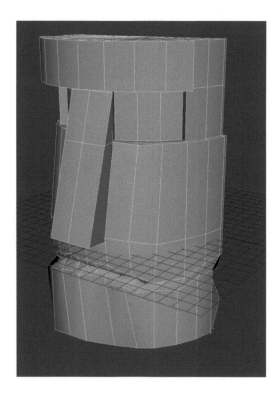

FIGURE 3.19   The Moai head.

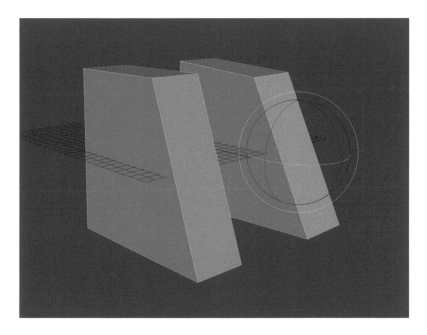

FIGURE 3.20   Extrusion of a face, followed by rotation.

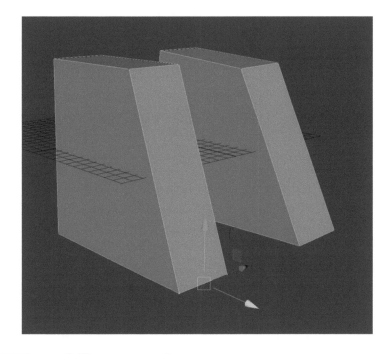

FIGURE 3.21   Pulling on two vertices.

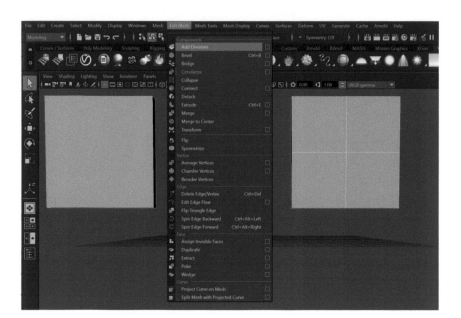

FIGURE 3.22   One level of subdivision.

the nose is not horizontal; in Figure 3.21, it is. Our nose was created using the second technique, but as the top of the nose is hidden by the forehead, it doesn't really matter.

Besides adding edge loops, the only operations used to turn Figure 3.18 into Figure 3.19 were vertex moves, face extrudes, face rotations, and the Add Divisions tool on the Edit Mesh dropdown. This last tool was used to add detail to the mouth. The way it works is shown in Figure 3.22. On the left cube, we have gone into face mode, then applied the tool. Note that if you pull up the settings of the tool, you can choose more than one level of subdivision. On the right of Figure 3.22, we see the result of applying the tool to the face of the cube on the left. After the subdivisions were added, vertices were pushed and pulled to make the mouth have an irregular shape. The reason we are doing this is so that later, the edges of the mouth will appear to be damaged by age.

SMOOTHING, THEN SCULPTING HIS FACE

Only two other things have been done to the Moai head. First, it was Smoothed several levels. This can be seen in Figure 3.23. This was done for the following reason: if an object is smoothed before sculpting, the

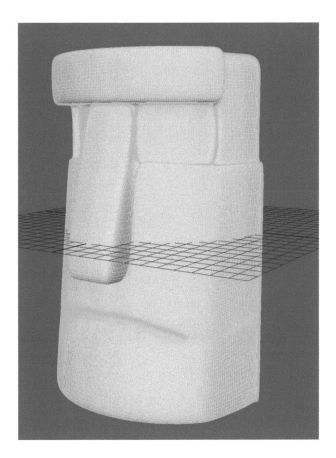

FIGURE 3.23   After some smoothing.

sculpting will be more organic because faces will have been subdivided; the point is that edges are used as bend points when sculpting, so the smaller the faces that border on these edges, the more graceful the sculpting. Second, in order to make it look aged, it has been sculpted by using the tool at: Surfaces → Sculpt Geometry Tool, as in Figure 3.24. The settings for that tool are in the right side of Figure 3.24. Several were adjusted in this example. The Radius(U) is the upper bound of how wide of an area the Sculpt tool will affect. The first two Operation settings control whether the tool makes an inward or outward dent. The Max. displacement setting controls the level of inward or outward dent that occurs when the left mouse button is held down. Figure 3.25 shows the result of using the tool; the longer striations were made by moving the cursor up and down; this is to simulate the aging of the stone artifact.

FIGURE 3.24   The Surface Sculpt tool.

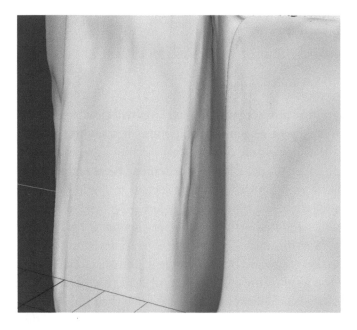

FIGURE 3.25   Results of sculpting with pen.

FIGURE 3.26   Using a pressure-sensitive pen to sculpt.

A Surface Pro was used to do the sculpting, as in Figure 3.26. This replaces the mouse and left-click. Interestingly, the "Max" in Max. displacement is actually a fixed amount unless a pen is used. With a pressure-sensitive pen, the maximum is only reached when full pressure is applied to the pen. Thus, a pressure-sensitive pen makes the sculpting faster by making it unnecessary to frequently stop to change the Max. displacement setting. We will take a closer look at sculpting in Chapter 4, and in particular, we will look at the new sculpting tools in Maya.

USING THE BRIDGE TOOL TO MAKE AN ARCH

We'll do a simple, fun example now. We'll make an archway and use it in a larger model later in this book. In Figure 3.27, two cubes have been made and they have been given 10 subdivisions along the Y axis. The easiest way to do this is to first create one cube of the right size and with the right divisions, then use Edit → Duplicate. In Figure 3.28, we have gone into object mode, shift-selected the two cubes, and used

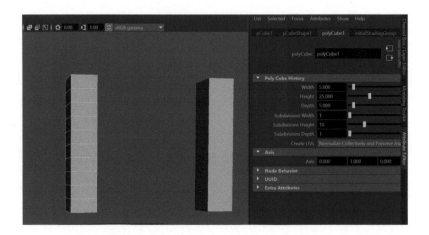

FIGURE 3.27 Two cubes for the archway.

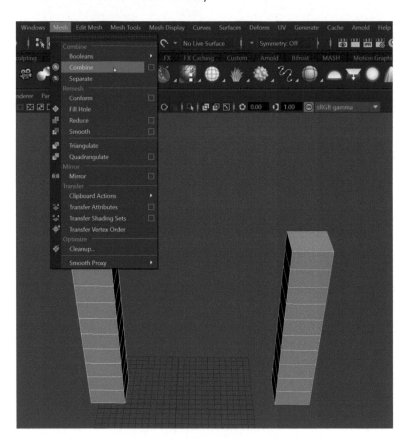

FIGURE 3.28 Combining the cubes into one object.

the tool at Mesh → Combine. The reason we are doing this is that the tool we are about to use to make the arch, the Bridge tool, only works on a single object. Although these two cubes are physically separated, they are now one object in the Maya database; they will move, rotate, and scale together. (Two combined objects can be separated again by selecting the combined object and then using the Separate tool in the Mesh dropdown.) In Figure 3.29, we have selected the right cube, right-clicked, gone into Face mode, then selected the top face; in the figure, we have already done this for the left cube. (If you have trouble going into Face mode by using this context-sensitive menu, you might need to go to Object mode first.) In Figure 3.30, we now use the Bridge tool with the two top faces selected. Note the settings of the radio buttons. Specifically, we must make sure the Smooth path + curve radio button or the Smooth path button is selected. Also, the number of Divisions is set to 20; this is so that we will have stones in the archway that are approximately the right size. By choosing an even number—20—we are assured of having a middle stone at the top of the archway. The result is in Figure 3.31.

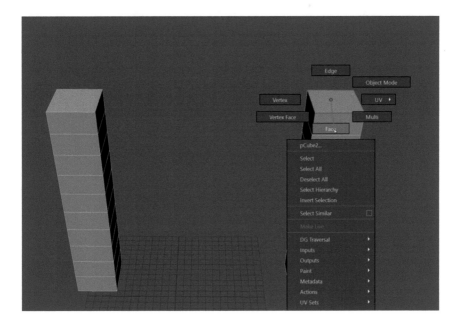

FIGURE 3.29   **Face mode for the two cubes.**

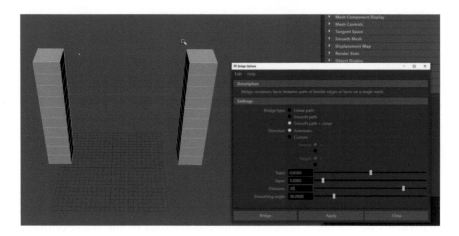

FIGURE 3.30   Settings for the Bridge tool.

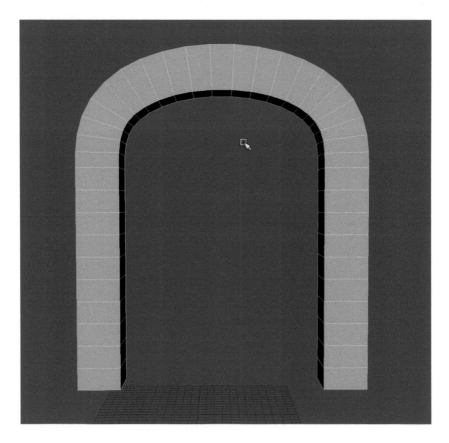

FIGURE 3.31   Result of the Bridge tool.

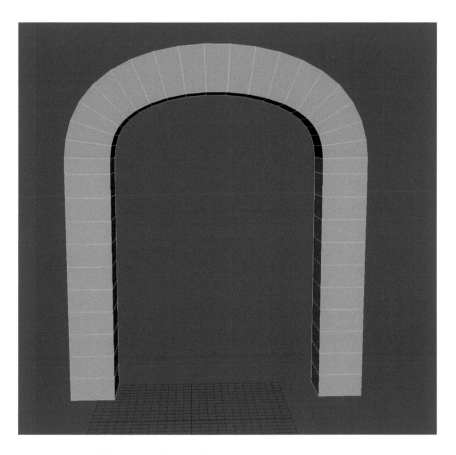

FIGURE 3.32   Selecting in Face mode.

Now, we'll do a couple of things to prep this archway so that it can be used for the orangerie rendering later in this book. First, we go into Face mode, hold down the Shift key, then swipe with the cursor, selecting the two vertical sections of the archway, as in Figure 3.32. When you shift-select the faces, the selection will grab all of the faces around the sides and backs of the two vertical sections. Then, we hit Mesh → Smooth. Finally, we use the Insert Edge Loop tool to add an edge between each stone on the top of the arch. This will be used to model the mortar between the stones. A stone material will be used for the larger faces on the top of the arch; a white mortar material will be used for the narrow faces. The final result is in Figure 3.33.

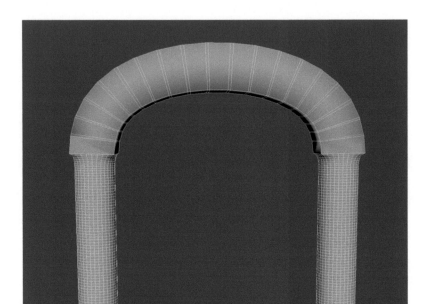

FIGURE 3.33   Smoothing the selected faces and inserting edge loops.

THE IMPORTANCE OF BEING PRECISE

Earlier in this chapter, we discussed the benefits of using a reference image to get the overall geometry, the relative scaling of components, and the details of a model correct. There are some other things that modelers can do to make sure that their work is precise and that they waste as little time as possible making multiple objects match each other in size and scale and line up properly with each other. We can also use one object primitive to help craft another object into a model.

First, we note that by going to Windows → Settings/Preferences → Preferences, we can set the units for a scene, as in Figure 3.34, where we have selected millimeters. This is a good way of making sure that a model built in one scene will import (as an .mb file) into another scene without having to do any rescaling. Just set the units to be identical in the two scenes.

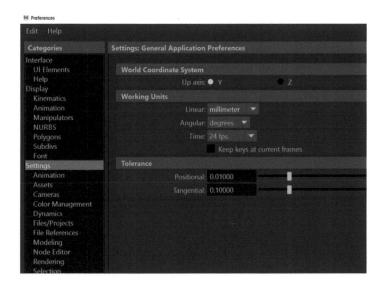

FIGURE 3.34   Selecting units.

Now, consider Figures 3.35 and 3.36. We have created a Pipe primitive and a Cylinder primitive with the same diameter. Having done this, it is now easy to line them up in 3-space, as in Figure 3.37. We can use the center vertex of the cylinder as a guide for extruding interior faces of the pipe; we know to stop the extrusion when we have reached the middle vertex of the cylinder. In this way, we extrude three different faces around the pipe to line up with the exact center of the cylinder; see Figures 3.37 and 3.38. The resulting geometry is in Figure 3.39. Note that we have gone into wireframe mode in Figure 3.38 so that we can spot the center of the cylinder. When we are done, we delete the cylinder. What we are doing is

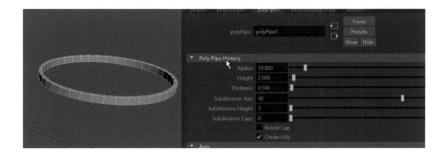

FIGURE 3.35   A Pipe primitive with a precise Radius.

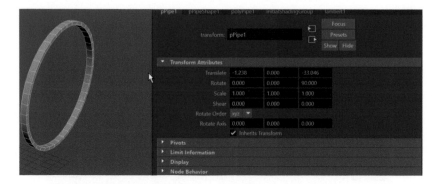

FIGURE 3.36   Rotating the pipe exactly 90°.

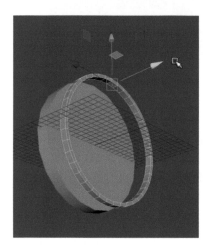

FIGURE 3.37   A Cylinder of the same diameter.

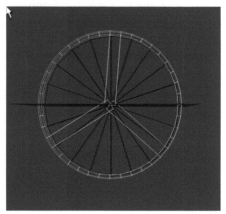

FIGURE 3.38   Extruding to the center.

making an alternative tabletop for the glass table we built earlier. The result is in Figure 3.40. Instead of the glass top being held up by a lip that goes around the table top, the glass is being held up by the three cross-pieces that meet in the center.

Now, consider Figure 3.41. This is the Snap Align Objects tool, and we begin by choosing the 2 Points to 2 Points alignment setting. We then go to the scene, right-click on each cube in turn, and go into Vertex mode. We then shift-select two vertices on each cube. After running the tool, the two sets of two vertices are lined up, as in Figure 3.42. If we also want the faces on the sides of the cubes to line up, we choose the 3 Points to 3

FIGURE 3.39   The resulting model.

FIGURE 3.40   The final table.

Points alignment setting; this gives us the result shown in Figure 3.43. There are a handful of different ways to line up objects with each other and with the axes of the 3D grid. Try going to the Modify dropdown and experimenting with the set of "Align" tools. But, as stated earlier, it's best to avoid alignment problems by not rotating objects in 3-space. Consider the bottom cube in Figure 3.41; most likely, there was never a reason to have it rotated in 3-space in the first place.

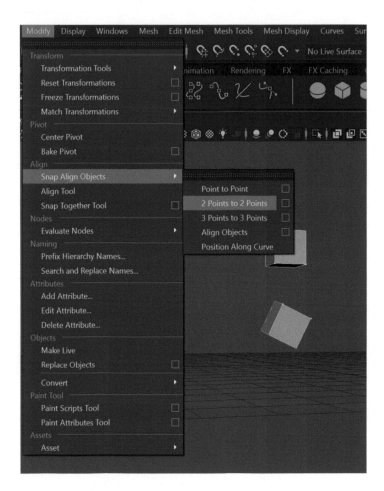

FIGURE 3.41   Snap Align tool with misaligned objects.

FIGURE 3.42   Two-point align.

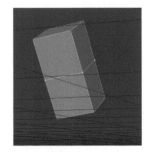

FIGURE 3.43   A three-point line-up.

IMAGE PLANES

We now discuss a nice tool for bringing reference images into a Maya scene. Many people prefer to bring reference images up in a separate application so that the Maya scene doesn't get cluttered. Most modelers, however, find that bringing an image into a scene makes it much easier to closely mimic the dimensions of the object. In Figure 3.44, we select the Free Image Plane tool. In Figure 3.45, we see the empty image plane on the left. At the bottom middle, the Image Plane tool is open, and we select an image from the file system of the computer. To the far right is the Attribute Editor for the Image Plane object; we clicked on the tiny yellow envelope icon to pull up the window at the bottom middle of the figure.

In Figure 3.46, we see what the image plane looks like after the image has been selected. The image plane can be moved around the scene freely, so we can use it as a modeling guide. Often, we create multiple image planes so that we have images of all sides of an object we are modeling. There is a website called the-blueprints.com that sells designs for thousands of items. These can be particularly useful for modeling objects that are engineered,

FIGURE 3.44   **Free image plane tool.**

FIGURE 3.45   Selecting image for image plane.

like cars. Another site is drawingdatabase.com, and their images are free. In Figure 3.47, we see a set of images from the drawingdatabase.com database. The four images in the figure could be separated with an image editor, then placed on four separate image planes. These planes could be positioned appropriately in 3-space, with the developing model in the center of them. It is very important to maintain the relative x/y scale of the images. Thus, the dimensions of the design images should be used to carefully scale the four image planes; if an image is 24 by 12, for example, we make sure that our image plane is twice as wide as it is tall.

FIGURE 3.46   Result of creating image plane.

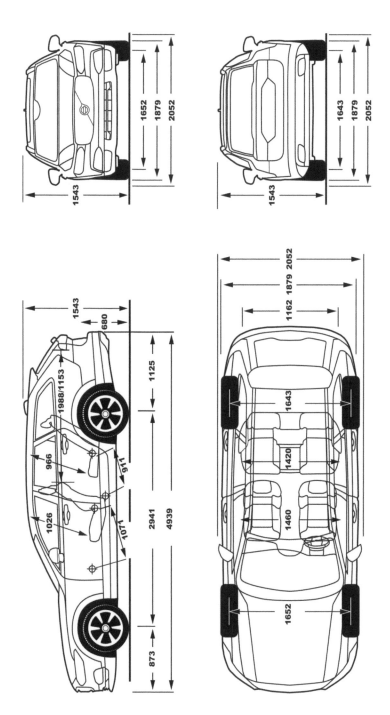

FIGURE 3.47   Blueprint from drawingdatabase.com.

A FINAL EXTRUSION EXAMPLE

Given the importance of the extrusion tool in polygon (and NURBS) modeling, we end with one more extrusion example. In Figure 3.48, we have set up our scene to perform an extrusion. The tall cube is at 90 degrees to the NURBS CV loop. The loop was drawn on the x-z plane in the top-left orthographic view; see Figure 3.49. In Figure 3.50, the cube

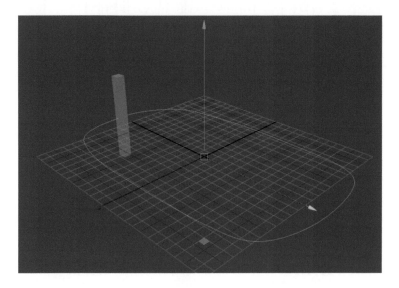

FIGURE 3.48   A perspective view of the setup.

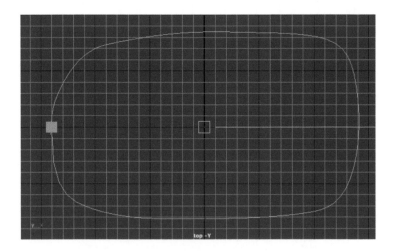

FIGURE 3.49   Setting up the poly extrude tool.

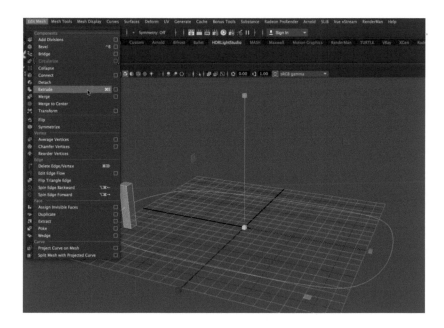

FIGURE 3.50 The Extrude tool.

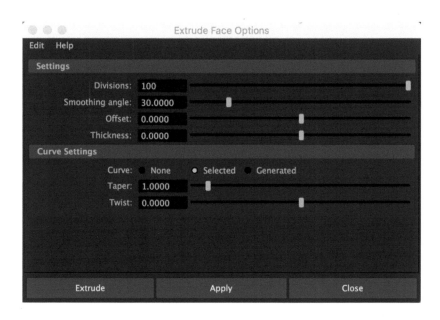

FIGURE 3.51 The Extrude tool settings.

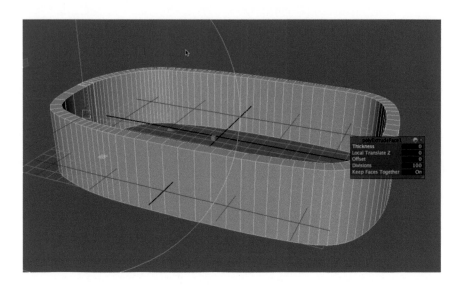

FIGURE 3.52   The resulting extrusion.

has been selected, then the loop shift-selected. Notice that in Figure 3.51, the number of divisions has been set to 100 to make the extrusion smooth. The result is in Figure 3.52. The extrusion tool can thus be used to make things like walls.

CHAPTER 4

Using the New(er) Sculpting Toolset in Maya in a Polygon Modeling Workflow

With examples: *A Moai head, a sun face, a stamped face, and a rock.*

I N RECENT YEARS, SCULPTING tools have become highly popular among 3D modelers. In this chapter, we look at the sculpting tools supported by Maya by stepping through some basic examples. We also begin to look at the use of materials in Maya.

ADVANCED SCULPTING IN MAYA

Sculpting has become an increasingly popular form of modeling. Sculpting, compared to using traditional polygon modeling tools, is in many ways a better intuitive match with the way an artist thinks. One way in which many 3D artists work is to first rough out the basic, overall shape of a model by using a 3D primitive like a sphere or a cube and manipulating it with traditional polygon tools like Boolean operations, extrusion, scaling, and edge loop insertion. Then, if the model needs to have organic aspects to it, such as areas with freeform curves, many modelers may, at this point, turn to using sculpting tools. Sometimes, a modeler will use sculpting tools from the beginning of the modeling process if the model is intrinsically organic. We have looked at a tool that has been in Maya for some time and is used for sculpting. But some years ago, Autodesk bought not just Maya (from Alias) but also a product called Mudbox, which is a dedicated sculpting modeler, often used to craft biped and quadruped characters, especially the faces of characters. Autodesk then began to incrementally move many of the sculpting tools found in Mudbox to Maya. These tools can be found by going to Mesh → Sculpting Tools. These provide a powerful, modern collection of polygon sculpting tools.

By going to Windows → General Editors → Content Browser, then going to the Examples tab and then choosing Modeling and then Sculpting Base Meshes, a number of sculpting starter models can be found. In Figure 4.1, we see the "BasicHead" model. To place the model in a Maya scene, right-click

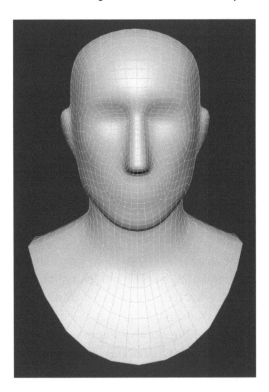

FIGURE 4.1   Basic head from Mudbox.

on the model in the Content Browser window and choose Import. Use the Attribute Editor (which can be pulled up by holding down the Control key and typing "a") to rescale it.

USING A LATTICE DEFORMER TO SET UP THE SCULPTING TASK

In Figure 4.2, the head has been selected and a deformer called Lattice is being created. By going to the Attribute Editor and using the second tab,

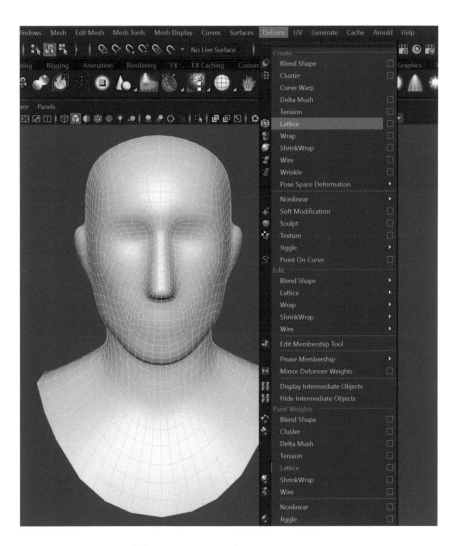

FIGURE 4.2   Lattice deformer to square face.

the number of control lines vertically left to right (S), horizontally (T), and vertically front to back (U) can be adjusted. I have chosen 2, 4, 2 in Figure 4.3. I have also right-clicked, pulled up a context-sensitive menu, and chosen Lattice Point. Now, by pulling on vertices on the Lattice deformer, the head can be deformed. The Lattice deformer is an extremely powerful and general-purpose tool and can be used in a wide variety of situations where a polygon model needs to be asymmetrically rescaled. The Lattice deformer should be added to our core, basic set of key polygon modeling tools that we began pulling together in Chapter 3.

In this example, as seen in Figure 4.4, the forehead and jaw are being pulled outward toward the viewer; the left side is being pulled to the left; the right side is being pulled to the right. This is the beginning stage of turning the Basic Head into a Moai head. In Figure 4.5, a second deformer has been created (with the head selected); it has 7 control lines horizontally (T = 7) and 3 control lines left to right (S = 3). It is being used to pull the

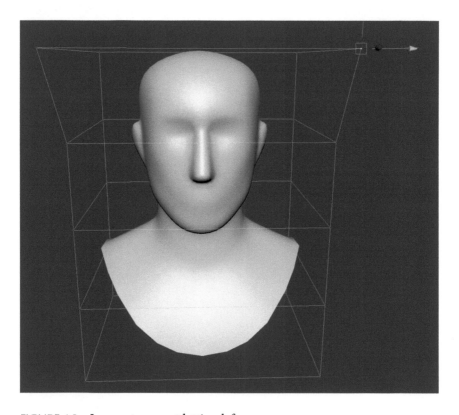

FIGURE 4.3   Low vertex count lattice deformer.

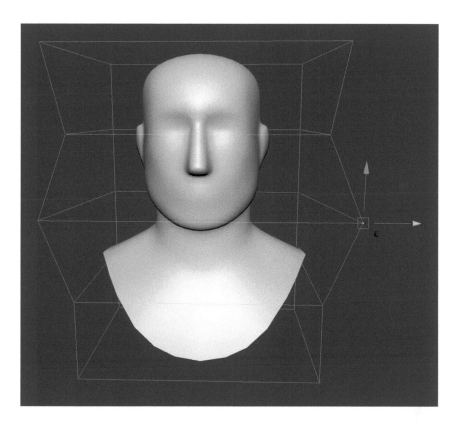

FIGURE 4.4   **After some lattice work.**

center of the jaw outward toward the viewer and upward, and to pull the left and right outside of the jaw further to the sides and outward toward the viewer. This squares the jaw. The forehead has also been pulled downward, and the nose is being squared by pulling outward on it. Notice that the S, T, and U values are chosen to give the correct points for pulling on the model, as well as to control the scope of a pull action. The magic of the Lattice deformer is that pulling on a vertex has a decreasing impact as we move further away from the vertex that is being pulled. Also, the more control lines there are in a given direction (top to bottom, left to right, and front to back), the smaller the area that will be affected when a vertex is pulled on. The reason a second Lattice deformer was used was to further limit the scope of impact of pulling on a given vertex. I often use Lattice deformers in the early stages of sculpting in order to rough out various areas that form the surface of the model.

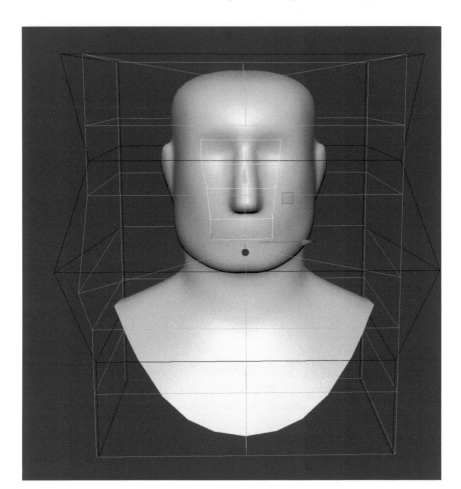

FIGURE 4.5   Squaring jaw and nose with two deformers.

SCULPTING THE MOAI HEAD

In Figure 4.6, we begin sculpting. It is very difficult to teach the sculpting tools because they are used in a freeform fashion. The best approach is to sit down with a base model, like the head, and experiment with the various tools in the Sculpting Tools dropdown. In our example, the Grab tool is being used first. It can be used to pull on an area of the surface of a model, thereby enlarging it in a controlled fashion. (We should note here that there are many tools in Maya that make organic changes to objects, in particular, where the impact of a tool is lessened as we move away from the position of the tool on

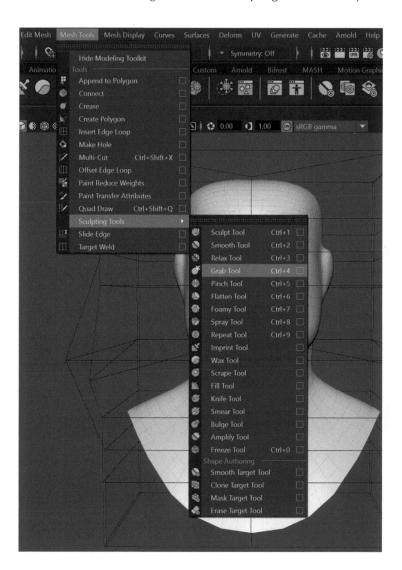

FIGURE 4.6   Sculpting tools—Grab tool.

the object's surface; the Lattice tool and some of the Sculpting Tools share this characteristic. Thus, we cannot cleanly separate the characteristics of the Sculpting Tools from the other tools provided by Maya.) The settings for the Grab tool are the size (the surface area that will be affected by the tool) and the strength (how far a section of the surface will be moved). The settings are in Figure 4.7. In Figure 4.8, the ears have been lengthened and widened.

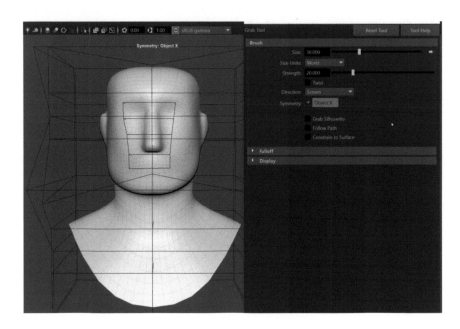

FIGURE 4.7   Size, Strength, and Symmetry settings for Grab tool.

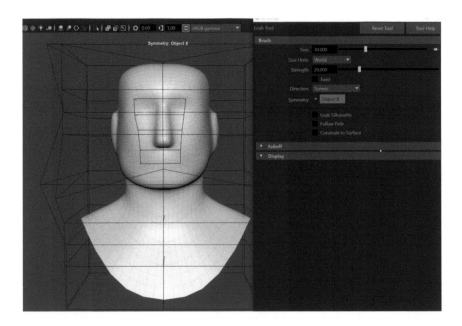

FIGURE 4.8   After using Grab tool on ears.

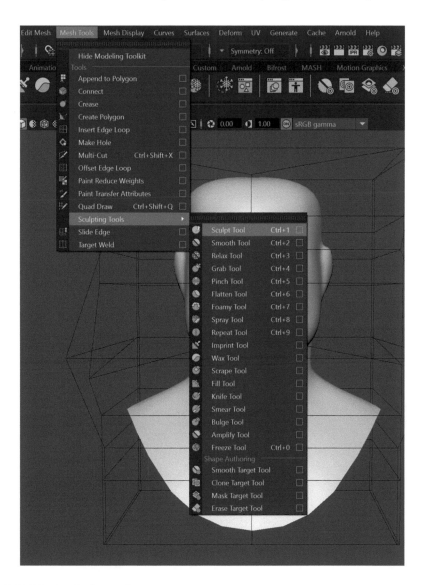

FIGURE 4.9   **Sculpt tool.**

In Figure 4.9, we select the most general purpose of the sculpting tools. It is simply called the Sculpt Tool. After selecting the tool, by right-clicking, a context-sensitive menu appears. In Figure 4.10, we choose Symmetry. Then, in Figure 4.11, the Symmetry Axis is chosen; it is X. The settings of this tool can be seen in Figure 4.12. The Size and the Strength are both set at 10. This tool is then used to give the result seen in Figure 4.12, where

FIGURE 4.10 Symmetry context-sensitive menu for sculpting.

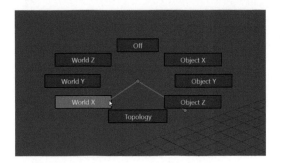

FIGURE 4.11 Choosing symmetry axis.

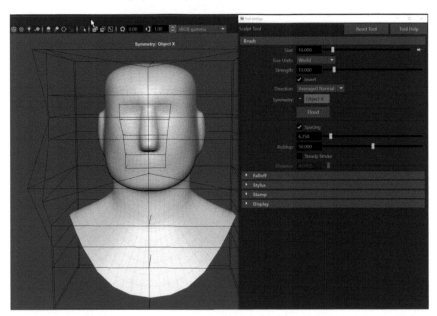

FIGURE 4.12 After sculpting nose.

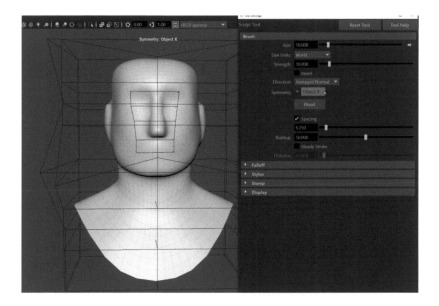

FIGURE 4.13   Inverting Sculpt tool for eyes.

the nose has been symmetrically enlarged. Notice that the Invert box is checked off; this tells the tool to pull outward and not push inward. In Figure 4.13, the box has been unchecked and the eyes have been enlarged inward by using the Sculpt tool.

The Sculpting tools are very forgiving, in that we can often use them to organically fix a problem rather than having to undo some number of steps, as we often find ourselves doing (by using the Control-Z key) with standard polygon tools. In Figure 4.14, we see that the process of enlarging the nose

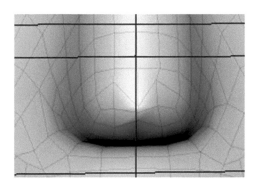

FIGURE 4.14   Problem with nose.

FIGURE 4.15   Smooth tool.

has resulted in the tip of it being pinched. In Figure 4.15, the Smooth Tool is selected. It is applied to the nose, with the result shown in Figure 4.16. Next, in Figure 4.17, the Knife Tool is selected. Its settings are in Figure 4.18. In Figure 4.19, we have used the Knife Tool to create a mouth. Our Moai head is unfinished, but Figure 4.20 shows what it looks like after some work with the Lattice deformer and a few Sculpting tools. We will return to sculpting later in this chapter, but for now, we turn to putting some stone on our Moai.

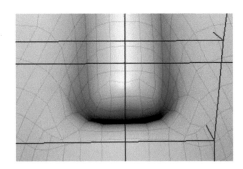

FIGURE 4.16   Fixed nose.

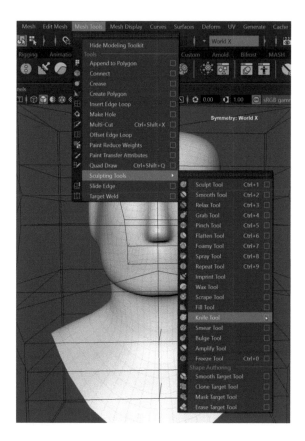

FIGURE 4.17   **Knife tool.**

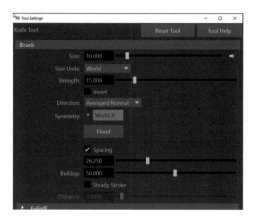

FIGURE 4.18   **Knife settings.**

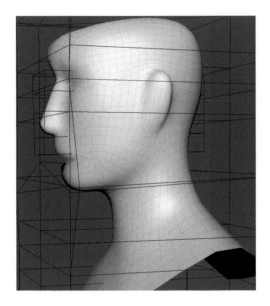

FIGURE 4.19   After making mouth.

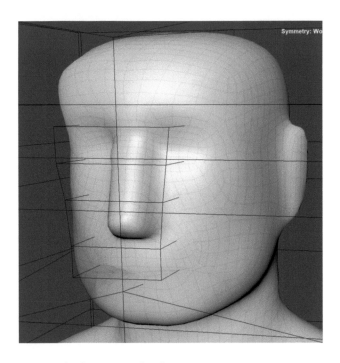

FIGURE 4.20   Roughed-out Moai head.

WORKING WITH AN ARNOLD MATERIAL

With Autodesk's purchase of Arnold, it is gaining popularity in the Maya world. I personally find its materials easier to work with than the materials of mental ray. Working with materials, however, in most rendering engines, is very similar. Although there are many attributes of material objects, there are two main steps to creating a material. First, we decide what the material should look like with respect to color. We might make it blue—or we might make it look like a brick wall. Second, we usually add something to the material to give it more depth. If we don't do this, our material will typically look very flat. For example, if we give our material a red brick color and do nothing else, our model ends up looking like it has a photograph of a brick wall plastered on it. To make that brick wall look more like a real brick wall, we have three choices in Maya: "normal," "bump," and "displacement" maps. We will look at these three techniques more closely and carefully compare them later in this book, but for now, we will choose bump mapping, which results in quicker renders than displacement maps, and yet produces very nice results for the most part.

There are countless materials from the real world that we could imagine mimicking in Maya. Consider every brick wall you have ever seen. Or every rock. Every kind of roof you have ever seen on a house. Or every street surface, cloth, leaf, or wood floor. The most common way of capturing a given material from the real world and turning it into a material inside an app like Maya is to use something called a "seamless texture" image file. It looks a lot like a photograph of something taken at exactly a right angle from the surface of the material. But there is one very major exception: a seamless texture must tile, without leaving any visible seams, left-right and top-bottom. There are many places on the Web where these can be purchased or sometimes downloaded for free. Generally, we need high-definition images, ones that are at least 4000 by 4000 pixels. (One thing to keep in mind, though, is that the more high def the images we use, the longer our render times will be.) By using seamless textures for the colors and bump maps of our materials, we can create virtually limitless numbers of different materials.

Some rendering plug-ins to applications like Maya come with a large number of material "presets" that save us the trouble of finding appropriate seamless textures and bump maps. Arnold for Maya only supplies a small number of presets, in particular, for glass and for a few reflective metals. One nice thing about a preset is that it also specifies all the other attributes of a material, so using a preset saves us a tremendous amount of time. But it is very difficult to create a 3D project without having to work directly with seamless textures.

Our workflow for putting a stone material on our Moai will be as follows. First, we will use a seamless texture image that looks like stone to create a Maya texture that is then applied to the color attribute of the material. In other words, a seamless texture image, one that wraps around top-bottom and left-right, is used to create a Maya texture, and then that texture serves as the color of the material being created. Then, we will use Photoshop to take our stone texture image and create from it a second seamless texture image that is grayscale. This texture image is used to create a second Maya texture, which is then used as the value of the bump map attribute of the material being created. The material is then applied to the object, in this case, our Moai head. Note that the second texture image, because it is grayscale, captures the changes in lightness and darkness in the original stone seamless texture image. The resulting bump map allows us to give our material a deeper sense of relief.

MAYA MATERIALS AND ARNOLD MATERIALS

There are two sets of materials that are of interest for us in Maya, using Arnold. Figures 4.21 and 4.22 show parts of the Hypershade. In Figure 4.21,

FIGURE 4.21   Native Maya materials.

FIGURE 4.22   Arnold materials.

we see legacy materials that have been in Maya for many years and predate the availability of the Arnold plug-in for the Maya interface; of particular interest here are the materials called Blinn, Lambert, Phong, and Phong E, as these work well with Arnold and have very general use when creating Maya projects. Figure 4.22 shows native Arnold materials. We can see from Figure 4.22 that various renderers, like VRay (chaosgroup.com), Maxwell (nextlimit.com), Octane (otoy.com), Redshift (redshift3d.com), Renderman (pixar.com), and Arnold, have their own native materials, and these renderers generally have their own native lights. In Chapter 8, we will see that there are some legacy Maya lights we can use with Arnold, as well as some native Arnold lights that are available with the Arnold plug-in to Maya. When using a renderer that is new to an application (like Arnold is to

Maya), it is better to use materials and lights that are native to the renderer (such as native Arnold materials and lights), rather than using materials and lights that pre-exist in an animation application; generally speaking, such legacy materials and lights only work properly if the application has been adjusted to allow their use with the newer renderer in question. It just happens that there are some legacy materials and lights in Maya that predate Arnold but do indeed work well with Arnold.

AN ARNOLD STANDARD MATERIAL

In Figure 4.23, we are in the Hypershade and are creating an Arnold Standard Surface material. This is the generic Arnold material that you will use over and over to create materials for your models. Remember that a material is part of a large collection of items, some data and some procedural, that is called a shader. Without a shader assigned to it, a model would just be a wireframe vector model with an infinitely thin—and invisible—surface. When light is shined on the surface of an object, it is the properties of the shader that make the object appear in a render. When an object is first created, Maya assigns a shader that contains a Lambert material (that is colored gray) to it. We then create new shaders and replace the default shader that is assigned to our objects. Shaders and materials are objects, as well.

Figure 4.24 is a composite image. On the right is the Attribute Editor for our Arnold material. The cursor shows us clicking on the checkered box to the right of the Color attribute of the material. In response to this click, the window on the left pops up. We use it to create a texture that will be used as the color of the Arnold material. We click on the item that is a bit more than halfway down, called File. We are going to create a file texture, which is a texture that is made from a seamless texture image. The texture is an object in Maya; the seamless texture image is a piece of data, like a JPG or TIFF; and the texture image is assigned to that texture object. It is the texture object that is then assigned as the value of the Color attribute of the Arnold material. The JPG in Figure 4.25 tiles left-right and top-bottom without leaving a seam. It's a little hard to tell because the image is fine grained, but if you look at it carefully, you can see this. The seamless property means that the shader can use this image and tile it however many times are necessary to cover the surface of an object. We can then adjust a large number of attributes of the shader (and the objects that make up the shader) to tailor the look of the rock. Figure 4.26 shows the properties of

FIGURE 4.23   Creating a standard Arnold material.

FIGURE 4.24   Creating a color for the material.

FIGURE 4.25   The seamless stone texture.

FIGURE 4.26   The resolution of the material.

the seamless texture. Note that it is rather low def; it is 1600 by 1600 pixels. The dpi is 96. When we use Photoshop to create a grayscale version of the seamless texture to use as a bump map, we will need these two pieces of information.

BUMP MAPPING AN ARNOLD MATERIAL

Figure 4.27 is another composite image. On the right is the Attribute Editor of the File Texture. We click on the yellow envelope icon and the window on the left pops up. We then locate the seamless texture image in the file system. Importantly, the seamless texture image *must* be placed in the

FIGURE 4.27   Using a seamless texture for the color.

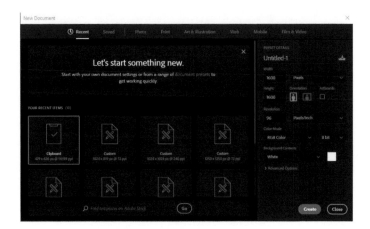

FIGURE 4.28   Creating a Photoshop project.

sourceimages folder *before* we select it. Maya then assigns the image to the File Texture, which has already been assigned as the Color attribute of the material.

Next, we create a Photoshop project—see Figure 4.28—with dimensions 1600 by 1600 with dpi 96. In Figure 4.29, we create a layer that is a Luminosity layer, and in Figure 4.30, we see what happens when we drag our rock seamless texture onto the Luminosity layer; it turns gray. We then

FIGURE 4.29   Creating a Luminosity layer.

FIGURE 4.30   The Luminosity layer as a bump map texture.

write this out as a JPG image and save it in sourceimages. Figure 4.31 is
another composite image. We have gone back to the window on the right
side of Figure 4.24 by selecting the material in the Hypershade (it is under
the Materials tab) and then going to the Attribute Editor. We have found
the Geometry menu, opened it up, and clicked on the checkerboard icon to
the right of the Bump Mapping attribute. This allows us to create another
File texture. We repeat the steps we used to assign the Color attribute of
the material. Only this time, instead of creating a colored File texture, we
create a File texture using the grayscale image. This new File texture is
then used as the Bump Mapping attribute of the material. We do not want

FIGURE 4.31   Assigning the bump map texture to the material.

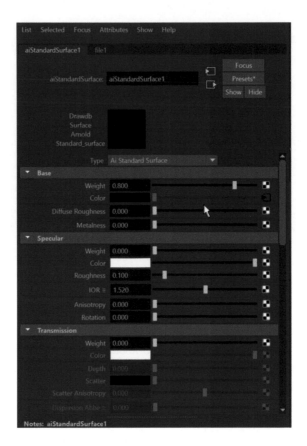

FIGURE 4.32 Lowering reflection of standard Arnold material.

our rock to be reflective like a polished floor, but rather dull, like rock. So, in Figure 4.32, we have made the Specular Weight 0 instead of 1. Specular refers to the highlights or bright spots of the material; by making it 0, we are ensuring that there will be no such highlights. Essentially, these attributes will tell the renderer to make the rock look dull when light hits it.

In Figure 4.33, we are back in the Hypershade and have gone to the Materials tab. We right-click on the Arnold material we just made. (Notice that to the left of the Arnold material is the goldish-brown material that was imported into Maya with the human head, and two materials over is the default Lambert material that Maya assigns to all new objects.) When we right-click, a context-sensitive menu pops up; we choose Assign Material to the Selection. (The human head in the Viewport must be selected when we do this.) Now the rock shader has been assigned to the human head.

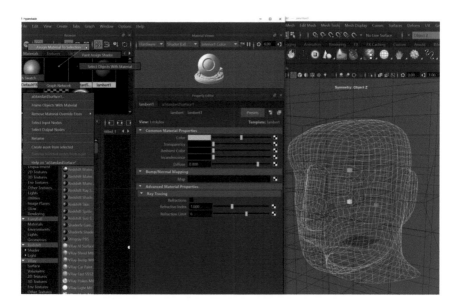

FIGURE 4.33   Assigning the material to the selected object.

TEST RENDERING

The resulting render is in Figure 4.34. Normally, it is necessary to perform numerous single-frame test renders during the process of putting materials on objects. The Viewport gives us a good idea of what wireframes look like, but not what a rendering will look like. This rendering was obtained by going to Windows → Rendering Editors → Render View, which makes the Render View window pop up. We then set the Renderer Selector to Arnold Renderer and click the rectangular white icon on the far top left of the window. This renders the human head with the default light bouncing off the Arnold rock material. The result is—well, terrible.

CHANGING THE TILING OF A MATERIAL

So, what's the problem? The most noticeable thing is that the rock granularity is too large. When a seamless texture image is used for the color and/or bump map of a shader, we usually have to rescale the tiling. In Figure 4.35, we are back in the Hypershade; we right-click, then select Graph Network. The graph in Figure 4.36 appears. Each box in the network is called a "node." The red-outlined box represents the Arnold material. We see that the Shader (the rightmost blue box) consists of the material (with the red outline), which has a color (the "stone-brown-black" file texture) and a bump map (which

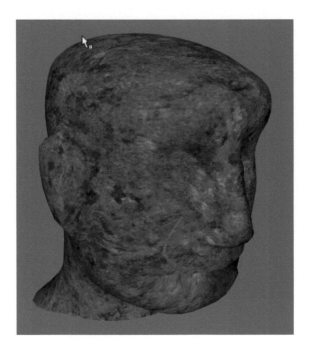

FIGURE 4.34 A rendering of the Moai.

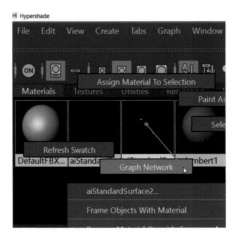

FIGURE 4.35 Pulling up the shader network of the stone material.

uses the grayscale bump map image). Both the color and the bump map have placement nodes. These nodes control tiling of the two seamless textures. In Figure 4.36, we have clicked on the placement node of the Color attribute and changed the tiling by setting the Repeat UV attributes to 4 and 4. We must

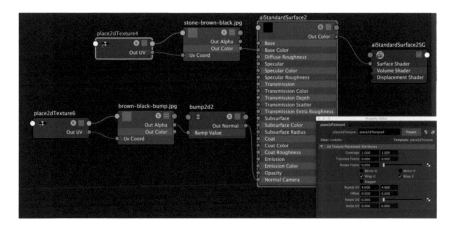

FIGURE 4.36   Selecting the placement node for the color of the stone material.

then click on the placement node for the bump map and set it to 4 and 4 as well. In the case where the bump map image is a grayscale version of the color image, they must be tiled (i.e., "repeated") identically. The resulting render is in Figure 4.37. This looks pretty good now.

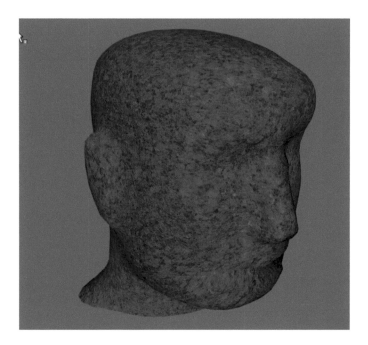

FIGURE 4.37   **A second rendering.**

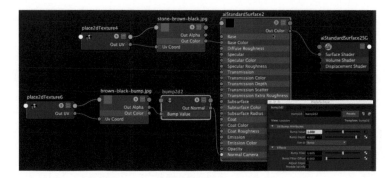

FIGURE 4.38   **Deepening the bump map.**

There are two things we could do to improve this material. One is to further refine the way the color texture and the bump map texture have been laid down; we will not do this here, but we will show this technique in a later example—it involves adjusting the (U, V) grid of the surface of the Moai. Here, we will consider the other problem: the rock doesn't look very textured; it seems smooth. To fix this, we will deepen the bump map. In Figure 4.38, we are back in the Hypershade, and this time, we have clicked on the bump map node itself (the green-outlined box). On the right of the figure is the Attribute Editor of this node. We then change the Bump Depth from 1 to 4. The resulting render is in Figure 4.39.

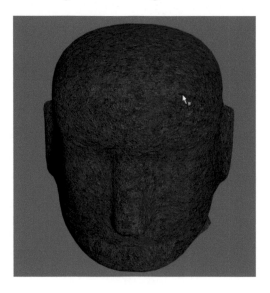

FIGURE 4.39   **A third render of the Moai head.**

ANOTHER POLYGON MODELING AND SCULPTING EXAMPLE

We are going to build a sun face, a popular form of southwestern art. In this example, we will highlight the Stamp tool available in Maya. We start out with a very short polygon cylinder (created from the Create dropdown menu). It has 20 for the value of the Subdivision Axis attribute on the third tab in the Attribute Editor of the cylinder. The Height of the cylinder is .1 and the radius is 2. The Subdivisions Height and Caps are both 1. With the cylinder selected, we have opened the Extrude tool by clicking on the box to the right of the Extrude tool's menu entry in the Main Menu; this reveals the settings of the Extrude tool. They are visible in the right-hand side of Figure 4.40, which is another composite figure.

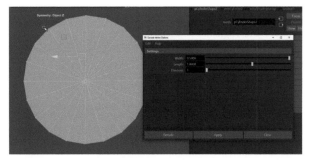

FIGURE 4.40   **Cylinder for sun face.**

With the settings of the tool set as in the figure, we run the tool by hitting Extrude. The result is in Figure 4.41. We then run the Extrude tool again, with the settings shown in Figure 4.42. The result can be seen in Figure 4.43. We then select this object and run the Mesh → Smooth tool. The result is in Figure 4.44.

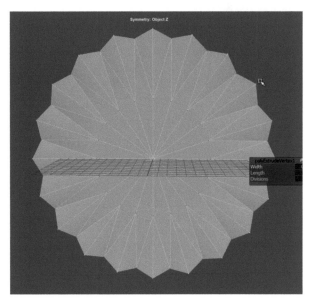

FIGURE 4.41   **Cylinder after extrusion.**

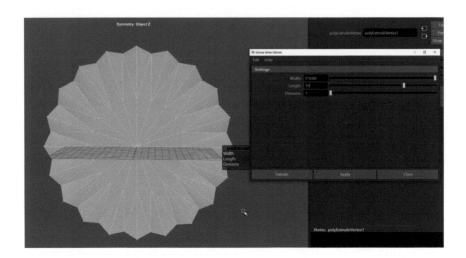

FIGURE 4.42   Setting up second extrusion.

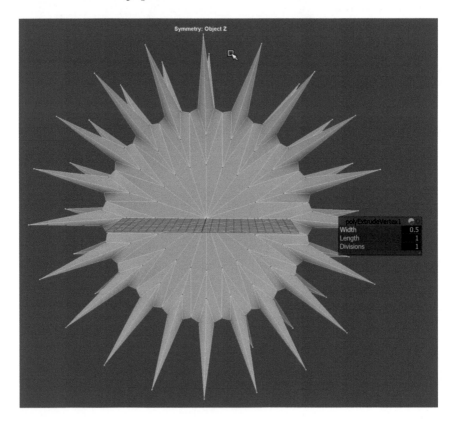

FIGURE 4.43   After second extrusion.

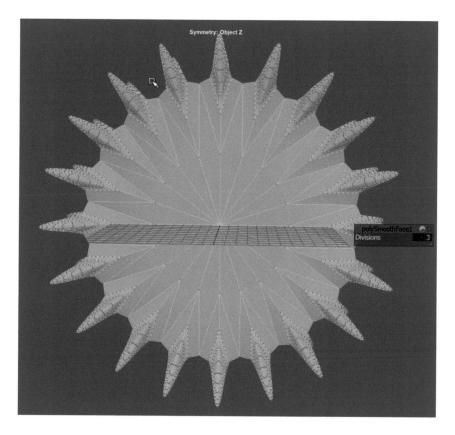

FIGURE 4.44   **After smoothing.**

BOOLEAN DIFFERENCE, THE COMBINE TOOL, AND SMOOTHING

Now, we do a little cleanup. It turns out that there is a back side to our sun face that we do not need, so in Figures 4.45 through 4.46, we select half of the sun face and delete it. Now, we will create a crescent moon by overlapping two very short cylinders (as in Figure 4.47), shift-selecting the one on the left and then the one on the right, and executing Mesh → Booleans → Difference. With all of the Boolean tools (Union, Difference, and Intersection), two things must be kept in mind. First, if two primitives (such as Cubes or Spheres) have been modified significantly since they were created, the Boolean tools might not behave as expected. Two, before Boolean tools are applied, it's a good idea if both primitives involved in the Boolean tool have a similar vertex/edge count.

FIGURE 4.45   Selecting back faces.

Finally, we might wonder why these are called Boolean tools. Boolean algebra involves operations that always result in one of two values, true or false. Equality is a Boolean operator. Two items are either equivalent or not. But addition is not a Boolean operator. Sometimes, we want to perform Boolean mathematics on sets of things. In this case, we are taking sets of objects, performing operations, and then seeing what is in the resulting set. Why do we call this Boolean? Look at it this way. For each item in the two sets, after we perform an operation, we are asking: Is this item in the resulting set? If we perform a Union, then everything in both operand sets is in the resulting set. If we perform a Difference,

FIGURE 4.46 After deleting back faces.

then only what is in the first operand set and not the second set is in the resulting set. If we perform an Intersection, only what is in both operand sets ends up in the resulting set. When we perform Boolean operations in Maya, we take two sets of points or vertices in 3-space, and then we perform a Boolean operation on the two sets. Then we look at the points (or vertices) that were in the original sets and ask: Which points or vertices are in the result and which ones are not? In other words, a Boolean yes/no decision must be made on determining which vertices/points and edges are in the result.

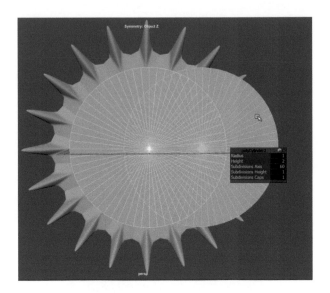

FIGURE 4.47   Setting up Boolean operation with two cylinders.

The moon can be seen in Figure 4.48. Now, we execute the tool Select →
All and then the tool Mesh → Combine. Our sun face is all one object now.
See Figure 4.49. We run Mesh → Smooth once or twice to get what we find
in Figure 4.50. Why once *or* twice? Because every time you run the Smooth

FIGURE 4.48   After Boolean subtraction, then smoothing.

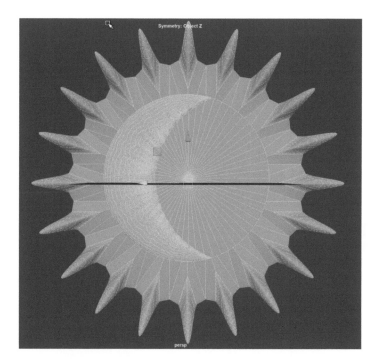

FIGURE 4.49   After adding a cylinder and combining all components.

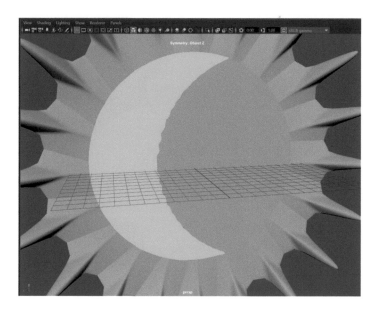

FIGURE 4.50   Smoothed moon for fine-grained imprint.

tool, you create many more polygons in your model. This can very quickly overwhelm the memory of your machine and create a scene that will take a very long time to render. Be careful smoothing!

SPECIALIZED SCULPTING

Now, we're going to do some specialized sculpting. We go back to the Mesh Tools → Sculpting Tools menu and pull up the settings of the Imprint Tool, as in the right half of Figure 4.51. Then we choose Import... We import an image of an eye, and then, in Figure 4.52, we choose Pick Stamp... and select the eye we just imported. Figure 4.53 is another composite figure. On

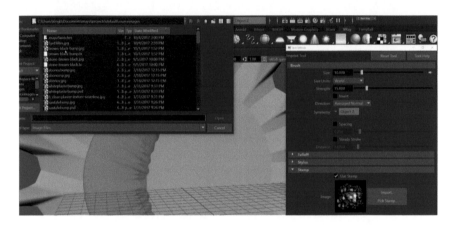

FIGURE 4.51   Selecting eye image for imprint.

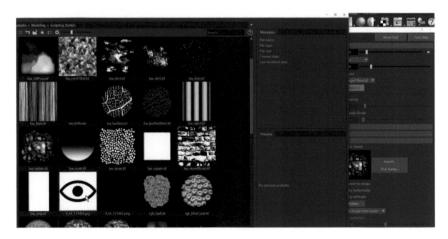

FIGURE 4.52   Eye image for imprint.

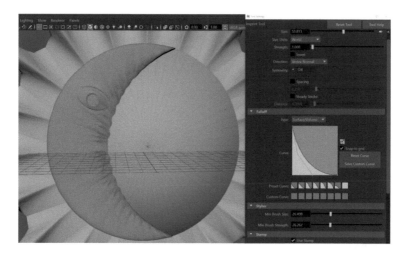

FIGURE 4.53   The imprinted eye.

the right, we have set the settings of the Imprint tool, choosing the Size and Strength, and the Stylus settings. In the left half of the image is the result of imprinting this eye image onto the moon. Figure 4.54 is a composite figure showing us imprinting a nose image. (When choosing an image for the

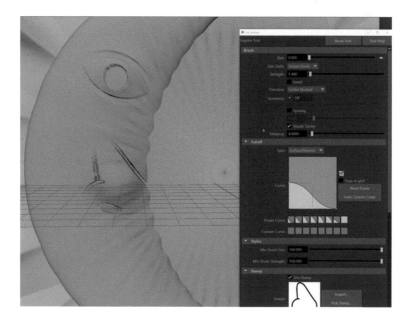

FIGURE 4.54   Imprinted nose.

Imprint tool, if we want a sharp, lined imprint to result, it's best to use an image with very sharp divisions between black and white areas, rather than using a grayscale image where there are many shades of gray.) In Figure 4.55, we have used the Knife Tool to cut a mouth in the moon.

We return to our sun face later in this book and put materials on it.

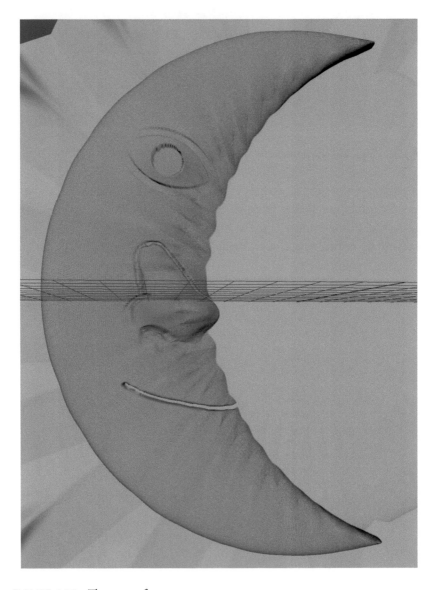

FIGURE 4.55   The moon face.

A STAMPED FACE

In Figure 4.56 is an image that was drawn using a painting tool; see Chapter 5. Note that this is a PNG image (PNG images support transparency), and the white area is actually transparent. Figure 4.57 shows the Imprint tool being used to stamp the human face into the face of a cube. The face of the cube has 300 by 300 subdivisions, so the stamping will be smooth; the more polygon faces, the smoother the edges of the stamp lines. An Arnold default material using the gold metal preset has been applied to the cube. The resulting render in Figure 4.57 was illuminated with an Arnold dome light.

FIGURE 4.56   The stamp for the face.

FIGURE 4.57 The stamped face in gold.

A ROCK

As a quick, final example, Figure 4.58 shows a Sphere that has been rescaled in two dimensions. It has a fairly high face count so that our sculpting will be smooth. The sculpting tool does not add faces to an object, and it uses edges as bend points, so it is necessary for us to have a large number of faces if we want the result to be smooth. We are making a rock. In Figure 4.58, we also see the settings of the Sculpt tool. We will vary whether the Invert box is checked off as we gently sculpt our rock. The result is in Figure 4.59. Next, with the rock selected, we choose UV → Spherical to redraw the uv grid, which has been altered by sculpting the rock. Since it started as a sphere and has only been modestly rescaled, this is a logical automatic uv rewriting selection to try first. It turns out that it will work well. We then use a seamless rock texture as the color of an Arnold standard material

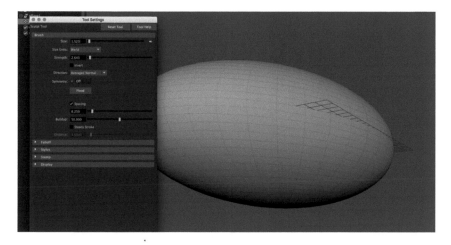

FIGURE 4.58   A rescaled sphere.

(as in Figure 4.60), lower the Specular Weight, and make the Specular Color of the material almost black so that the rock will not have shiny spots. We also give it a bump map value of .2. (We create a grayscale version of the rock texture to use as a bump map.) We apply the material, with the texture tiled 4 by 4, and we get the rock seen in the render of Figure 4.61.

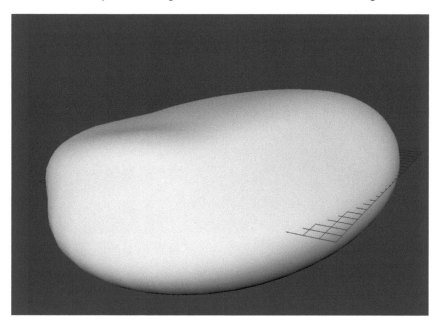

FIGURE 4.59   A sculpted rock.

FIGURE 4.60   **A rock texture.**

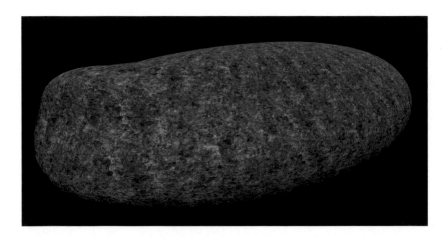

FIGURE 4.61   **A rendered rock.**

CHAPTER 5

Advanced Materials Techniques

Using Arnold Mix Materials and Photoshop

With examples: *Comparing normal/bump/displacement maps, three grunge materials, fixing the uv grid in order to repair a model of the Mona Lisa, repairing the uv grid of the sculpted Moai, painting on a canvas, using a projection texture, and human skin.*

THIS CHAPTER IS DEVOTED to working with materials. The overriding issue is the same as with modeling: given the complex materials systems supported by Maya and the Arnold renderer, what should the beginner focus on? We look at the work that must be done outside of Maya (generally with Photoshop), ways to create materials that will lead to photorealistic renderings, and some tradeoffs between getting some tasks done entirely in Maya or partly in Photoshop.

PREPPING MATERIALS OUTSIDE OF MAYA AND "GRUNGING" MATERIALS

Bad materials can ruin beautiful modeling, so it's worth the time to carefully craft materials. Often, one can't do the entire job of creating materials within Maya. We will use Photoshop to help prep textures that will be used to create materials. There are now a number of full-featured image-editing applications available that are much cheaper than Photoshop. These include OnOne (on1.com), Affinity Photo (affinity. serif.com), and Luminar (skylum.com), all of which run on both Macs and Windows. Another option for Macs is Pixelmator (pixelmator.com). An option for Windows is Corel Paintshop (paintshoppro.com). A free alternative for both Macs and Windows is GIMP (gimp.org). Essentially, we will use a pixel-based (as opposed to vector-based) image editing tool to create a seamlessly tileable image either to be used as the color of a material or to give the material a better sense of depth via a normal, bump, or displacement map. A central focus will be on creating materials that look aged or damaged, and, again, we will use Photoshop to prep a texture in order to create a "grunged" material. We will also look at working entirely within Maya to age or damage a material.

NORMAL VS. BUMP VS. DISPLACEMENT MAPPING

We begin with a comparison of three different techniques for making a material look more natural by increasing its sense of depth. First, there are essentially two ways to create an image that might be used to give a material its color: manipulating a photograph to make it tileable or creating a tileable image with a drawing or painting program. Starting with a photograph-based image is more likely to produce realistic renderings. As noted earlier, if you simply use a seamless texture as the color of a model, it will look like that photograph or drawn/painted image has been laid down on the model. The way to take a seamless image and use it as the basis of a photorealistic material is by manipulating not just the color of the material, but other attributes of the material as well. The goal is to eventually obtain a photorealistic rendering that makes the model in question appear to have much more detailed geometry (i.e., many more faces contributing to its apparent surface relief) than it actually has. We should say upfront, though, that any technique for doing this will increase render time, so, in gaming systems, which require real-time rendering in response to user input, compromises are often made. In real-time rendering, an image might be used to replace substantive surface detail (such as using an image to replace a door or window on a house), without any accompanying technique to make the "fake" detail look more realistic.

Let's step back and consider the relationship between materials and the other aspects of creating a photorealistic rendering from a wireframe model. As noted earlier, every renderer typically comes with its own set of materials, and, in fact, a renderer typically has its own set of lights as well. But two things are shared across most renderer/materials/lighting applications. First, they generally use the same sorts of seamless textures. Second, they use more or less the same techniques for giving a color texture a better sense of depth. These are normal, bump, and displacement mapping.

Using any of these techniques increases render time by adding to the computations that must be performed by the renderer. The decision as to which of these three techniques to use often comes down to a tradeoff between compute time while rendering, the ease of working with the technique, and the quality of the result. Normal mapping is often the quickest to calculate, but sometimes the most difficult to work with. Displacement mapping generally increases render time the most, but often provides the most realistic results. A common compromise between the two is bump mapping; it is quicker to compute than displacement mapping, but in many 3D apps is easier to work with than normal maps. When it comes to the quality of the result, it is difficult to rate normal mapping as better than bump mapping or vice versa. But, in particular with Maya, bump mapping is easier to work with and so often leads to better results on the part of the beginner.

Figure 5.1 shows the creation of an Arnold standard material in the Hypershade. We are going to model an outdoor flooring material. We will use the texture image in Figure 5.2 as the color of our material. Next, we will examine a normal map, then a bump map, then a displacement map being applied to this material. As a lookahead, with respect to render time, the displacement map took longer than the bump map, which took longer than the normal map. In all three cases, the basic attributes of the material, as shown in Figure 5.3, have been set to identical values; these include the Base Weight, Color (whose value is the seamless texture in Figure 5.2), and various Specular attributes, which have been set to give the material a dull look. For the sake of comparison, Figure 5.4 is a render of a face of a cube

FIGURE 5.1   Creating an Arnold standard material.

with this material on it, but with no normal, bump, or displacement map being used.

Figures 5.5 through 5.7 show the creation of a normal map, along with the corresponding render. Figures 5.8 through 5.10 show the creation of a bump map, along with the corresponding render. (Figure 5.11 is the Hypershade graph for the material, without any bump, normal, or displacement map applied.) And Figures 5.12 through 5.14 show the creation of a displacement map, along with the corresponding render.

There is a subtle difference between Figures 5.5 and 5.8, which show the attribute editors of the normal map and the bump map. This has to do with the somewhat unintuitive way in which Arnold supports normal maps in

FIGURE 5.2   A seamless texture.

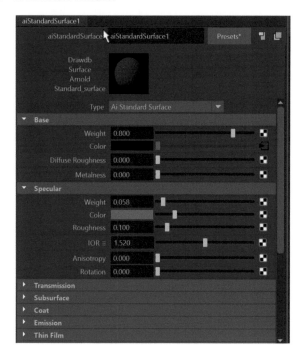

FIGURE 5.3   Using the texture as a color.

FIGURE 5.4   Rendering the colored material.

FIGURE 5.5   Creating a normal map.

FIGURE 5.6 The brick texture transformed to a normal map.

Maya. With an Arnold material, a normal map uses settings that are labeled for bump mapping, except that the Use As attribute is set to Tangent Space Normals. In other words, from a terminology perspective, Arnold considers normal maps to be a kind of bump map.

It is also important to take note of the difference among the images used for normal, bump, and displacement mapping. For our displacement mapping, the original color texture image is used. For the bump map, we use a grayscale image. The normal map, however, looks a bit bizarre, as it is a bluish-purple. Why is this? To answer this, we must consider the difference between these three kinds of maps. This will also, to some extent, explain the differences in render time.

Let's start with bump mapping, as we have discussed it earlier in this book. It is a technique that has been around for a long time. It is essentially

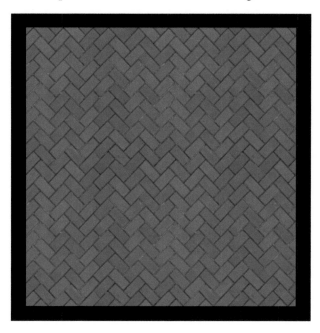

FIGURE 5.7 Rendering the normal mapped material.

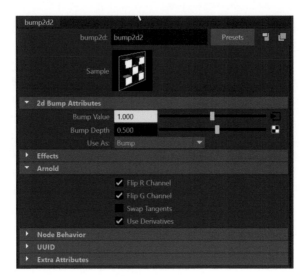

FIGURE 5.8   Creating a bump map.

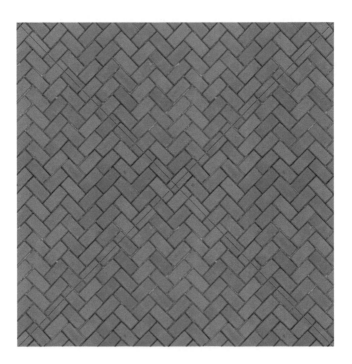

FIGURE 5.9   The brick texture transformed to a bump map.

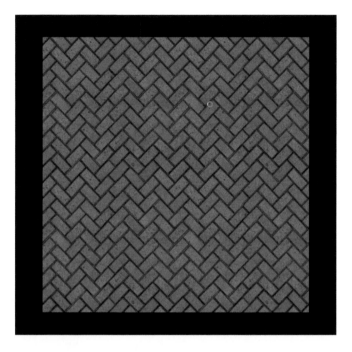

FIGURE 5.10 Rendering the bump-mapped material.

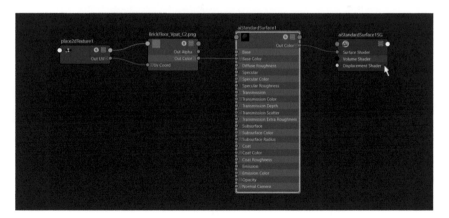

FIGURE 5.11 The Hypershade graph for the colored material.

a way of creating a light effect. It is very simple: a darker area on the bump map grayscale image results in a deeper appearance on the surface of the model, a lighter area on the bump map image results in the appearance of raised geometry. In general, the darker the coloring on the grayscale bump map image, the deeper the geometry of the surface appears to be.

FIGURE 5.12   Assigning a displacement map.

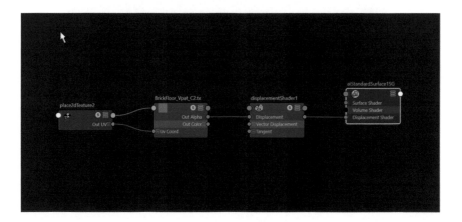

FIGURE 5.13   The Hypershade with the displacement map.

The renderer is using the bump map image as a way of deciding how to accentuate the apparent darkness or lightness of the color of the material; this makes the material appear to have a greater surface relief.

Next, we consider normal maps. This is a newer technique. Again, we are simulating surface detail by using a lighting technique. But in this case, we are using RGB information—which is why the normal map image appears to be somewhere in the blue-to-purple color range. A surface normal is an imaginary line that is at 90 degrees to the orientation of the slope at any given point on the surface of an object. If the surface is completely level, all

FIGURE 5.14   The resulting render with a displacement map.

the normals are parallel. There are actually multiple kinds of normal maps, and they use differing algorithms. In our Arnold example, we are using the most common form, a Tangent Space normal technique. The normal map tells the renderer the apparent angle of light bouncing off a surface, rather than the apparent depth of a point on the surface of the model, as with a bump map. In other words, an RGB value is used to tell the renderer the slope of a face at a given point, that is, how steep the face is. (And, of course, we are only simulating the angle of light reflections and the depth of various areas on the surface of the model.)

Displacement maps are a very different sort of thing. Rather than simulating (or "faking") the detailed texture of the surface of a model, the renderer calculates what the surface would look like if it actually had the detailed surface suggested by the seamless texture. If a point on the surface is dark because it is in shadow, the geometry is altered internally so that it is indeed mathematically indented. It is obvious why this takes so much time to render: we are literally creating more detailed surface geometry at render time, instead of creating it in our model at modeling time. In comparison, bump maps and normal maps only mimic surface detail.

FIGURE 5.15 Bump map versus displacement map.

Notice the extreme difference between the normal, bump, and displacement renders in Figures 5.7, 5.10, and 5.14, respectively. In this case, the bump map looks better than the normal map—but keep in mind that the significant superiority of the bump map is to some extent an artifact of the herringbone brick texture being used and the idiosyncrasies of the Arnold materials and renderer. More significantly, the displacement map looks far better than the other two. It has created a very realistic brick effect, and this is the sort of result that one commonly gets with displacement mapping.

Another example of the difference between bump mapping and displacement mapping can be seen in Figure 5.15. This is a render that was created with mental ray using native mental ray materials. The image is a NURBS curve that has been revolved into a surface using the Revolve tool under the Surfaces dropdown. It has no true surface detail whatsoever: the grooves in the top of the glass, the stem, and the base are all simulated. The glass chalice with a bump map is on the left and the glass chalice with a displacement map is on the right. We see that the displacement map makes it appear that the chalice actually has the grooves cut into it. This makes sense, as the renderer is, in effect, creating this geometry at render time.

Finally, we should point out that there are programs that will generate bump and normal maps from texture images. One that I have used in the past is CrazyBump (crazybump.com).

CREATING TWO "GRUNGE" MATERIALS USING AN ARNOLD MIX MATERIAL

In a very general sense, there are two approaches one might take to "grunging" or aging a material to give a model a neglected look. We could make use of a specialized material that allows us to blend two materials together to create a new material. Or, we could use a single standard material, but also use an image editor to mix two textures together and use the resulting new texture as the color of a material.

Let's consider the first approach: creating a "grunge" material with the Arnold Mix material. In Figure 5.16, we create a Mix material for

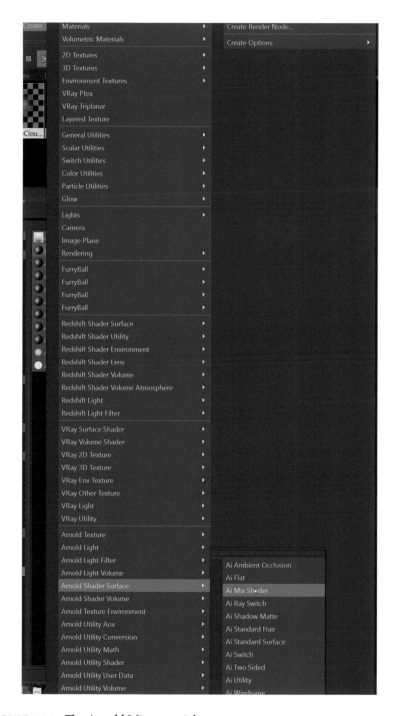

FIGURE 5.16 The Arnold Mix material.

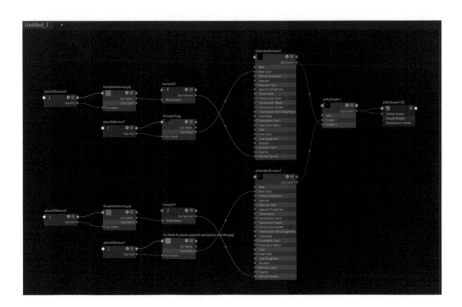

FIGURE 5.17   The two component materials.

the Arnold renderer. A view of this material in the Hypershade appears in Figure 5.17. The way the Mix material works is that we first create the Mix material, then assign two standard materials to it; these standard materials are the two materials we are "mixing." In Figure 5.17, we see that the two participating materials are created by using very different File textures as their colors. The top material uses a black-blue splotchy texture image that can be seen in Figure 5.18. The bottom material uses a powder-blue plaster texture image; it can be seen in Figure 5.19. Our goal is to create a grunged material that looks a lot like the texture in Figure 5.19, but with it appearing damaged or aged by mixing it with a material that looks like Figure 5.18.

Figures 5.19 and 5.20 show us the two textures that are used as the color and the bump map of the bottom material in Figure 5.17. This is a blue plaster material with a corresponding grayscale bump map. Our goal is to create a grunged version of the blue plaster material. So, since we want the resulting Mix material to appear to be an aged plaster, we will use the grayscale bump map image created from the blue plaster texture as the bump map texture for both materials. Indeed, in Figure 5.17, the same bump map is being used for both materials that are being mixed.

FIGURE 5.18   A "grunge" seamless texture.

FIGURE 5.19   A plaster seamless texture.

FIGURE 5.20 The bump map texture.

But what mechanism is used to mix two materials into a new, Mix material? There are two ways to control the mixing in Arnold. One is to use a slider to control the degree to which each material is used in the mixed result. This tends to produce a homogeneous look. But we want to create a material that is blotchy and not homogeneous, as an aged material almost never ages uniformly. So, we will not use the mix slider. In Figure 5.21, we use the second way to mix two materials together using a Mix material: a texture has been assigned as the value of the Mix attribute of the Mix material. It can be seen at the bottom of Figure 5.21. To demonstrate how this works, we start with a checkerboard material. In Figure 5.22, we see that the checkerboard has been assigned two colors: black and white. Importantly, it is the pattern and relative lightness/darkness of the colors in the mix texture, not the actual colors themselves, that control the way the two materials are blended together. Since black and white are at the two extremes of the light-to-dark spectrum, we get a very distinct result, as seen in Figure 5.23.

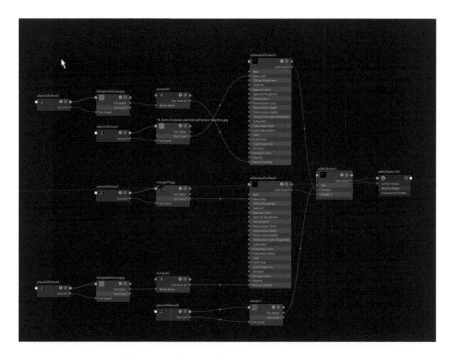

FIGURE 5.21   Using a texture to mix the two materials.

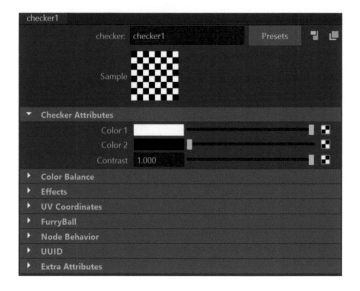

FIGURE 5.22   The mix attributes.

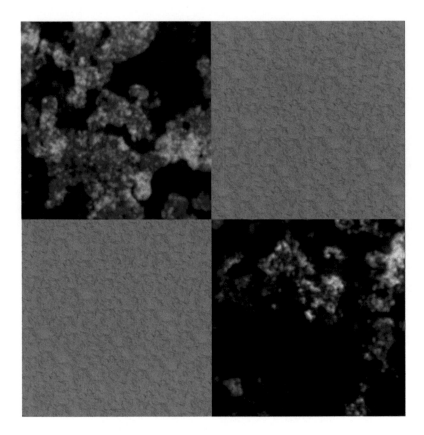

FIGURE 5.23   The resulting Mix material.

Now, we will use this technique to produce a truly grunged material. In Figure 5.24, we use the same two base materials to create the Mix material, the blue plaster and the black-and-green organic-looking material. But this time, as we see in Figure 5.25, we are using the native Noise texture that comes with Maya. The result is in Figure 5.26; we see that the noise material has created a blotchy look, much like plaster that has been aged. As an alternative, we could substitute the native Noise texture for an organic-looking texture to use as the value of the Mix attribute. Specifically, we could replace the Noise texture with the seamless texture shown in Figure 5.27; it is an image of stained or rusty metal. The resulting Mix material is seen in Figure 5.28.

There are a number of attributes in the Noise texture that can be adjusted to change the appearance of the Noise texture; we see these attributes

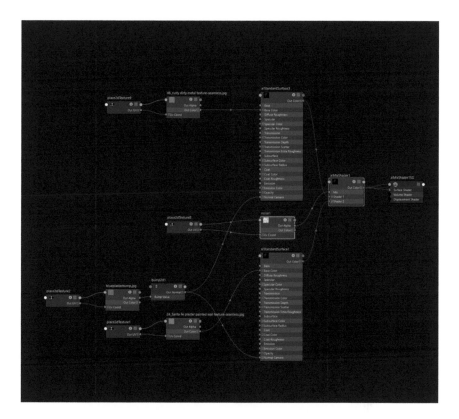

FIGURE 5.24   Using an organic texture pattern as a mixer.

in Figure 5.25. This means that using this native texture, rather than a texture image (such as the one in Figure 5.27), gives us much more control over the appearance of the resulting Mix material. The point is that the texture shown in Figure 5.25 is a *procedural* texture, created by a piece of software, while the texture in Figure 5.27 is a *bitmapped image*. Thus, the Noise texture is in general a superior choice for the Mix attribute value, as we can tailor the Noise texture to vary significantly in its appearance. In general, applications like Maya support two kinds of textures: procedural and image. Most materials are created by using images, but procedural textures, since they are very flexible, can be far more useful as colors, as normal/bump/displacement maps, and as the Mix attribute of an Arnold Mix material. (There are a handful of very useful procedural textures in Maya. The Checker texture is a procedural texture.)

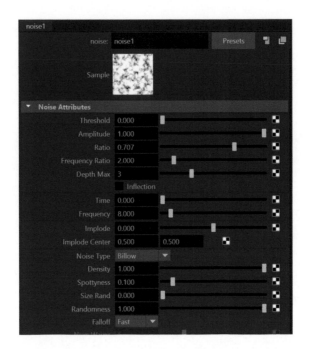

FIGURE 5.25 The mix attributes.

FIGURE 5.26 The resulting alternative mix material.

FIGURE 5.27   The stained seamless texture.

FIGURE 5.28   The alternative resulting Mix material.

CREATING A "GRUNGE" TEXTURE IN PHOTOSHOP AND ASSIGNING IT TO AN ARNOLD MATERIAL

Mix materials in Arnold (and similar materials in other renderers) are a relatively new thing. An older, well-established technique is to use an image editor like Photoshop to create a grunged texture that can be used as the color of a material and (perhaps in an adapted form) as a normal or bump map. Consider Figure 5.29, where we have a moss texture that is 1000 by 1000 pixels. In Figure 5.30, we create a Photoshop project that is 3000 by 3000 pixels—enough to tile the seamless moss texture 3 by 3 times. It is also important that the Photoshop project have the same resolution as the image we are tiling; in this case, 72. We see this tiling in Figures 5.31 and 5.32. At this point, we write the tiled texture out as a PNG and then create a Photoshop project with this PNG. We do this because PNG images contain transparency information, and we are going to want a transparent area around the splotch we are going to make. The reason for tiling it 3 by 3 is to make sure we have a large enough cutout. This is something that one needs to think about when prepping textures in an image editor. When textures are preprocessed before loading them into Maya, they are often tiled in the image editor, and in this case, it's important to do some rough calculations to determine how much tiling is necessary, given the real-world size of the objects we are modeling. In this case, we might conclude that the splotch we are going to put on the wall of a building needs to be of such size as to warrant 3 by 3 tiling.

FIGURE 5.29 An organic "moss" material.

FIGURE 5.30   Creating a Photoshop project for tiling.

FIGURE 5.31   Tiling in Photoshop.

FIGURE 5.32 The tiled moss texture.

To create the cutout, we must verify a couple of important Photoshop settings. First, as in Figure 5.33, the Vector Mask → Reveal All selection must be made. As in Figure 5.34, we verify that Paths on the Window dropdown is checked. Now, we will create a mask that will be used to create the cutout. In Figure 5.35, the Pen tool is selected; in Figure 5.36, the Freeform Pen tool is chosen. This Pen tool is used to draw an irregular, connected shape, as in Figure 5.37 (look closely). Then, at the lower right-hand part of the Photoshop interface, the Mask tool is clicked on, as in Figure 5.38. This creates the cutout. But we don't want a sharp perimeter on our blotch of moss. In Figure 5.39, the Mask is chosen. We see what the cutout looks like in Figure 5.40. With the Mask selected, the Feathering slider is adjusted to get the desired result, as in Figure 5.41. The result is in Figure 5.42. The checkerboard background around the cutout tells us that this part is transparent. This image is written out as a PNG.

The next step is to create a new Photoshop project that is the size of the texture we want to grunge and has the same Resolution as the image we will use as the base layer for the Photoshop project; in this case, it is 240. (The texture image has a resolution of 240.) The project is being created in

FIGURE 5.33   Creating a vector mask.

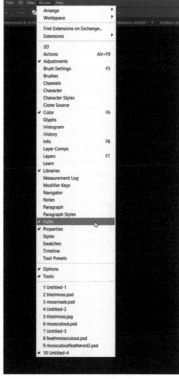

Figure 5.43. This might again require some tiling, depending on the necessary size of this texture. We see in Figures 5.44 and 5.45 that two layers have been initialized, one for the brown tile texture image and the second for the mossy splotch. In Figure 5.46, the cutout, with its surrounding transparent perimeter, is dragged on top of the brown tile texture to create the second layer. We now have a grunged tiled texture to use as the color of an Arnold standard material to put on a floor or wall. In an actual project, we probably would have tiled the brown tile texture some number of times within Photoshop before putting the splotch over it.

FIGURE 5.34   Selecting the path attribute.

FIGURE 5.35   Selecting the Pen tool.

FIGURE 5.36 Selecting the freeform pen tool.

FIGURE 5.37   The drawn mask path.

We'll now make a variation of this same blotched effect. In Figures 5.47 and 5.48, we create a 5 by 5 tiling of our moss texture. In Figure 5.49, we make the Mask for a new cutout, as seen in Figure 5.50. This image is then written out as a PNG. We create a new Photoshop project, using the seamless texture in Figure 5.51 as the base layer. Again, we drag the cutout onto the base layer, as in Figure 5.52. In Figure 5.53, we show the Hypershade window for an Arnold material that uses this new texture as its color. We use the bump map texture for the texture shown in Figure 5.51 as the bump map for the material, since we want the grunged material to look like it is a white plaster that has been stained. The final effect is in Figure 5.54. In this case, the Specular attributes of the material have been left high enough to allow for some white speckling in the green part of the

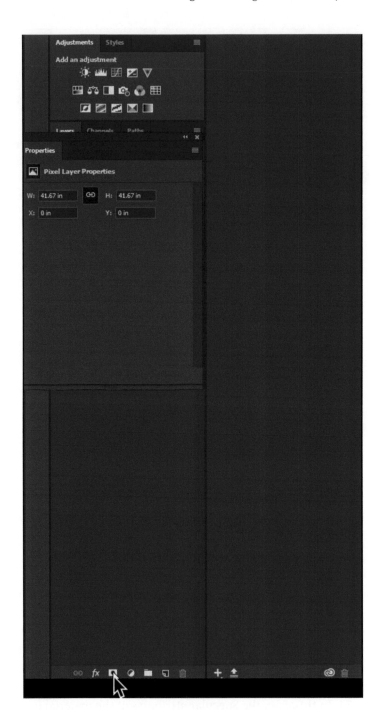

FIGURE 5.38   Creating a mask.

FIGURE 5.39 **Selecting the cutout layer.**

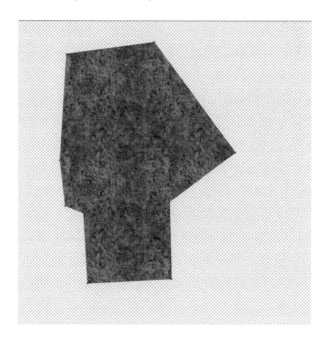

FIGURE 5.40 **The cutout.**

FIGURE 5.41   Adjusting the feathering.

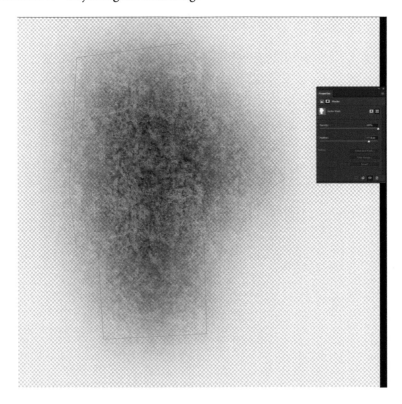

FIGURE 5.42   The resulting fuzzy moss patch.

FIGURE 5.43   Creating a Photoshop project for the layered texture.

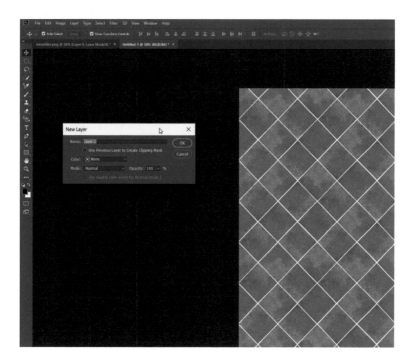

FIGURE 5.44   Creating a second layer.

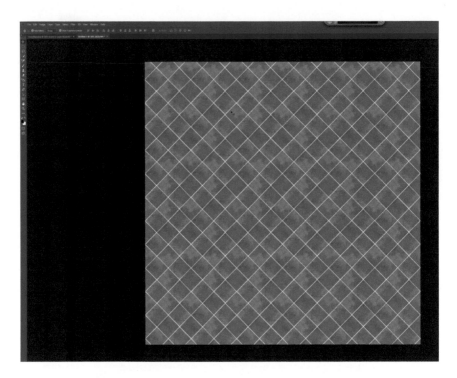

FIGURE 5.45 The base texture.

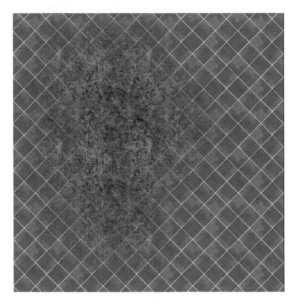

FIGURE 5.46 The layered "grunged" texture.

FIGURE 5.47   Creating a Photoshop project for tiling.

FIGURE 5.48   The tiled texture.

FIGURE 5.49   **The mask layer.**

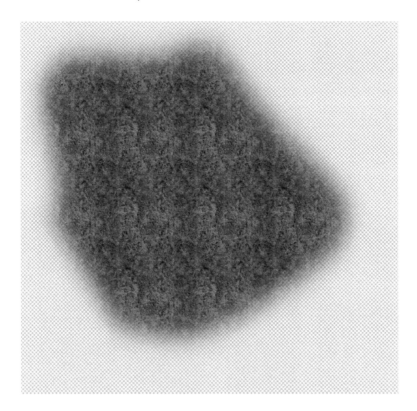

FIGURE 5.50   **The fuzzy mask.**

FIGURE 5.51   The base texture.

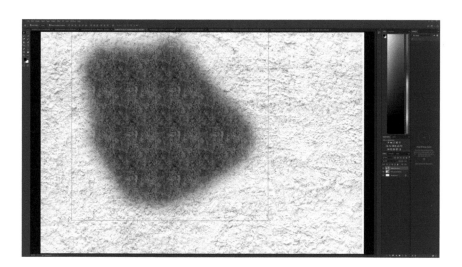

FIGURE 5.52   The layered texture image.

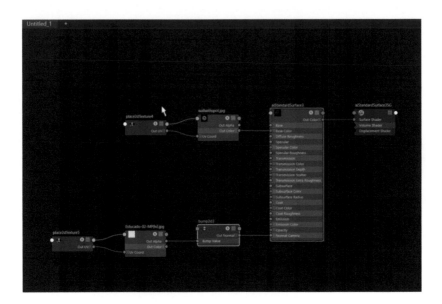

FIGURE 5.53 **A Mix material.**

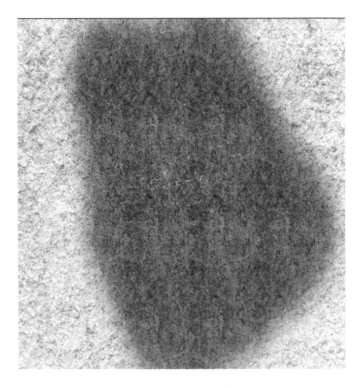

FIGURE 5.54 The resulting Mix material applied.

material; this makes the blotching look a little more realistic, as it simulates some of the underlying white plaster showing through.

CREATING ANOTHER ARNOLD MIX MATERIAL

Now, we do one more quick example using an Arnold Mix material. In Figure 5.55, we have an Arnold Mix material. One of the two components is a material with the moss as its color, but the white plaster as its bump map. The other material is a white plaster with the white plaster bump map. The Noise texture is used as the mixing attribute of the Mix material. The result is in Figure 5.56. The attributes of the Noise texture must be adjusted to get the right look.

USING THE UV EDITOR TO UNWRAP A BOX TEXTURE TO CREATE A "BOX" MATERIAL

We have already discussed the uv grid, the two-dimensional grid on the surface of every Maya object that controls the way materials are laid down. There is a special window available in the Windows dropdown (under Modeling) that gives us access to the UV Editor. The face(s) of any object that is/are selected in the Viewport will be shown in the UV Editor, along with its uv grid. The UV Editor allows us to adjust the uv grid so that we can alter the way a material appears.

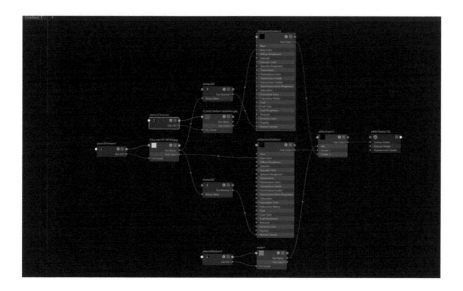

FIGURE 5.55 An Arnold Mix material.

FIGURE 5.56   The resulting Mix material.

In Figure 5.57, we have six Arnold materials that have been created, each with a different color. In Figure 5.58, we see a cube that has a single color on each face, with all six colors being used. With all six faces of the cube selected, we open the UV Editor; the result is in Figure 5.59. In Figure 5.60, we use the Image → UV Snapshot tool to create an image of the uv map of the cube. Figure 5.61 shows the settings for this tool; importantly, we are exporting a PNG image, as it has crucial transparency information. Note that this image does *not* have any colors in it. The image is simply a line drawing, with a transparent background. (It was not really necessary to color the cube in Figure 5.58, as all we need is the uv map, not the colors of the materials.) In Figure 5.62, this image has been imported into an Affinity Photo project and each face has been recolored. (Only this coloring

FIGURE 5.57   Colored materials for the cube.

FIGURE 5.58   The colored box.

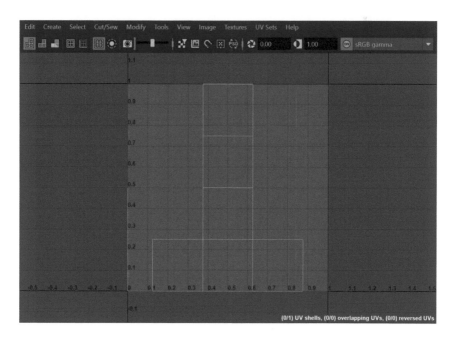

FIGURE 5.59   Unfolding the box.

FIGURE 5.60   Getting a snapshot of the texture.

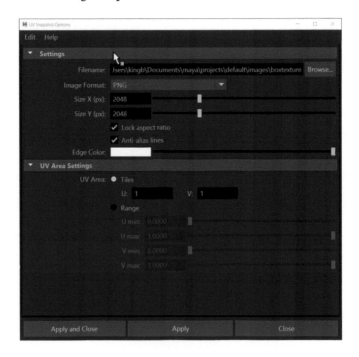

FIGURE 5.61   Exporting the texture as a image.

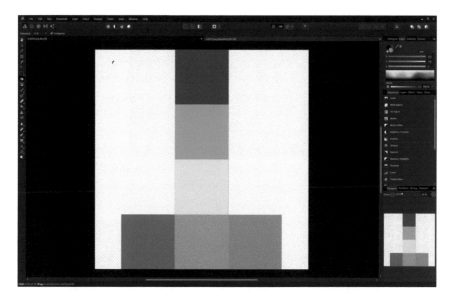

FIGURE 5.62   The unfolded texture image in Affinity Photo.

phase is necessary.) In Figures 5.63 and 5.64, this image is exported as a Photoshop project (because Maya can read Photoshop files).

In Figure 5.65, we have imported this Photoshop image into Maya and used it as the color of a material; this material has been assigned to a new cube. In Figure 5.66, we see the old cube, on the right, with the new cube on the left. Note that the old cube was manually assigned colors, which is

FIGURE 5.63   Creating a Photoshop project of the unfolded texture.

FIGURE 5.64   Selected Photoshop in Affinity Photo.

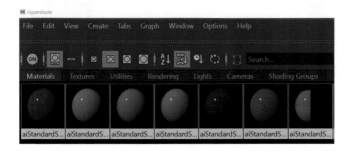

FIGURE 5.65   The resulting Maya material.

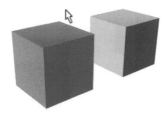

FIGURE 5.66   The box material applied to the cube.

tedious. But the new cube was assigned a single material, in one step; it worked because we created an unfolded cube image, with transparency information around the "T" shape of the unfolded cube as the template for the new texture. Now, we can easily color a cube any time we want.

USING THE UV EDITOR TO FIX A UV GRID

In the next two examples, we look at using the UV Editor to repair the way a material lies down on a model. In Figure 5.67, we have a square plane that

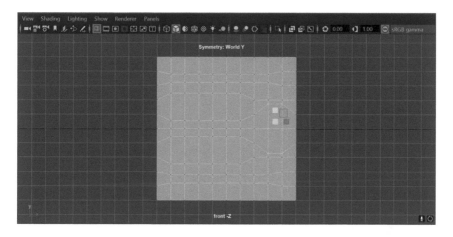

FIGURE 5.67   Messing up the uv grid.

is broken up into a number of faces, and we are looking at its uv grid in the UV Editor. We are also moving vertices around in order to disrupt that grid. There are Move and Scale tools that manipulate the uv grid; they can be accessed by first going into Vertex mode in the UV Editor (with a right-click in the UV Editor), then going to Tools → Move. (You can then switch between the Move and Scale tools by hitting the R and W keys.) Next, in Figure 5.68, the checkerboard texture is used as the color of a material. It is assigned to the plane in the Viewport. The resulting render is in Figure 5.69. In Figure 5.70, with the plane selected, UV → Automatic is chosen. The resulting render is in Figure 5.71.

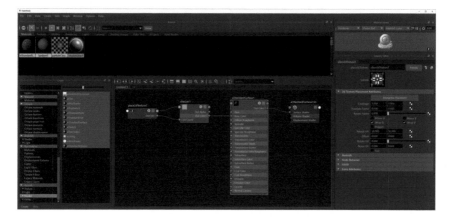

FIGURE 5.68   The Hypershade with the checkerboard material.

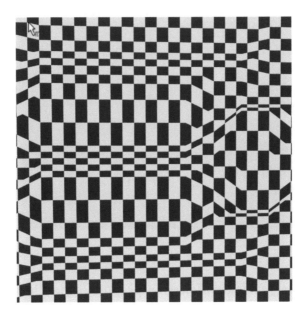

FIGURE 5.69 The resulting box face.

The point is that one often begins a modeling process with regularly shaped Maya solids. These solids are manipulated to create new shapes. Because the initial uv grid is engineered around the original location of vertices in the object, the process of manipulating an object can cause the uv grid to become very irregular. If the model isn't very organic, and in particular, if the model has large, flat sides to it, such as those in an indoor or outdoor architectural model, the Automatic and Planar tools on the UV menu can often transform a messy surface into one with a nice, regular uv grid that allows a material to go on smoothly.

USING THE UV EDITOR TO REFINE THE LAYOUT OF A MATERIAL ON A BOX PAINTING CANVAS

Next, we consider a painting that has been mounted on a canvas with no frame. The goal is to get the painting to wrap around the edges of the canvas properly. The canvas object is a flattened cube with a total of six faces. In Figure 5.72, we have created a material by assigning as its color a JPG of the Mona Lisa. Then, we shift-select the front of the canvas, the top and bottom, and the right- and left-side faces of the canvas object (in the Viewport of the main window) and assign the material to them. Maya then

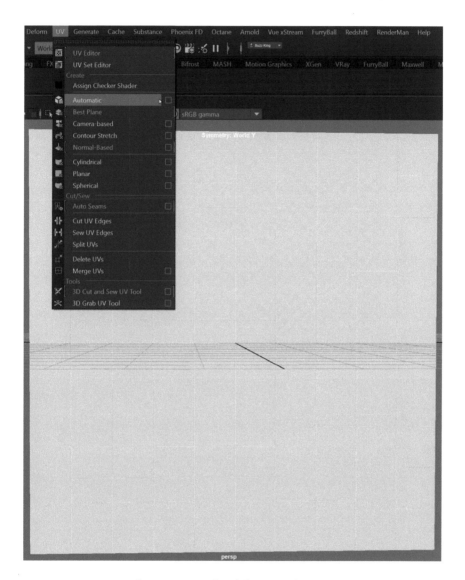

FIGURE 5.70   Using the Automatic fix of the uv grid.

places the Mona Lisa on these five faces of the canvas object. As it turns out, the front of the canvas looks good, but the assignment operation does not properly put the top, bottom, left, and right portions of the Mona Lisa on the corresponding parts of the canvas object. Figure 5.73 shows the breakdown of the uv grid for the canvas object. The large, central square face in the uv grid corresponds to the main portion of the Mona Lisa image,

FIGURE 5.71 The resulting render of the fixed box face.

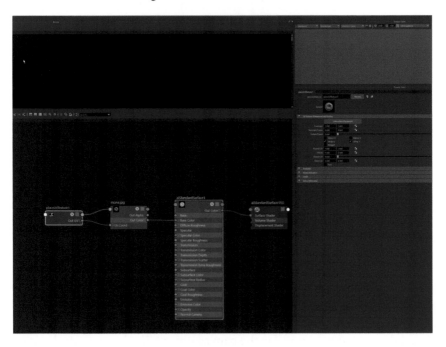

FIGURE 5.72 A cube with a Mona Lisa material on it.

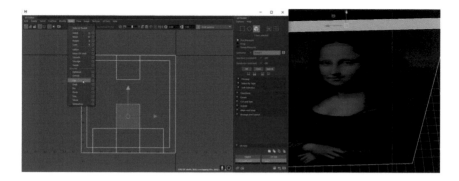

FIGURE 5.73   Cutting a section of the Mona Lisa uv grid.

that is, the large face showing in the right-hand side of Figure 5.73, which is how the canvas object appears in the Viewport. The top, bottom, left, and right faces of the canvas object correspond to elongated areas in the uv grid that are in the top, bottom, left, and right of the uv grid.

In other words, the uv grid corresponds to the canvas object just as we might guess—but with a significant exception. There are four extra faces in the uv grid, and they are square; one of them is highlighted in the left side of Figure 5.73. The problem is that when we select the top face of the canvas object (as in Figure 5.73), it is the orange square in the left side of Figure 5.73 that is highlighted. This means that the top portion of the Mona Lisa is in the wrong place. We want to relocate this square part of the uv grid to the top of the Mona Lisa.

By going to Tools → Cut, we can separate rectangles from the uv grid. We have selected the orange square in the UV Editor and then selected the Move tool. In Figure 5.74, we have then selected the Cut tool; this cuts out a rectangle. It has then been moved with the Move tool to the part of the uv

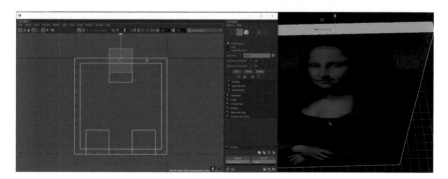

FIGURE 5.74   Moving a section of the uv grid.

FIGURE 5.75   Rescaling the moved uv section.

grid that represents the top face of the canvas cube. The scale tool is used to reshape the cutout cube to match the shape of the top of the canvas cube. Again, the part we cut out and moved represents the uv grid for the top of the Mona Lisa image. The result of the rescaling is in Figure 5.75. We now select the top of the canvas cube in the Viewport (see the right-hand side of Figure 5.76), and, with the appropriate part of the UV Editor grid selected, we assign the material to the selection. We have to repeat this procedure for the bottom, left, and right sides of the Mona Lisa canvas object. In Figure 5.77, we see the result: the five faces of the canvas cube that have the Mona Lisa on them are now correct. Figure 5.78 is a closeup of a render: it shows that the Mona Lisa now wraps around the top of the canvas properly.

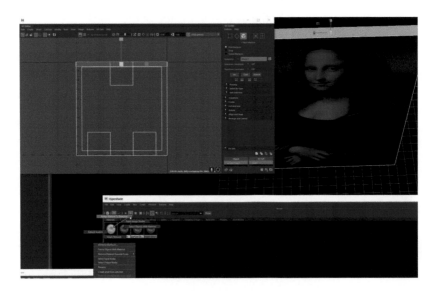

FIGURE 5.76   Assigning the uv section to the top of the box.

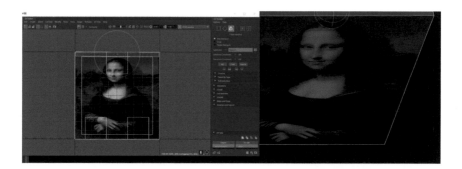

FIGURE 5.77 The resulting render.

FIGURE 5.78 A closeup of the repaired Mona Lisa box.

USING THE UV EDITOR TO FIX A LOCALIZED UV MAP PROBLEM

Figures 5.79 through 5.85 show the Moai created earlier. When it was rendered, I noticed a defect in the top of the left ear; see Figure 5.80

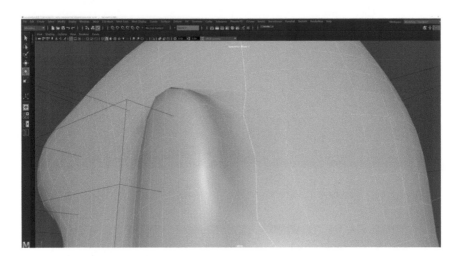

FIGURE 5.79   The Moai's ear.

for the render and note that it is not obvious in the prerendered model in Figure 5.79. This is why it is so important to do test renders before assuming that a model is perfect. Figure 5.81 shows the UV Editor being opened with the Moai head in the Viewport selected. In Figure 5.82, the

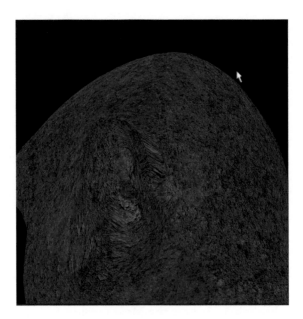

FIGURE 5.80   The rendered ear with a flaw.

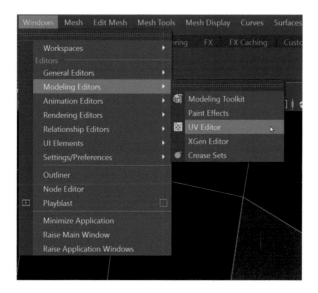

FIGURE 5.81   The uv Editor.

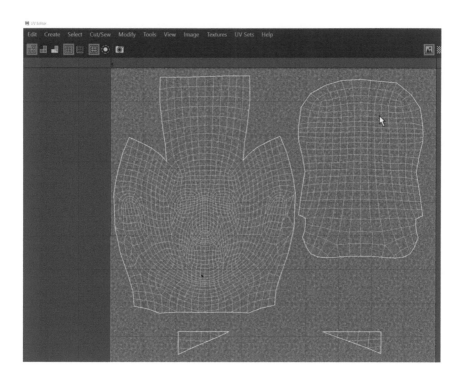

FIGURE 5.82   The uv map of the head.

damaged uv grid can be seen in the center of the uv map, near the right edge of the left section, which shows the uv map for the face. This must have happened while a sculpting tool was being used to form the ear. In Figure 5.83, the Move tool has been used (in Vertex mode) to reposition vertices in order to make the grid more even. With an organic model like a sculpted head, it isn't necessary to be absolutely perfect. The resulting render in Figure 5.84 is much improved. Note that in Figure 5.85, we see a Copy UVs to UV Set tool that can be used to create a new uv map; this allows us to keep multiple uv grids for a single model. This is useful if a model demands different uv mappings for different materials, which is a common need. We might, for example, want to build a different uv map if we were going to make the Moai out of sculpted wood.

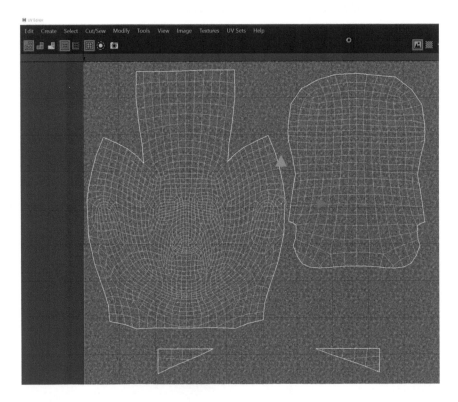

FIGURE 5.83   Repairing the uv grid.

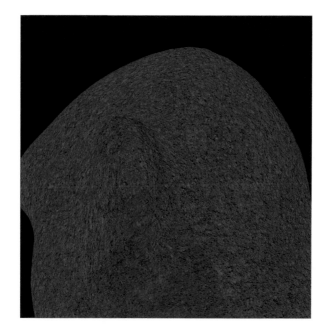

FIGURE 5.84   The new render.

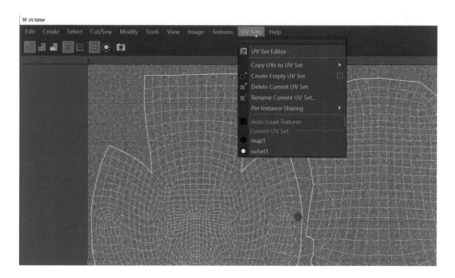

FIGURE 5.85   The repaired uv map.

THE PAINT UTILITY

There is a painting engine in Maya that is called Artisan; it is the same engine that was used to implement the new(er) sculpting tools that we looked at earlier in this book. The painting tools allow you to paint on a canvas, on a surface in a scene, or in the scene itself. There are also effects within the Windows → General Editors → Content Browser → Paint Effects that can be painted into a scene as 3D objects. These include various plant and tree objects. They appear to be polygon geometry, but they are not a form of polygon geometry that Maya can render; to actually render them, they must be converted to standard polygon geometry by going to Modify → Convert → Paint Effects to Polygons. In the same place in the Content Browser are a number of sample paint brushes, like airbrushes, pencils, and pastels. These are used for creating 2D paint effects. In this example, we look at using the canvas to paint.

In Figure 5.86, we open the Paint Effects toolset from within the Viewport. With the toolset opened, we open an image in Figure 5.87,

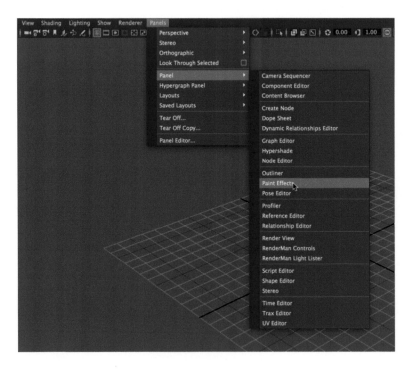

FIGURE 5.86   Opening the paint canvas.

read in a seamless texture from the computer's file system, and place it on the canvas. It is a yellow plaster pattern; see Figure 5.88. In Figure 5.89, we select a brush. We've left out a few steps, but the painted result appears in Figure 5.90. Earlier in this chapter, we looked at using Photoshop to create a layered texture. Now we see that there is another option: we can paint directly on a texture on the Canvas, then write it back out and use it as a new texture—one that appears to have had graffiti painted on it.

FIGURE 5.87   Opening an image file.

FIGURE 5.88   The tileable texture on the canvas.

FIGURE 5.89 Selecting a brush.

FIGURE 5.90 The grafittied texture.

A NOTE ON TEXTURES

There are three different ways that Maya can apply a texture to the surface of an object. As a reminder, we first create a material. Then, often, a texture is used as the color and/or bump/normal/displacement map of the material. And often, the value of the texture is a seamless texture file. In this book, when we create textures to be used in the definition of materials, we are assuming that these are "normal" textures, which is one of the three application methods. In Figure 5.91, we see that there is a radio button that can be set, and it will then control what kind of application method will be associated with the next texture object when it is created. An alternative is to make the decision by right-clicking (instead of left-clicking) when the texture is created (see Figure 5.92); this ignores the radio button setting. To clarify one aspect of the terminology in these images: 2D Normal in Figure 5.91 is the same as Create texture in Figure 5.92. Perhaps the reason for the lack of the word "normal" in Figure 5.92 is that normal is the default—and the textures we create in this book are all normal textures. (The only exception is the brief example immediately below.)

Stencil is a special case, and we will not be covering it in this book. It refers to a technique whereby a mask is used to remove part of a texture; this allows us to control what part of the texture is visible on an object. More relevant to this book is the distinction between normal and projection textures. When normal is chosen, the texture is applied to the uv space of the surface of the object. When projection is chosen, instead of the uv grid of the object's surface controlling how the texture is laid down on the object, the user can manually resize the texture when laying it down. In other words, with a normal texture, if we want to change how the texture appears on the object, we change the uv grid on the object. But if we use a projection texture, we alter the way the texture is laid down by manipulating the texture itself.

Figure 5.93 shows the graph (in the Hypershade) of a material that has a projection texture assigned to it. Notice the extra node: projection1. In Figure 5.94, this material has been applied to the surface that is shown in the image and the Interactive Placement button has been hit. This causes the square icon for the interactive rescaling tool at the left of the image to pop up. It can be used to manually rescale the texture. Figure 5.95 is a render with the rescaling tool set as is shown in Figure 5.94. In Figure 5.96, the tiling has been enlarged using the Scale tool; the resulting render is in Figure 5.97. Again, the tiling has been enlarged by expanding the tool so

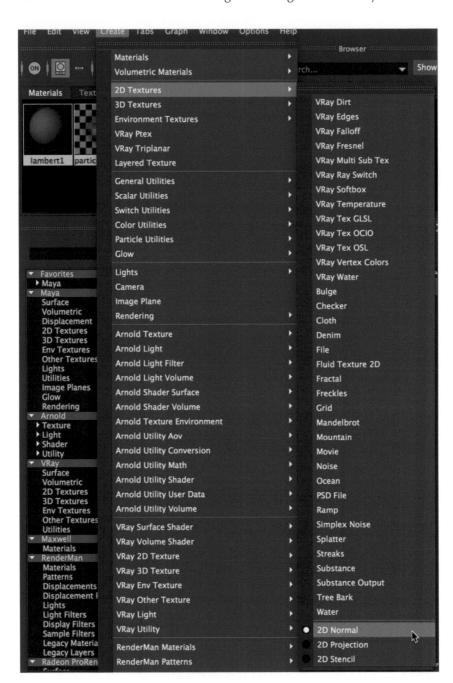

FIGURE 5.91 Three ways to apply a texture.

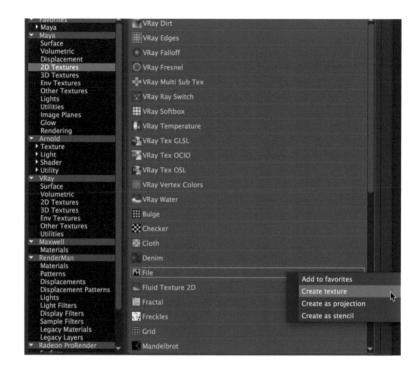

FIGURE 5.92   Another way to choose the application method.

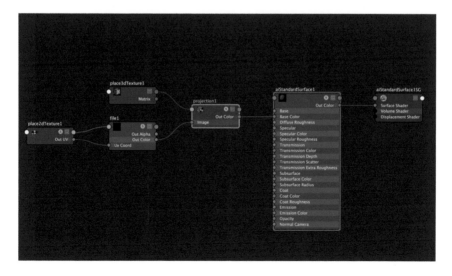

FIGURE 5.93   A projection texture as the color of a material.

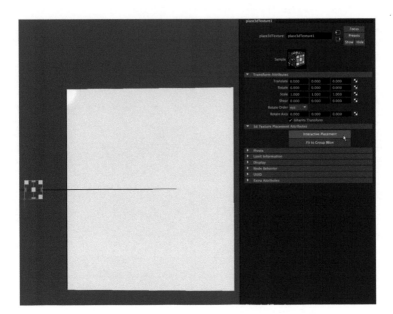

FIGURE 5.94   Rescaling a projection texture.

FIGURE 5.95   A render before rescaling the texture.

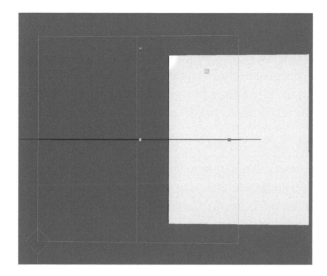

FIGURE 5.96   **Rescaling the texture.**

FIGURE 5.97   **A render after rescaling the texture.**

that the texture is applied only one time, instead of being tiled many times top to bottom and left to right. Using a projection texture makes sense when a surface is flat and rectangular, like the wall of a house; a projection texture does not give us the flexibility we have when manipulating normal textures with the UV Editor, but it does give us a very quick and intuitive way to rescale textures on simple surfaces.

SKIN: AN ARNOLD STANDARD MATERIAL PRESET

One of the presets that can be selected for the Arnold Standard material is Skin. Its attributes are shown in Figure 5.98. In Figure 5.99, we see the human head model from the Content Browser. It has had the skin preset material assigned to it. The render almost has a glow to it. What we see in this material has to do with a few of its attributes, in particular, its Specular and Subsurface attributes. This second group of attributes is used to model real-world substances that trap light, like skin and wax. Rather than all of the light bouncing off the object, some of it is caught below the surface; this is referred to as "subsurface scattering" or SSS. The weight under Subsurface is set to 1, meaning that the SSS value is high.

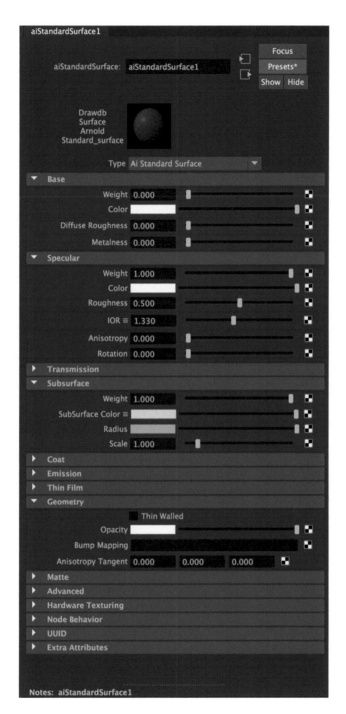

FIGURE 5.98   The Skin preset for Arnold.

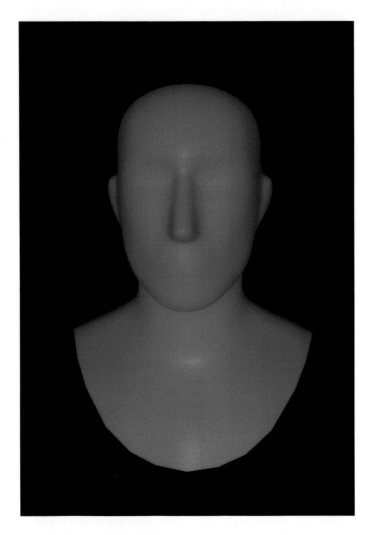

FIGURE 5.99 **Arnold skin rendered.**

CHAPTER 6

Advanced Design Techniques

Modeling, Composition, Lighting, and Materials

With examples: *A saguaro cactus, a church, a courtyard, cloth curtains, a flag, a balcony box, a pool room, a mailbox, a cabana, a new way to create our glass table, repair tools, Vray hair, Maya fur, and Modo subdivision.*

T HIS CHAPTER INTRODUCES A number of topics that the beginner should master in order to get the most out of Maya. We use specific examples to illustrate both low-level and high-level design decisions. These include scene-level composition, the contrasting ways that polygon and NURBS modeling can be used, and the importance of proper lighting and shadows. We also consider the dramatic impact that the choice of materials has on the overall look and feel of a scene.

MODELING A CACTUS WITH "BOX" MODELING AND WITH NURBS

There are many different ways to construct a given model. A common question (with Maya) is whether to use polygon or NURBS modeling. The simple answer is that it is up to the modeler. Whatever will produce the model you want is the way you should do it, and, of course, it's fine to mix polygon and NURBS modeling in the same model or scene. But it is important to remember that the two forms of modeling are extremely different, and you don't want to be simulating polygon modeling while doing NURBS modeling, or vice versa. In our first example in this chapter, we look at two ways to model a saguaro cactus. First, we use polygon modeling, and then we use NURBS modeling. In each case, we try to use an approach that highlights the given modeling paradigm in a natural way. For polygon modeling, we take a "box" modeling approach, which is essentially a technique whereby we start with one cube and then incrementally add more cubes until we have roughed out the shape we desire; then, we smooth or refine it. For NURBS modeling, we start with lines and then move them through 3-space in order to create surfaces. The polygon modeling approach is an incremental one; the NURBS approach is a bottom-up approach, in that we begin with non-3D objects and build them up into 3D objects. We say that box modeling is incremental, rather than top down, because it does not take one cube and make a model out of it, as is common with polygon modeling; rather, we keep adding cubes until we are done.

Figure 6.1 is a Saguaro cactus that we will use as a reference image. (It is taken from bonanza.com, which sells seeds for an incredible range

FIGURE 6.1   A saguaro cactus.

of plant life.) Figure 6.2 shows the use of an Image Plane to pull the photo into Maya so that we can build our model in front of it. We begin with the creation of the trunk of the cactus—but not by using box modeling. In Figure 6.3, a single cube is scaled up the trunk of the cactus; the spacing of the segments is engineered to allow for the branching off of an arm of the correct width at the right height. In Figure 6.4, the bottom of the trunk is flared out

FIGURE 6.2 **Importing the cactus image into Maya.**

FIGURE 6.3 **Beginning the box model.**

FIGURE 6.4   Shaping the bottom of the cactus.

by pulling on vertices. In Figure 6.5, vertices are pulled in and out in order to give the trunk a more organic shape.

Now comes the box modeling process. In Figures 6.6 through 6.11, one of those divisions in the trunk is extruded (a face extrusion), rotated (a face rotation), then extruded again, then rotated once more, and extruded again. This process is repeated until, in Figure 6.12,

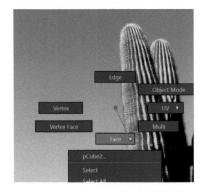

FIGURE 6.5   Shaping the cactus trunk.

FIGURE 6.6   Working with faces while box modelling.

FIGURE 6.7 **Extruding a face to make an arm.**

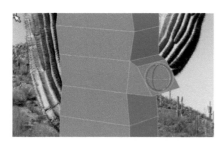

FIGURE 6.8 **Rotating the face upward.**

FIGURE 6.9 **Extruding the arm.**

FIGURE 6.10 **Making the next box.**

FIGURE 6.11 Extruding the rotated face upward.

the arm is seen. Figure 6.13 shows the cactus after using the Mesh → Smooth command.

Notice that the arm was constructed out of a series of boxes, thus the name of the technique. This is in contradistinction with the construction of the trunk, which is top down; we create a single cube and then reshape it into the trunk. Importantly, when we created the cube for the trunk, we sectioned it in

FIGURE 6.12   The box model.

a way that would give us vertices and
edges that could be manipulated to
give the trunk an organic shape, as
well as giving us a division of the
appropriate size for creating an arm.

FIGURE 6.13   Smoothing the model.

Creating a Cactus with Nonuniform Rational Basis Spline Modeling

In Figures 6.14 and 6.15, we create a few NURBS circles with varying
diameter. They are placed above each other, and then, in Figure 6.16, we
loft between them by shift-selecting all of them in a series and then hitting
the loft tool. If one or more of the circles are turned upside down, the
resulting loft will be significantly distorted, so we must remember that two-
dimensional primitives like circles have tops and bottoms. In Figures 6.17
and 6.18, a NURBS circle is placed parallel to the trunk; the circle and then
the trunk are shift-selected. Next, Surfaces → Project Curve on Surface is
chosen. This creates a loop on the trunk, which will be used to root an
arm. If the circle isn't properly placed parallel to the trunk, the projected
loop might be highly distorted in shape; it can take several tries to get this
right. In Figure 6.19, multiple other circles, with varying diameters, have

FIGURE 6.14   Beginning the NURBS model—the circumference.

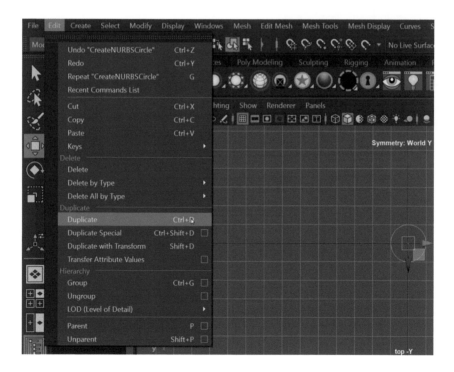

FIGURE 6.15   A second loop for lofting.

FIGURE 6.17 **Projecting a circle on the trunk for an arm.**

FIGURE 6.16 Lofting through multiple loops.

been placed above each other and displaced left to right. Then, the circles are shift-selected in a series, starting with the circle that has been projected onto the trunk, and, in Figure 6.20, Surfaces → Loft is chosen. Since the first circle (which after projection probably isn't a true circle anymore) is on the trunk

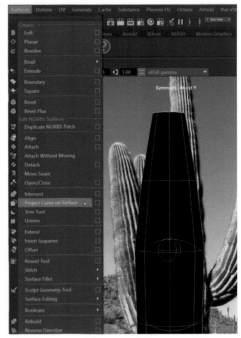

FIGURE 6.18 The lofted trunk.

of the cactus, the resulting arm is rooted in the trunk. The lofted result is in Figure 6.21. (It does need smoothing.) This same technique can be used to attach an arm or leg to a character.

In Figures 6.22 through 6.24, an alternative approach to creating the branch is shown. In this approach, after the circle is projected onto the trunk, the Create → Curve Tools → CV Curve Tool is used to draw a line perpendicular to the loop on the trunk. The curve is drawn upward and outward from the trunk. The circle and then the line

FIGURE 6.19   Multiple loops for the arm.

FIGURE 6.20   Lofting the arm through multiple loops.

FIGURE 6.21 The lofted arm.

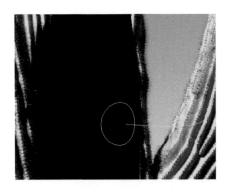

FIGURE 6.22 Creating an arm by extruding a loop along a path.

FIGURE 6.23 Extruding the arm.

FIGURE 6.24   The extruded arm.

are shift-selected, and the Surfaces → Extrude tool is chosen. This creates an arm that is much smoother.

CREATING A MODERNISTIC CATHEDRAL

We will look at modeling a modernistic cathedral; we will consider some low-level modeling techniques, the overall composition of the cathedral, and the use of reuse in constructing a large scene.

First, we consider some issues having to do with lights and shadows. Indoor architectural scenes are a good venue for beginning 3D modelers. There are no organic objects like trees, rocks, and hillsides inside buildings, for the most part. It's perfectly natural for an indoor scene to have no grunged materials (although we will look at some in this chapter). An indoor scene is contained, with no need for extensive city or natural environments. An indoor scene can be built out of relatively flat surfaces that are easy to put materials on. There are also countless architectural textures available online for creating walls, ceilings, floors, rugs, carpets, cement, glass, steel—all the objects you need to put materials on in an interior scene. Indoor scenes also provide contained environments that simplify the process of lighting a scene. And, when modeling objects that are made by humans and not nature, one can make heavy use of reuse. You don't want to copy the same tree 50 times, but a building might have 50 identical arches or windows.

LIGHTING AND RENDERING

We will look in more detail at Arnold lighting and rendering in Chapter 8, but a brief discussion of lighting and rendering will help us understand the modeling and design process a little better. The renderer simulates the movement of light through a scene as it bounces (reflects) off objects. When light hits the material on an object, the only way for the renderer to "see" the object is if light reflects off it. Of course, the material on the surface of the object is really just some mathematical properties that have been assigned to the surface; again, rendering only simulates the movement of light. When light hits an object, it might bounce off sharply, like it does off car paint, or it might bounce off in a highly diffuse way because it hits a rough surface like sandpaper or a soft material like carpet. In this second case, many smaller rays reflect off and go in different directions. Light also refracts through transparent materials like glass, water, and plastic. What the renderer does is follow rays (or photons) of light as they move through the scene. It calculates the brightness and number of reflected and refracted rays by looking at the properties of the materials on the surfaces of objects.

You cannot completely ignore lighting until after you have done your wireframe modeling and put materials on objects. This is for two reasons. One, lights might well be part of your modeling job: rooms have lamps and the outdoors has a sun. The other reason affects beginners more than experienced modelers: it will be hard to evaluate the geometry of your models until you put materials on them and then shine light on them. Periodically during the modeling process, the beginner should put a highly reflective material on a model and then shine a bright light on it—perhaps by using a Directional light—to see how the model is shaped.

Lights and Shadows

Let's start our discussion of the church scene with lighting. There are two main approaches to lighting that are commonly used in 3D modeling. The first is to use a lighting paradigm that is fashioned after live-action movie making, where there is (1) a main light shining directly on the scene, but probably coming from a slight angle, along with (2) fill-in lights that come in from the sides and softly add light to areas that are not properly lit by the main light, with (3) a very soft backlight that creates a silhouette around the central objects and people in the scene.

The second approach is simply to place light sources where they would be in the real world. An outdoor scene might have a Directional light simulating the sun. An indoor scene might have overhead light fixtures with lights in them, along with light coming in through windows. An outdoor scene or an indoor scene with a large window might use an environmental light that provides a bluish horizon, along with a dome of ambient light. In Arnold, this sort of light is called a Sky Dome light, and we will look at them again in Chapter 8. This second approach, that of placing lights in a scene in a natural way, is far more popular, and it is what we are using in the church scene.

But whatever lighting technique is used, it's bad to wash out all shadows. It is tempting to light up a scene very aggressively so that we can see everything. However, it's important to remember that shadows root objects in a scene. An object that sits on the ground or the floor will appear to be floating if it does not cast a shadow that starts where the object meets the floor or ground. Consider Figure 6.25. There are two chairs on a balcony. The one on the left is casting shadows and is clearly sitting on the balcony deck. The one on the right is not casting shadows—and it seems to be floating. (In Maya, one of the attributes of an object is whether it casts shadows, and it can be turned off; that is how the chair on the right has been made shadowless.) Internal shadows, or shadows cast by parts of an object onto itself, bring out the detailed geometry of the object. Shadows also help us visually discern the relative position of objects. It can be difficult to set up the lighting in a scene in a fashion that allows all the objects in the scene to be seen without either washing out some objects with too much light and/or washing out shadows, which leaves the objects in the scene floating. The beginner can expect to spend some time working with the lights in a scene to get them right.

Consider our second lighting scheme, the one where we place lights where they would be naturally. One problem is that this technique sometimes doesn't work optimally because a scene inside a 3D application is inherently artificial: the renderer cannot allow light to move throughout the scene the way it does in nature because this would involve an almost infinite set of calculations. The renderer will calculate the movement of

FIGURE 6.25   Shadows vs. no shadows.

light only so far, as it reflects (both sharply and in a diffuse way) and refracts through a scene. At some point, the renderer has to stop calculating the movement of light in order to make the rendering process tractable. Thus, it is often the case that small areas remain dark, when in the real world, they would be lit up. This is one reason many renderers support something called "global illumination," which tries, within the finite limitations of the renderer, to simulate the movement of light into small or out-of-the-way areas. Arnold does this. Often, global illumination consists of a final pass at the entire scene, where the renderer looks for dark spots and fills them in with light.

In our cathedral scene in Figure 6.26, we have the following light sources: there is sun coming in through the right-side arches, which contain clear glass windows. There is also sunlight coming in through the skylight that runs down the length of the ceiling. This sunlight is simulated with an Arnold Physical Sky light. There are also lights contained in the two long light fixtures on the ceiling. Interestingly, these are modeled with Arnold mesh lights that allow us to turn objects of

FIGURE 6.26   Creating a modernistic cathedral.

arbitrary shape into light sources. These light sources sit inside the clear glass fixtures that are mounted to the ceiling; the mesh lights appear white in the rendering. There are also two small lights, one underneath the gold dome at the front of the cathedral, and one underneath the arch that is halfway between the small altar table and the gold dome. Finally, there is light coming through the stained-glass windows—apparently.

Yes, apparently, but not really. This gets to the heart of our design process. When we begin to model a scene, we want to have a vision of what it will look like, with major criteria being the overall feeling of the scene, combined with what in the scene should catch the viewer's eye. In this case, we are looking for something vast, with a big feeling to it. We are also looking to highlight a few things, in particular the skylight, the highly reflective gold cross, and the stained-glass windows. But the stained-glass windows are not made of glass. They are actually images of real stained-glass windows that have lights in front of them, shining directly on them. Consider the stained-glass window on the left. It is really just a material that has as its color a texture, which in turn consists of an image of a stained-glass window; that image is tiled 1 by 1. (The plane that the material has been applied to has the exact same dimensions as the stained-glass window image.) And there is a light, with the same dimensions as the image, only a few pixels away from it, shining directly on the object. This gives the illusion of the opposite—that there is light coming *through* the stained-glass image. The kind of light that was used is called an "area" light, which is light emanating at 90 degrees from a rectangle. We will cover lights in more detail in Chapter 8.

COLOR

Let's consider a couple of other design issues in this scene. Colors affect the emotional feeling of a scene. Bright yellows and oranges can make a scene feel hot and stressful. Blues and soft lights—as in our church scene—make a scene more calming. We also have to be careful not to introduce so many colors that a scene becomes noisy. The brown of the pews and the floor was chosen to add to the soft, calming effect. The reflective white trim was chosen to highlight the overall shape of the room and to accentuate the curved ceiling and the lines where the walls meet. The ornate white trim and matching arches give us a grandiose feeling. The stained-glass windows are very colorful, and this draws our eyes to them, but it might be that the scene would feel softer if there weren't so many colors and shapes in the stained-glass windows; perhaps I overdid it with the stained-glass windows.

SCALE

Scale is an important issue. It's a good idea to include objects that give the viewer a subconscious sense of scale. The pews tell us how high the ceiling is—so do the arches, which are presumably engineered for a human to pass through. The microphone stand at the front of the room, along with the table and the two chairs, tell us the relative size of a human compared to the room.

MODELING CONSIDERATIONS

Let's consider how some of the objects in the scene were made. First of all, we note that all of the modeling in this scene is straightforward and quite doable by the beginner. Consider Figure 6.27. A common problem is creating a wall that meets the curved arches properly: we cannot simply make a straight wall; it needs to have curves in it. The wall at the top of the image had a flat bottom originally; what I did was grab some vertices with the Move tool and pull them up, as shown in the figure. These vertices were then tucked inside the tops of the arches. This leads us to create a lot of

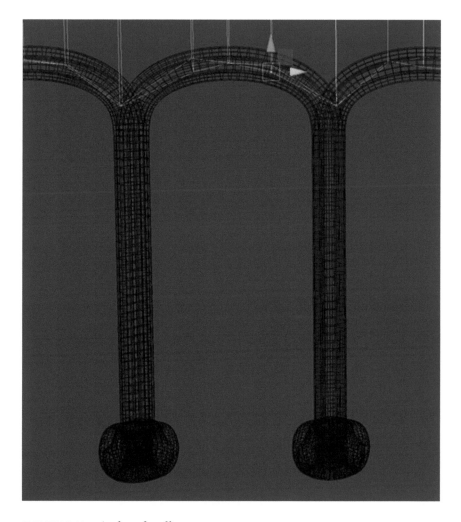

FIGURE 6.27 **Arch and wall segments.**

vertical subdivisions in the wall—see the figure—so that there are enough vertices to allow us to hide all of the top of the wall. Also, the modeler should keep reuse in mind: I created a segment that consisted of three arches plus some connecting wall and then duplicated this until I had the entire side of the cathedral built.

As for the arches themselves, they consist of two sets of four parallel cylinders each that have been joined with the Bridge tool; see Figure 6.28. This gives the impression of perfectly bent cylinders; in other words, a perfect arch. The bases of the arches have been made out of tori that have

FIGURE 6.28 Bent cylinders—a arch.

been reshaped with Lattice deformers. Note that the tori were reshaped in such a way that two of them could be placed at 90 degrees to each other, as in the right-hand side of Figure 6.29.

The arched ceilings and the skylight have been made with planes warped with a bend deformer. The three ceiling segments and the skylight are all duplicated from the same bent plane. See Figure 6.30. The pews were made with polygon cubes and smoothed with beveling. See Figure 6.31. The light fixtures were made with beveled cubes. See Figure 6.32. The wheelchair ramp was made by using two bend deformers to warp the ramp in two dimensions. See Figures 6.33 and 6.34. The mesh lights in the ceiling fixtures are also beveled cubes and are brown in Figure 6.35.

If we look at Figure 6.36, we see the red icons for the area lights on the right and left walls; the lights are facing the stained-glass window images. We also see round area lights on the circular stained-glass windows. (All of the stained-glass windows were bump-mapped with grayscale versions of the stained-glass window images in order to give them better depth.)

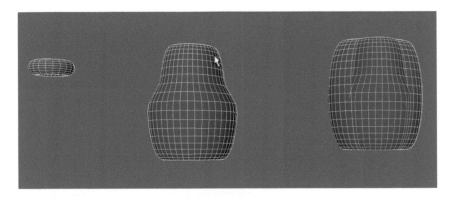

FIGURE 6.29 Two shaped toruses for arch bases.

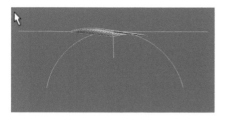

FIGURE 6.30   **A ceiling section.**

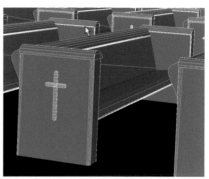

FIGURE 6.31   **The pews.**

FIGURE 6.32   **A light fixture.**

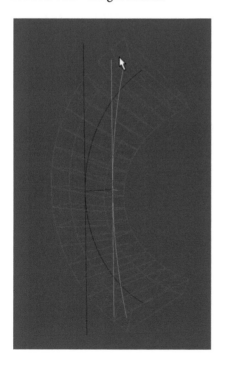

FIGURE 6.33   **Bending a bridge.**

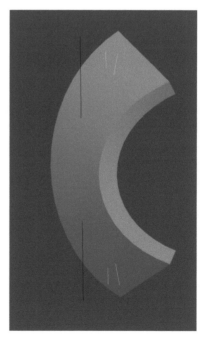

FIGURE 6.34   **The Bridge.**

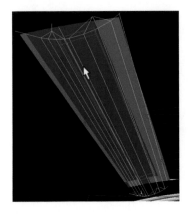

FIGURE 6.35 Creating mesh lights.

The arched trim where the ceiling meets the front wall to the right and left of the altar were made out of the same curved sections (created with a bend deformer) that make up the ceiling and the skylight; for the arched trim, there are two curved sections, and they were simply compressed from front to back so that they would be very narrow. This way, there was no problem in fitting the curved trim to the shape of the ceiling—because they were made out of the same pieces of geometry. The ones that were used for trim were not only made thin, they were also beveled.

Finally, note the very significant use of reuse. Consider the pews; the arches; the bases of the arches; and the bent cube that was used to make the ceiling pieces, the skylight, and the trim along the top of the front wall. Also, consider the trim along the right and left side walls, where they meet the ceiling: they are made out of the same four-cylinder construction as the arches, except that they were not bridged; they were left straight.

FIGURE 6.36 The church.

The Indoor Courtyard

Consider Figure 6.37. It's a lesson in reuse: a single balcony unit has been duplicated a number of times to enable the construction of a large scene. The walls, floor, and ceiling are flat. The doors—there are three identical sets of double doors—are made out of polygon cubes. The railings on the balconies are polygon cylinders warped with a bend deformer, and in a moment, we will take a close look at the balcony unit. The ceiling has glass skylights, which use the glass preset for the Arnold standard material. The outside blue light was created with Arnold → Lights → Physical Sky. This is the only light in the scene except for the soft lights emanating from behind the curtains of some of the balcony units. The floor was created with an Arnold standard material, with the Specular Weight set at 1 and the Specular color set to a plain white in order to create the highly reflective polished flooring. The walls were created with an Arnold standard material; by clicking on the place texture nodes for the color and the bump map of the material, we can see that there is an attribute called Stagger that was checked off. This attribute can sometimes help with a texture whose pattern seems to jump out at the viewer by offsetting the tiling of the texture; it was used here to minimize the appearance of repetition in the stone pattern—but it is still easy to see the repeating pattern in the stone texture. Also, in the wooden ceiling panels, the texture

FIGURE 6.37 **An indoor courtyard.**

(and bump map) was rotated 90 degrees for the beams that run front to back in the rendering in order to make the grain in the wood point in the right direction. The same technique was used on the door panels. (The Rotate Frame attribute is above the Stagger checkbox.)

Let's take a closer look at the balcony units. First, we consider how the curtains were made. In Figure 6.38, a series of NURBS CV curves has been created. The placement of the CVs is shown in Figure 6.39; they are in red, and this illustrates that simply moving over two grid positions and then alternately moving up or down two grid positions before left-clicking for each CV creates a smooth series of curves. In Figure 6.40, the curve series is

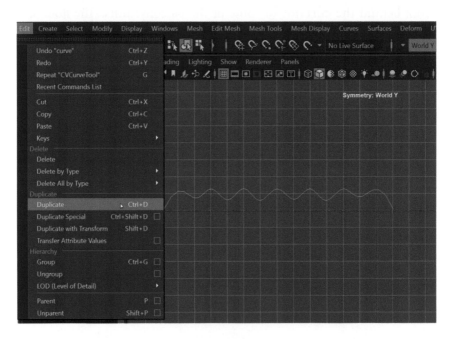

FIGURE 6.38 A NURBS curve for the curtains.

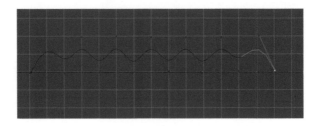

FIGURE 6.39 How the curve was made.

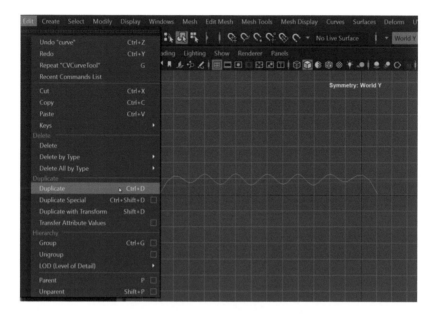

FIGURE 6.40   Duplicating the curve for lofting.

duplicated. We loft between them in Figure 6.41, and the result is in Figure 6.42. Figure 6.43 shows the curtain from multiple perspectives, three of them orthographic. As we have said previously, leaving objects lying flat in some planes makes it easier to line them up with other objects later on. In Figure 6.44, a rod (a polygon cylinder) has been inserted. We want to make cloth out of the curtain, and to do this, we must first convert it to polygon geometry, as in Figure 6.45. The result is in Figure 6.46. In Figure 6.47, it is turned into nCloth.

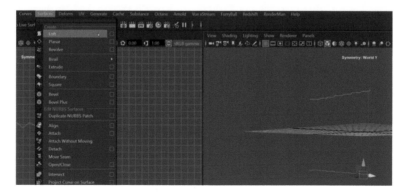

FIGURE 6.41   Lofting the curtain.

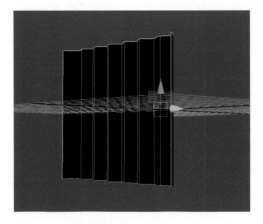

FIGURE 6.42   The resulting NURBS surface.

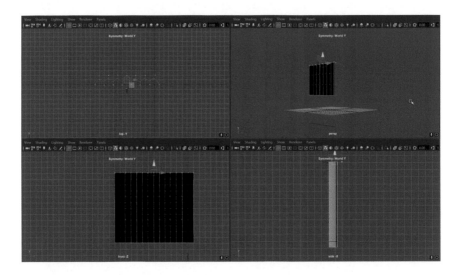

FIGURE 6.43   The curtain in profile.

It's useful to learn to make nCloth hang differently from frame to frame, even though we will not use this in our courtyard scene. Figure 6.48 shows an important tool that can be used to keep cloth objects constrained to polygon objects in a scene, such as by forcing a flag that is flapping in the wind to remain attached to a flagpole, or, in this case, keeping a curtain constrained to a curtain rod. It is a component-to-component constraint tool. The user selects vertices, edges, or faces on one object (the cloth), then

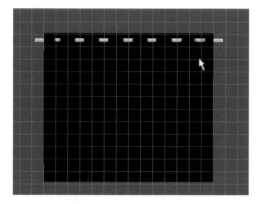

FIGURE 6.44   Putting a rod through the curtain.

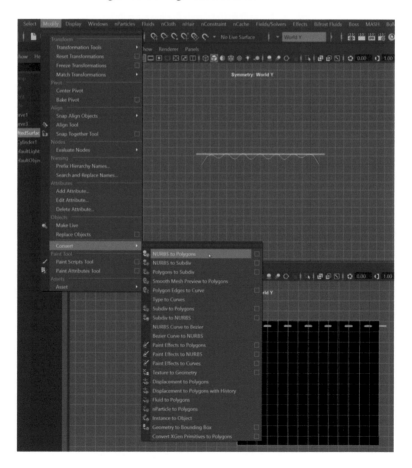

FIGURE 6.45   Turning the NURBS surface into a polygon object.

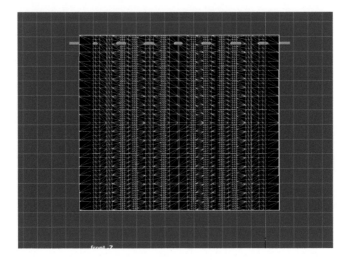

FIGURE 6.46   The resulting (noisy) polygon object.

selects corresponding vertices, edges, or faces on the other object (the pole or the rod), and then uses the tool to constrain the two sets of components to each other. The constraint isn't rigid and how far the components can move away from each other while animated can be adjusted. The distance between the two sets of components can be varied from frame to frame by applying a field to it; remember that the vertices of the cloth are particles, so they can be affected by fields. So, in Figure 6.49, the curtain has been selected and the Main Menu Selector has been set to FX. Then Fields/Solvers → Gravity has been chosen, and we have selected the box to the right of the menu item in order to pull up the gravity settings. The gravity is set to 0.1. Note that only the objects that have been selected when a field is created are actually affected by that field. Figure 6.49 also shows an Air field—a very strong one—being applied to the curtain. Notice that it is moving horizontally with respect to the ground (–1 along the Y axis). Now, in Figure 6.50, we have gone into vertex mode on both the rod and the curtains, selected all the vertices on the curtain and the vertices at the two ends of the rod, and chosen nConstraint → Component to Component. Again, this causes the curtain to remain close to the vertices along the rod, with the distance varying due to the Air field. Now, in Figure 6.51, we run the simulation (by hitting the Play arrow), and the result is the curtain moving gently. Figure 6.52 is a composite image. On the left it shows us using the Outliner to select the constraint, which is an object, and on the

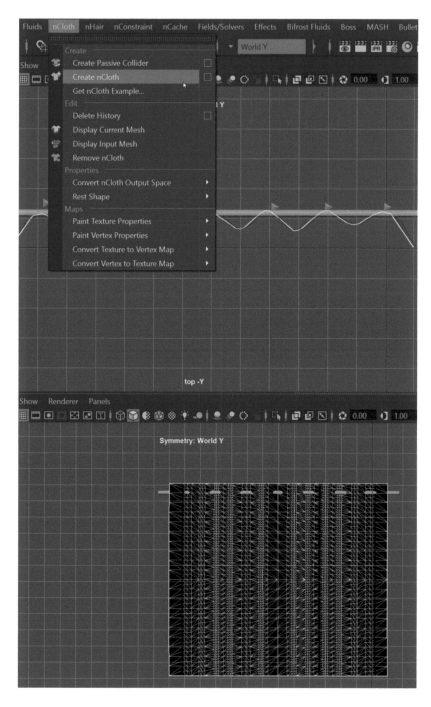

FIGURE 6.47 Turning the curtain into cloth.

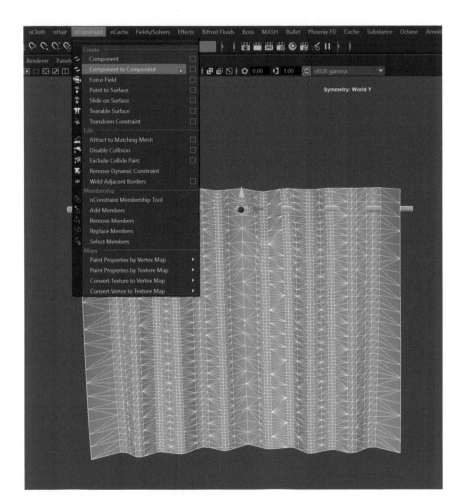

FIGURE 6.48 The constrain component-to-component tool.

far right, we have adjusted its attributes. In the middle of Figure 6.52, we see the result—the curtain moving more aggressively in the wind.

In Figure 6.53, we have created an Arnold standard material, right-clicked on its icon in the Hypershade, and pulled up its graph network. The bump map node has been selected with a right-click and a file texture for the bump map has been created. We have chosen the cloth texture, which is a procedural texture native to Maya. The color of the material was made blue by using the Maya color wheel. The tiling node in the material's graph in the Hypershade has been selected, and in Figure 6.54, we tile it densely. In Figure 6.55, the uv grid for the curtain is being rewritten. As it turns out,

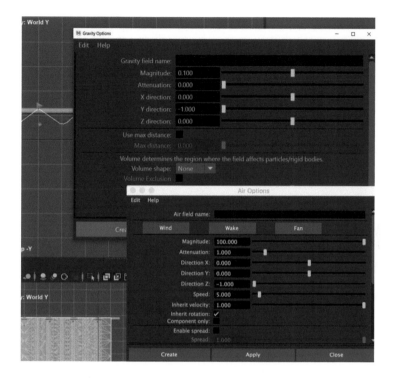

FIGURE 6.49   Putting a gravity field and wind on the curtain copy.

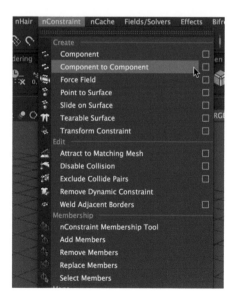

FIGURE 6.50   Constraining the curtain to the rod.

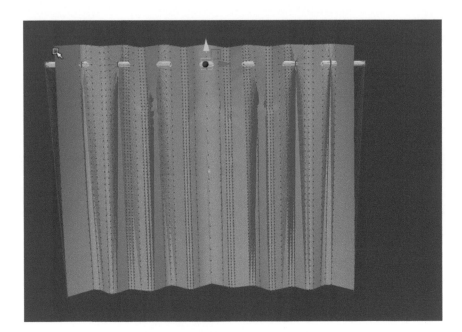

FIGURE 6.51   The curtain animated.

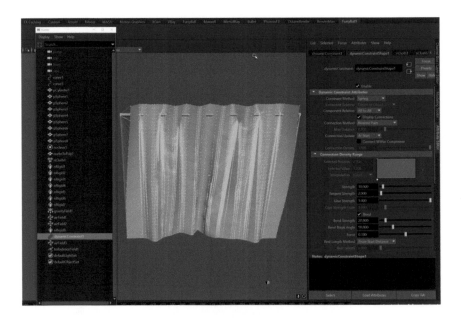

FIGURE 6.52   Adjusting the constraints.

FIGURE 6.53   Putting a cloth bump on the curtains.

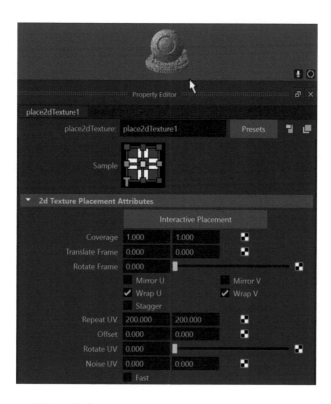

FIGURE 6.54   Tiling the bump map.

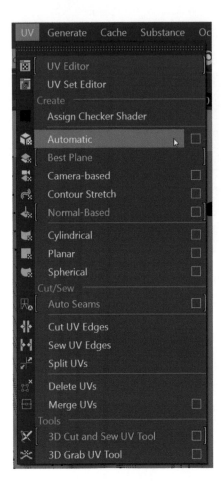

FIGURE 6.55　Cleaning up the uv map.

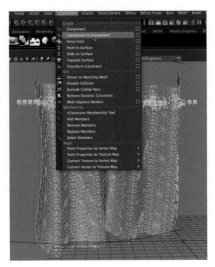

FIGURE 6.56 **An alternative constraint pattern.**

FIGURE 6.57　The curtain rendered.

the process of converting a NURBS surface to a polygon object often badly damages the uv grid, as was the case in this example.

In Figure 6.56, we show an alternative way to constrain the curtain rod to the curtain. In this case, we select all of the vertices of the rod that go through the top of the curtain, along with only the vertices of the curtain that happen to be near the rod (rather than all the vertices in the curtain). The simulation is then run, and a single-frame render of it appears in Figure 6.57. By constraining only the vertices of the curtain that are near the rod, the bottom of the curtain moves more freely when the simulation is run.

We step away from our balcony example briefly to consider another

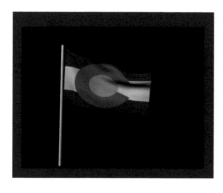

FIGURE 6.58   A flag.

cloth model. A flag can be seen in Figure 6.58. A polygon plane with many vertices was created. (If we wanted to make a stiff cloth, perhaps like the sails on an old sailing ship, we would have lowered the vertex density.) Our flag model was created with the same dimensions as the Colorado state flag. Then a material was created, and a JPEG of the Colorado flag was used as the color. It was tiled once. The top left vertex of the flag was constrained to a vertex high on the pole, and the bottom left vertex of the flag was similarly constrained. The flag was turned to nCloth. With the flag selected, and with the Main Menu Selector set to FX, we chose Fields/Solvers → Turbulence and set the Magnitude to 10. The result of the subsequent simulation is in the figure.

Getting back to our courtyard scene, we see in Figure 6.59 one of the balcony units, shown from the back of the scene. The green colored material is on the

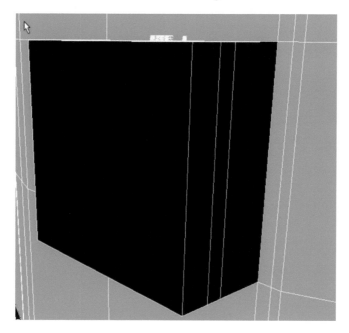

FIGURE 6.59   A balcony box.

backs of the four walls of the courtyard; in Figure 6.59, we see one of those walls. The black box contains a double curtain (you can see part of it poking through the top in the figure—the curtain is white). At the front of the box, and in front of the curtain, is the glass and wood frame of the window (they cannot be seen in this image). The material for the curtain has been made partially transparent, and behind the curtain is a light that is shining outward and into the courtyard. The black box is used to contain the light shining through the curtain so that it doesn't shine outward from the back of the scene and then bleed into the top of the scene through the glass in the ceiling. This way, each balcony unit creates light that shines outward but doesn't add any indirect light to the scene. Creating modeling units like this is also a good modeling practice; the balcony unit is all set now to be reused in another scene, and we can be sure that its light will be appropriately contained.

A POOL ROOM

Figure 6.60 shows an indoor pool room. Like all the scenes and models in this book, this is a scene that can be built by a beginning student of Maya. All materials in the scene are Arnold standard materials. The goal is to create a scene that has an open, bright feeling to it and that renders in a photorealistic fashion. Thus, the focus is on materials and lights. There are four light sources: first, an Arnold Physical Sky light shining through the windows from the outside and with the light colored blue, and second, a very bright

FIGURE 6.60 **A pool room.**

Arnold Area light the same width and length of the pool, shining down on the pool from just barely above the water. This gives the light blue water a very bright look. (This same technique—applying a light directly on a very specific region of a scene in order to give it a glow—was used to illuminate the stained-glass windows of the cathedral we modeled earlier.) The water also has a bump map made out of a grayscale version of a rippled water texture. The water material was made reflective with bright white specular highlights so that the windows would reflect in it. The third and fourth lights are identically sized back-to-back Arnold Area lights of the same depth and width as the ceiling. They sit just below the ceiling and parallel to it. One shines downward and is bright; the other shines upward and is much softer. It serves to illuminate the ceiling. (Note that instead of using two back-to-back area lights, I could have used a mesh light in the shape of a very thin cube, but it would have been difficult to get bright light shining downward and a soft light shining upward.) There is a dark ring around the ceiling; this is the area between the two lights. This dark ring looks natural, as there is often a dark border between perpendicular surfaces in architectural scenes.

The openings for the rectangular windows were made by using the Mesh Tools → Insert Edge Loop tool to create edges parallel and perpendicular to the ceiling that line up with the left, right, top, and bottom of each window. Since they are edge loops, these edges wrap all around the scene, but where they intersect, they create faces that have the dimensions of the various rectangular windows. These faces were then deleted from the walls—which are planes. (Mesh Tools → Multi-Cut could have been used to create edges that are only on a given wall and do not wrap around the scene, but the Edge Loop tool is simple to use, and the extra edges do no harm.)

The hole for the circular window was created by placing a cylinder of the proper width at a 90-degree angle to the wall, with it intersecting with the wall, then shift-selecting the back wall and the window and choosing Mesh → Booleans → Difference. The reason that Boolean operators were not used to create the rectangular windows is because repeated Boolean operators on a given piece of geometry tends to create bizarre effects. The Boolean tools in Maya often exhibit strange effects and should be avoided as much as possible—they are very unreliable. Since there is only one circular window, its creation with a Boolean operator did not create strange modeling effects, but, indeed, when I tried to create the rectangular windows by using a Boolean (with a cube instead of a cylinder), the scene literally blew up when I was in the middle of creating the holes for the windows.

All materials have been given bump maps, with the bump map on the wood siding set to 0.2 depth and the rest of the bump maps set to much smaller values. The seamless texture used for the glass on the balcony is a slightly opaque glass, with a corresponding rough bump map made with an organic material that has been converted to grayscale. The rest of the windows were made with the Arnold preset glass material of the Arnold standard material. The ladder for the pool was created with a Bend deformer; the material is the Arnold chrome preset with its attributes adjusted to make it more reflective.

The colors in the scene were chosen to accentuate blues. The raw wood siding was chosen as the texture for the color of the walls because it is a neutral color that would not detract heavily from the blues in the scene, and because it bumps nicely.

Figure 6.61 shows how much the materials of a scene impact its feel. This is the grunged version of the same scene. The only changes to the geometry are the broken glass on the railing (created by using the Mesh Tools → Multi-Cut tool to insert some edges and then deleting faces), the broken railing (which has fallen into the water), the leaning over of one of the railings of the ladder, the tilting of an air vent, the knocking over of the poolside furniture, and the dropping of the bottom stair rail to the floor. Everything else was done simply by changing materials. Figure 6.62 shows another version of this scene, with the addition of a plant in the pool (from the Maya Content Browser) and blobs added to the pool texture.

FIGURE 6.61 **An aged pool room.**

FIGURE 6.62   **A grunged pool room.**

A MAILBOX

The next model is meant to convey one specific principle: it's best to have a plan of how a model will be built—before beginning the modeling process. In Figure 6.63, we have a cube that is of the approximate dimensions of a mailbox. And, most importantly, there is a single edge loop down the center of the cube and around the middle of the cube; these were created by setting the Width and Height Subdivision attributes to 2. In Figure 6.64, we choose the Bevel tool, and in Figure 6.65, we go into Edge mode with a right-click on the mailbox. In Figure 6.66, the Segments setting of this tool is set to 7. Then, with the edge going down the top middle of the mailbox selected, we hit the Bevel button in Figure 6.66—and the basic shape of the mailbox appears; see Figure 6.67. Note that it was the original setting of the subdivisions of the box that allowed us to create the curved shape of the mailbox with a single bevel command; this is the key element in our plan for creating the mailbox—to create a cube with the dimensions of a mailbox and then to create edges exactly—and only—where they are needed.

In Figure 6.68, we begin to set up the creation of the lid by duplicating the mailbox, as seen in Figure 6.69. In Figure 6.70, a cube has been overlaid on the copy of the mailbox; the cube, then the duplicate mailbox, have been shift-selected, then a Boolean difference has been used to create the lid. The result is shown in Figure 6.71. (An alternative would have been

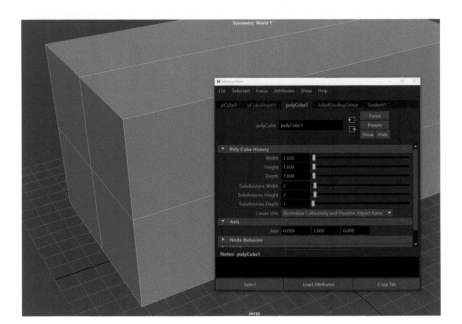

FIGURE 6.63   A box with an edge down the middle.

FIGURE 6.64   Beveling the mailbox top.

to simply rescale the duplicate to be very short, then delete the four faces on one side of the shortened box; given the sometimes-strange behavior of the Boolean tools, this might have been a safer approach.) In Figure 6.72, the mailbox lid has been scaled up slightly in two dimensions so that it can fit over the mailbox. The resulting rescaled lid is in Figure 6.73. In Figure 6.74, the pivot point of the lid has been moved down to the bottom of it by using the D key in combination with the Move tool; by rotating it 180 degrees, it will open from the top. Figure 6.75 shows the lid closed and the pivot point at the bottom of the lid. Figure 6.76 is another look at the rotation of the lid, which can be used to keyframe its animation; this figure also shows that the lid indeed fits nicely over the mailbox. Figure 6.77 shows the transforms

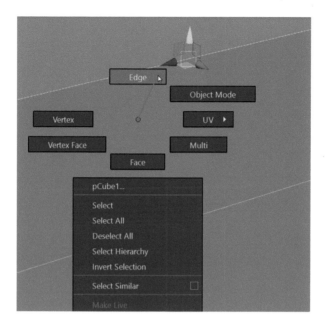

FIGURE 6.65 **Selecting the edge for bevelling.**

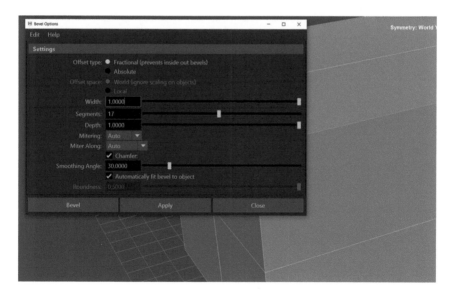

FIGURE 6.66 **The bevel settings.**

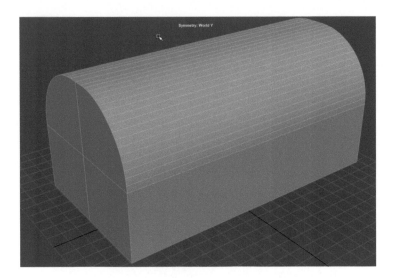

FIGURE 6.67   The resuliting bevelling.

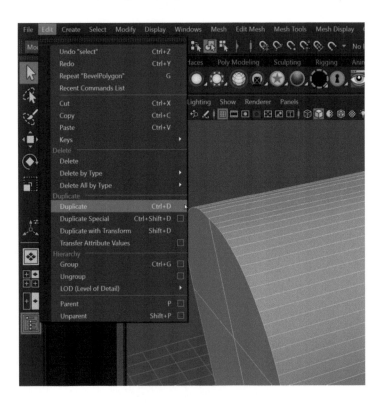

FIGURE 6.68   Duplicating the box to make the lid.

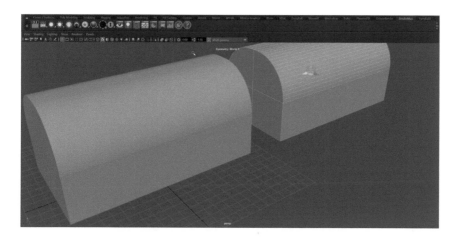

FIGURE 6.69　Two mailboxes.

FIGURE 6.70　Using a boolean to create the lid.

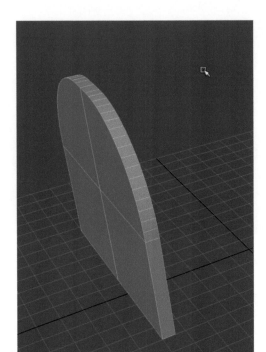

FIGURE 6.71   The resulting lid.

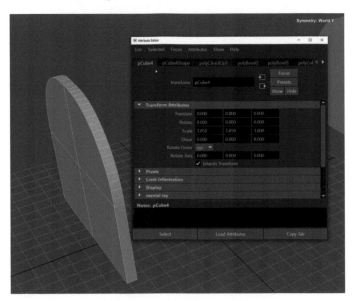

FIGURE 6.72   Slightly scaling the lid up in two dimensions.

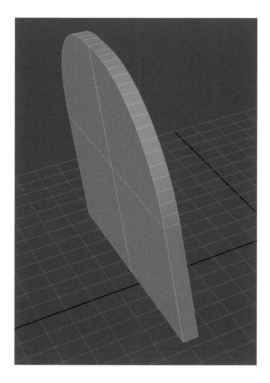

FIGURE 6.73   The scaled-up lid.

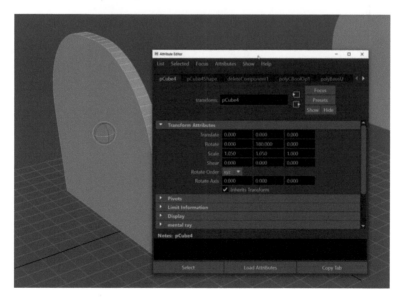

FIGURE 6.74   Rotating the lid from the middle.

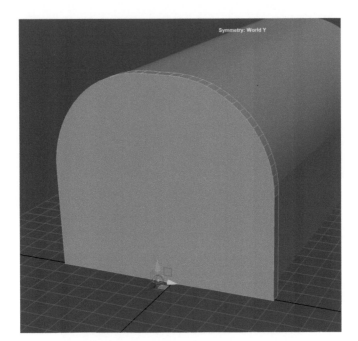

FIGURE 6.75 **Moving the pivot point of the lid.**

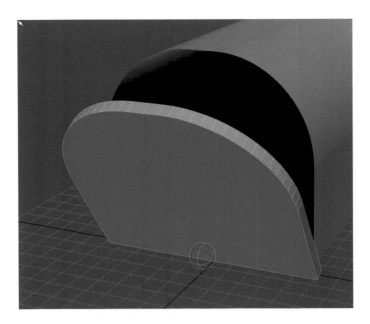

FIGURE 6.76 **Rotating the lid from the bottom.**

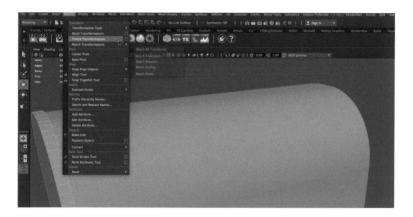

FIGURE 6.77   Resetting transforms on lid.

being reset on the mailbox lid; now, its Scale attributes are (1,1,1) and, more importantly, the Rotate attributes on the lid are (0,0,0)—that means that if we change them to (45,0,0), the mailbox lid will be open exactly 45 degrees.

In Figure 6.78, we begin to create the handle for the lid. A stretched cube is given a number of horizontal divisions because we are going to use a Bend

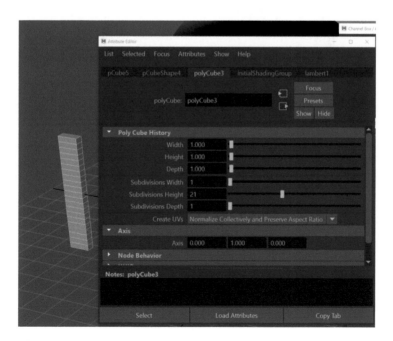

FIGURE 6.78   Creating the handle with divisions for bending.

deformer on it—and the deformer uses edges as bend points. The use of the deformer is shown in Figures 6.79 through 6.82. Note that in Figure 6.80, the translation point of the deformer is moved so that the handle will bend at the end and not the middle. (The same technique was used to create the rounded sides of the pool ladder previously discussed in this chapter.) In Figure 6.82, we duplicate the bent handle because the original will change shape if it or the Bend deformer is moved. The handle is then parented to the lid with the middle mouse button, as shown in Figure 6.83. An Arnold standard material with a black color has been assigned to the mailbox, and the final render is in Figure 6.84.

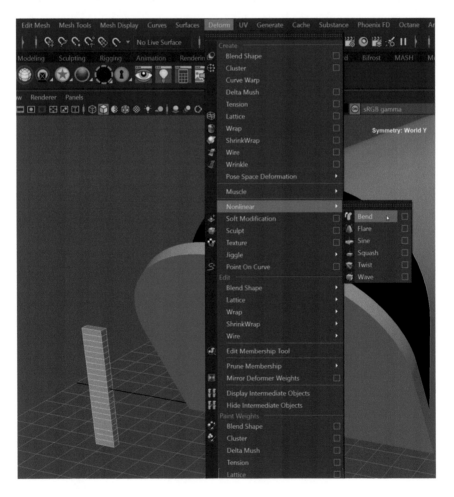

FIGURE 6.79 Using a bend deformer.

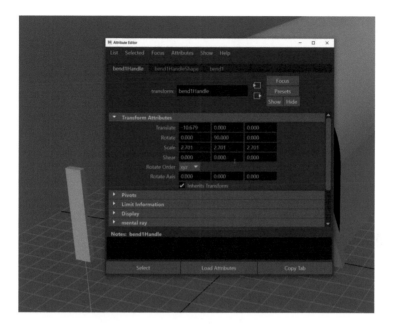

FIGURE 6.80   Repositioning the bend deformer.

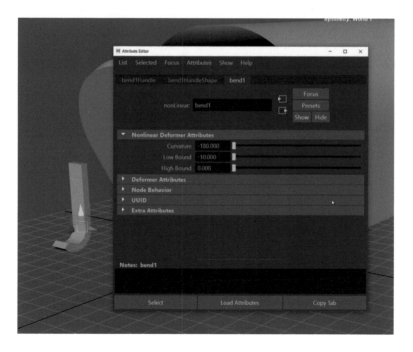

FIGURE 6.81   Bending the handle.

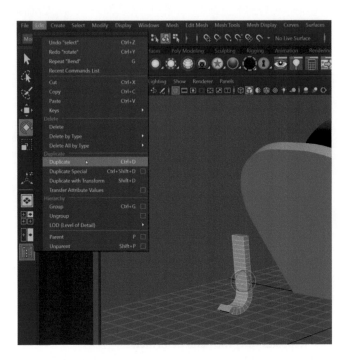

FIGURE 6.82 Creating a duplicate not tied to the deformer.

FIGURE 6.83 The finished mailbox.

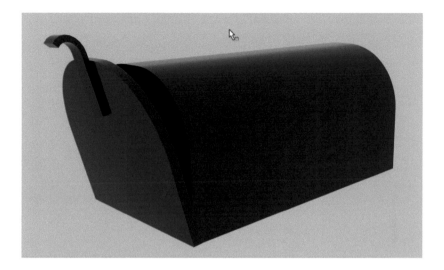

FIGURE 6.84   The mailbox render.

THE GIANT CABANA

Figures 6.85 through 6.87 are renders of a cabana. The only difference is the materials used for the arches; one is painted cement, another is metal, and the third is rock. The goal of this scene was not to be photorealistic: the scene is intended to be somewhat fanciful. The yellow/orange sky is meant to accentuate this. For scale, human models were introduced to the scene so that the viewer would immediately and intuitively see how big the cabana is. When constructing an outdoor scene, it is often necessary

FIGURE 6.85   The giant cabana.

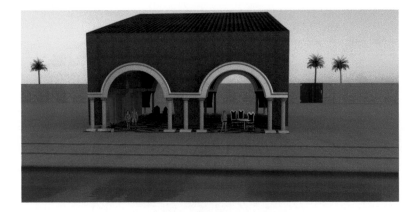

FIGURE 6.86   The giant cabana with gold arches.

FIGURE 6.87   The giant cabana with stone arches.

to introduce objects that enclose the scene; in this case, a wall sits behind the cabana, blocking off the horizon and eliminating the need to model whatever might be behind the cabana. Palm trees are added to give a sense of depth. The water was made highly reflective to give the scene a calm feel.

SOME REPAIR TOOLS

When first learning to model with an application like Maya, one should resist the urge to stick with a model that has gotten out of hand. You have to be willing to start over with a new plan. However, there are times when small artifacts on models emerge that need to be fixed and can be fixed in a

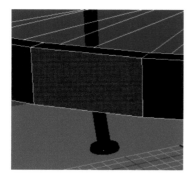 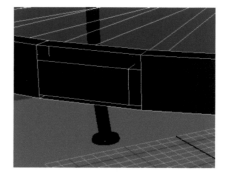

FIGURE 6.88 A face on a table edge.   FIGURE 6.89 The face removed.

very localized fashion. A common problem is a missing face. In Figure 6.88, a face that will be removed has been selected from the perimeter of our round glass table; the result is in Figure 6.89. Then, with a right-click, we pull up a context-sensitive menu and choose Edge mode; see Figure 6.90. The edges to the right and left of the hole are shift-selected and the Bridge tool is engaged, as in Figure 6.91. The patched table is in Figure 6.92. This creates a flat face, just like the original one.

Another common problem is a sharp, nonorganic spot in a polygon model. Rather than using the Smoothing tool, which is extremely

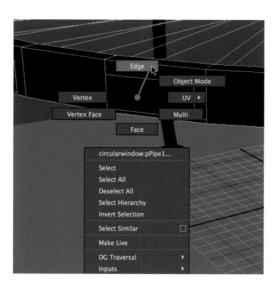

FIGURE 6.90 **Edge mode.**

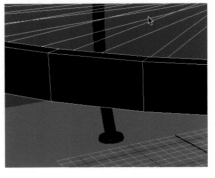

FIGURE 6.91 The Bridge tool.

FIGURE 6.92 The face replaced.

difficult to use in a localized fashion without creating strange geometry around the perimeter of the smoothed area, it's better to use a more precise tool. In Figure 6.93, we are looking at the top of the left ear of the Moai. The edge in red is problematic because it creates a sharp line in a rendering; see Figure 6.94. In Figure 6.95, we see a very useful tool—Slide

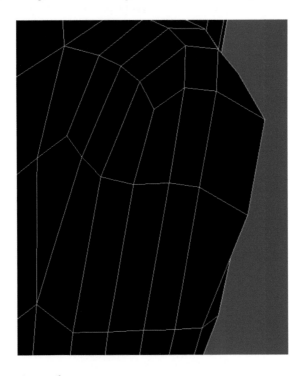

FIGURE 6.93 A angular ear.

FIGURE 6.94   A render of the angular ear.

Edge. The reason it is so useful is that it moves an edge along the contour of a wireframe, rather than moving it in a straight line, like the Move tool would do. In Figure 6.96, our problem edge has been slid along the ear, removing the sharp angle along the top of the ear. The improved render is in Figure 6.97.

Next, we look at a tool that, like the tool shown in Figure 6.91, can fill in a missing face. But, also like the Bridge tool, it creates a flat face—which will be a problem. In Figure 6.98, a face has been removed from a model. In Figure 6.99, the Merge

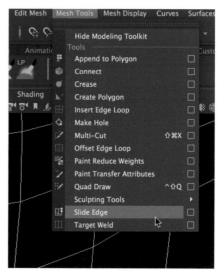

FIGURE 6.95   The Slide Edge tool.

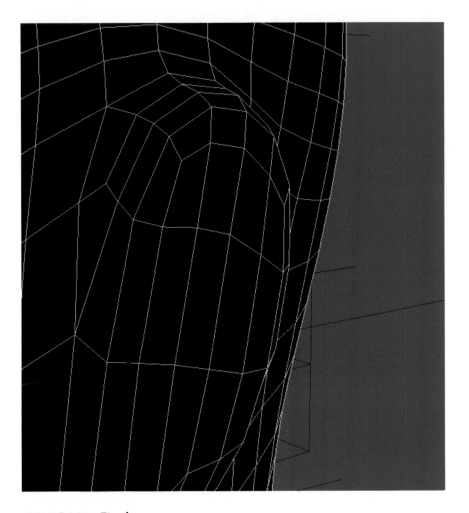

FIGURE 6.96 **Fixed ear.**

to Center tool is used to fill in the missing face. The resulting, somewhat odd, result is in Figure 6.99. If we step back and look at the repaired model in Figure 6.100, we see that indeed, the result needs some work, as we have created a flat spot on the head of our Moai. This can be fixed by first using the Move tool in vertex mode to lift the center vertex in the fixed patch up a bit along the Y axis. We then use the Slide Edge tool to slide the three edges (shift-selected together) that are at the right of the fixed spot to the middle, to meet the single vertex. (The three edges will snap in place to meet the

FIGURE 6.97   **Render of fixed ear.**

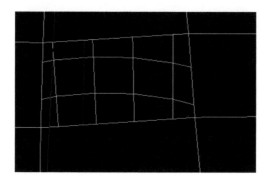

FIGURE 6.98   **A missing face on a head.**

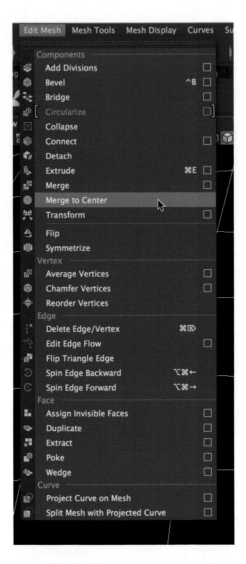

FIGURE 6.99   Merge to Center tool.

center vertex.) Finally, we slide the three edges at the left of the fixed spot to the vertex in the middle. The result isn't perfect, but it removes the obvious flat spot. The completed fix is in Figure 6.101. By lifting the center vertex up and then sliding the edges on either side of it over to meet the vertex, we almost fully restore the curvature of the skull.

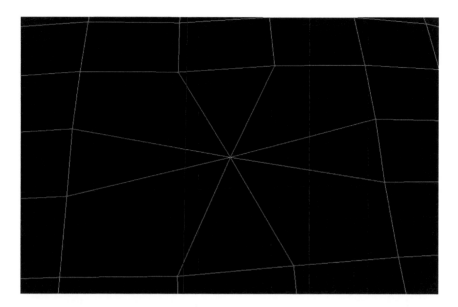

FIGURE 6.100   The filled in hole.

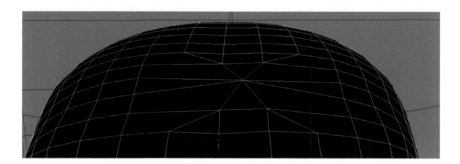

FIGURE 6.101   The completed fix.

VRAY HAIR

We look at an option offered by a very popular renderer: Vray. It is a largely CPU-driven renderer, and along with a number of other renderers, it will be discussed in Chapter 8. In Figure 6.102, we see our Moai head. Vray, sold by chaosgroup.com, installs into Maya as a plug-in. It adds some options to the Create menu. In Figure 6.103, we create Vray fur (hair) with the appropriate faces of the skull preselected. In Figure 6.104, we see the

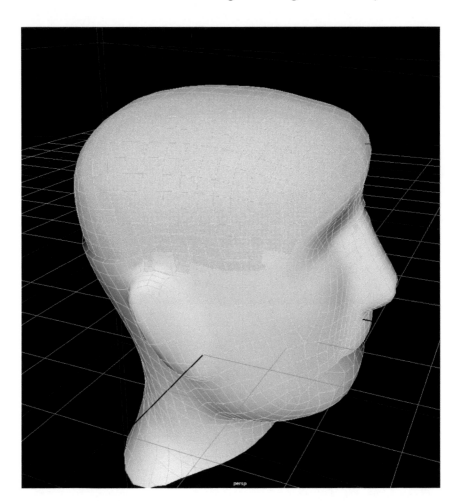

FIGURE 6.102   Selecting scalp area.

default Vray hair. In Figure 6.105, we select it in the Outliner, and in Figure 6.106, we adjust its attributes. The final rendering is in Figure 6.107. The fur renders quickly (with Vray) and can be tailored to resemble a wide variety of fur types.

Maya has a native fur primitive, but it does not render with Arnold. It does, however, render with the little-used, substandard Maya Software Renderer, which ships with Maya. A quick look at the native Maya fur shelf and attributes and a render appear in Figures 6.108 through 6.110. The Maya fur, which is being deprecated by Autodesk, rendered beautifully in the now-dead renderer mental ray.

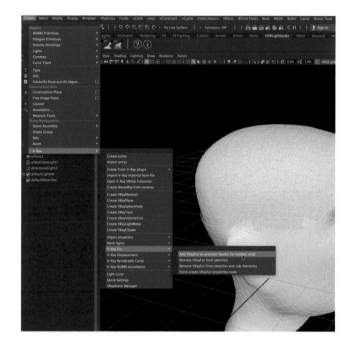

FIGURE 6.103   Creating Vray hair.

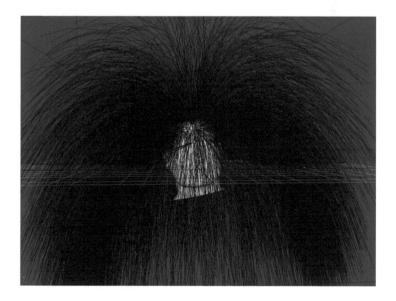

FIGURE 6.104   The default hair.

FIGURE 6.105 The outliner with Vray hair.

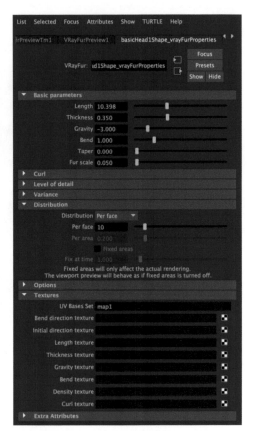

FIGURE 6.106 Adjusting the Vray hair attributes.

SUBDIVISION IN FOUNDRY MODO

We will take a quick look at another 3D modeling application, sold by The Foundry. It is called Modo and it has a modest, but long-time, loyal user base. (We will look at a couple of other 3D applications later in this book, namely Cinema 4D and Houdini; see Chapter 7 on animation.) The reason we're looking at Modo here is that it has a feature that is reminiscent of both Maya's Smooth polygon command and a form of modeling that Maya used to support: subdivision. Until several versions of Maya ago, this third form of modeling was often considered a compromise between NURBS and polygon modeling because, although it was a polygon form of modeling and did not use curved lines, it allowed a polygon model to be easily smoothed. What subdivision in Maya supported was a

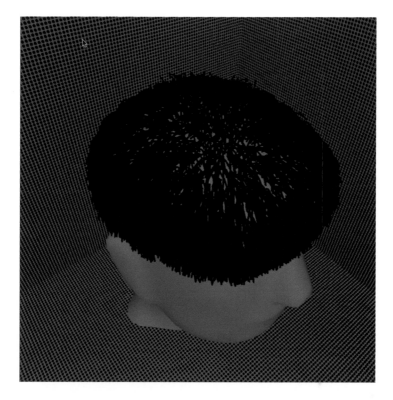

FIGURE 6.107 **The Vray hair render.**

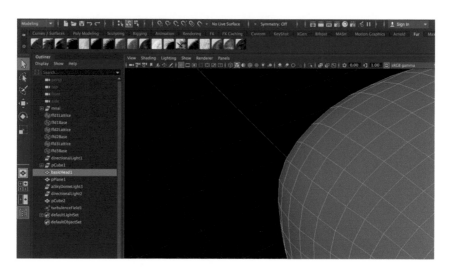

FIGURE 6.108 **The Maya fur shelf.**

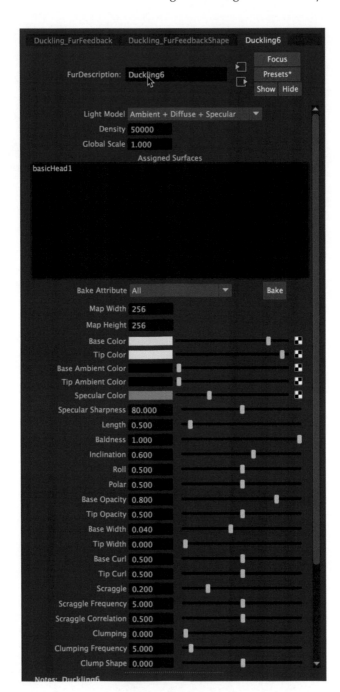

FIGURE 6.109 The fur attributes.

FIGURE 6.110   Maya Software render of fur.

form of polygon modeling where each polygon could be continuously subdivided until an object was smooth; this explanation is a bit of an oversimplification, but it's close enough for our purposes. Essentially, the idea was to allow a model created with straight lines to be smoothed by increasing the polygon count. Since it was a recursive algorithm, subdivision could quickly smooth an object. The interesting thing is that Modo has a subdivision algorithm included in its polygon modeler, and it works a bit like Maya's polygon Smooth tool. This is because the Smooth tool in Maya is a very simple form of subdivision, without the extensive tool support that came with subdivision when it was directly supported by Maya with a full-blown modeling toolset. (The reason the Maya folks got rid of subdivision isn't clear, but I found it to be poorly integrated into the rest of Maya—and it was tricky to use. I did not like teaching it.)

In Modo, there is also a form of subdivision supported. Interestingly, it can be engaged as a completely logical operation, in that it does not permanently change the internal geometry of the model. Thus, a user can toggle between using subdivision and not using it. A common way to use subdivision in Modo is to create a polygon model and selectively apply subdivision to the model to surgically smooth the surface of the model. The way to control how subdivision smooths a model is by carefully inserting edges to control the behavior of the subdivision tool. And, again, this is similar to the Smooth tool in Maya—it is highly sensitive to the location of edges on the surface of the object being smoothed.

To see how subdivision works in Modo, consider Figure 6.111. We see three cubes within the Modo workspace. Note the set of polygon primitive tools on the left side of the interface; the cube tool is highlighted because we use it to create a cube. We click on the tool, then, while holding the Control key down, we click and drag; this creates a cube of equal dimensions. See Figure 6.112. Here, we have clicked on Edge and then selected the Add Loop tool. This tool has been used on the left and middle cubes in Figure 6.111. (The right-hand cube is untouched.) On the left cube, we have added three edge loops all around the cube, in much the same way the Maya Insert Edge Loop tool works. In Figure 6.113, we have hit the Tab key—which engages the subdivision tool. Notice how differently the subdivision tool has behaved on these three cubes. The right one has turned almost into a sphere. The left one

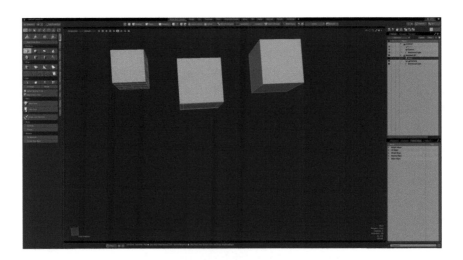

FIGURE 6.111   The Modo interface and 3 cubes.

FIGURE 6.112   Modo's edge loop tool.

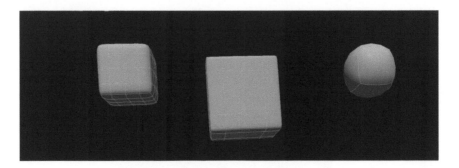

FIGURE 6.113   Modo's subdivision tool.

is somewhat rounded. The middle one has modestly smoothed edges. It all has to do with the location of the added edge loops. Essentially, the less you want an edge of an object smoothed, the closer you want to have an extra loop of edges near the object's physical edge (where the perpendicular faces meet).

There is another way to add edges to a Modo object. Figure 6.114 shows another cube. In Figure 6.115, we see the Bevel tool. Again, we select it,

FIGURE 6.114   **Another Modo cube.**

FIGURE 6.115   The Modo bevel tool.

FIGURE 6.116 The bevel tool applied.

FIGURE 6.117 The cube subdivided.

then we select our object—and Modo bevels the six faces of the cube. By dragging the mouse, we can move the new edges closer or further from the object's physical edges. In Figure 6.116, we see the Bevel tool applied. And in Figure 6.117, we see what happens if we hit the Tab key and engage the subdivision tool. Remember that if we hit the Tab key again, the cube returns to its appearance in Figure 6.116.

As a final note, the subdivision modeling capability that used to be in Maya was very extensive, as it came with a number of specialized tools for manipulating subdivision objects, in much the same way that there are special polygon and special NURBS modeling tools. But in Modo, the use of subdivision is more restricted and—in my opinion—far easier to use, as it is blended in with its polygon modeling capability rather than being a completely separate modeling capability.

CHAPTER 7

Animation

Particle Dynamics, Collisions, Forces, Blend Shape, Key-framing, Skeletons, and Scripting

With examples: *A keyframed camera in an orangerie, a moving mouth, the bones of a simple leg, the bones of a simple fish, a human skeleton and skin, balls colliding with a bowl, rain hitting the ground, a car hitting the blocks of a wall, a car smashing a wall into fragments, a door rotating and closing to a sound, a car on a motion path, using Vue to create natural terrain, hair moving in a wind, a Cinema 4D motion graphics bomb, and Houdini water and fire.*

THIS CHAPTER LOOKS AT adding motion to a scene. Maya supports a very broad range of tools for animation: keyframing, skeletons, particle and rigid object physics, fields (such as gravity), motion paths, and blend shape. As always, we take a concrete approach by stepping through basic tutorials on how to use these tools.

SIMULATING THE PHYSICS OF THE REAL WORLD

3D modeling and animation applications like Maya contain sophisticated engines that simulate Newtonian physics. Here is an important term:

"elastic" collisions. This refers to collisions where there is no loss of energy after two or more objects collide and rebound; that is, the total kinetic energy in the system remains the same after impact. To create realistic simulations, it's important that an animation application be able to handle nonelastic collisions—which significantly complicates the simulation process. One of the key tasks of physics engines in applications like Maya is to (a) calculate the changes in trajectory of rigid objects and/ or particles as they hit each other, (b) while taking into account the loss of energy (which dissipates in the form of friction) after these objects and/ or particles rebound, (c) while very roughly taking into account what effect the overall shapes of these objects and/or particles have on their trajectories after impact. Applications like Maya do a pretty good job of (a) and (b), that is, of calculating the results of nonelastic collisions, but they only approximate how the shapes of objects and particles affect nonelastic collisions. Applications like Maya also provide very little support for naturally modeling the potential fragmentation of objects when they collide. Importantly, particles in Maya can collide with each other; in the past, this was not true for Maya particles.

To calculate collisions, animation applications typically break 3-space up into partitions. When there are two moving objects and/or particles, a first cut calculation is made to determine whether these two objects/particles will ever enter the same partition. If not, then they will not influence each other and any calculations relating to their possible collision can be terminated. Next, if objects/particles might indeed come close to each other, the 3D application places bounding containers around the objects/particles; these could be as simple as spheres or (rescaled) cubes. Often, as is the case with Maya, the user can control the shape of the bounding container to some extent. Also, some particles do not have any geometry associated with them and their appearance is calculated at render time; this means that the bounding containers also have no geometry and they are treated as if they are as small as can be simulated. Once the objects/particles are in motion and bounding containers have been placed around them, the application performs calculations to determine if these bounding containers might collide. This is a simpler calculation than determining if the objects themselves will collide, as the bounding containers have geometrically regular shapes. It could be that the process does not go into any more detail with respect to the overall geometry of the two objects/ particles; in other words, the application essentially calculates the effects of the impact of the bounding containers, not the objects themselves. As an aside, these same bounding containers can be used to determine if one object/ particle might be concealed visually behind another object as it moves and thus will not need to be rendered.

TWO DYNAMICS ENGINES

There are two very powerful dynamics engines in Maya that simulate the physics of the real world, and both of them were added to Maya in relatively recent years. They are nDynamics and the Bullet system. To make sure that the Bullet system is loaded when Maya is running, go to Windows → Settings/Preferences → Plugin Manager and check the bullet.bundle. It loads as an FX Main Menu dropdown, and there is a Shelf tab for it, as well.

nDynamics is associated with a trademarked "Nucleus" technology owned by Autodesk. It supports multiple forms of objects, including nCloth, nParticles, nHair, and body collisions. (nCloth is essentially a particle system created out of the vertices of polygon geometry. The particles are programmed to remain near each other physically.) All of these objects can interact with fields, such as gravity and airflow.

The Bullet engine simulates the collision of objects in an extremely realistic fashion, and it allows objects to come under the influence of fields like gravity. It also allows objects to be impacted by natural phenomena like friction and the rebounding qualities of substances. (The ultimate rebounding substance in the real world is rubber, and its discovery in the Americas by Westerners revolutionized industry and manufacturing.) It supports both hard and soft bodies, although we look only at hard bodies in this book. While it is a separate physics engine that installs in Maya as a plug-in, it is nicely integrated with the wireframe geometry system of Maya.

We will look at both of these systems in Maya in the examples in this chapter. But we end this overview with a crucial point: what makes particle systems (nDynamics in Maya) so powerfully realistic is the fact that they allow the animator to have direct control over the movement of groups of particles, but at the same time allow each particle to behave semi-independently. This controlled form of randomness is how chaotic systems like clouds, smoke, fire, and water are able to look so realistic.

THE LIVE-ACTION METAPHOR

Maya supports a number of tools and facilities that can be used to animate models in a scene. We noted in Chapter 1 that Maya uses a live-action metaphor. It's important to be aware that when modeling in the Viewport, even before creating a single camera, the user is actually modeling through the perspective of the "default" camera. Remember: when tumbling, panning, and dollying, the user is moving the camera, not the scene.

Often, users will not create a camera until they begin the process of animating a scene. However, it can simplify the process of evaluating a scene from multiple perspectives by creating cameras during the modeling process. You can change the camera you are looking through by going to Panels → Perspective in the Viewport Settings; all cameras that the user has created will appear in the Perspective list. Our first example of animation demands that we create a camera, because we are going to keyframe the camera, and you cannot keyframe the default camera. First, we use the Create dropdown to make a camera (not one with an aim; we will look at this later). Then, we set the scene up for animation. We use an orangerie as our example scene, as seen in Figure 7.1. This is an Arnold render. The trees inside the building are from the Content Browser, and they have been converted from paint effects to polygon geometry for rendering. (In case you are wondering, an orangerie is traditionally a building where fruit trees were kept in the winter in England. The word itself is French.)

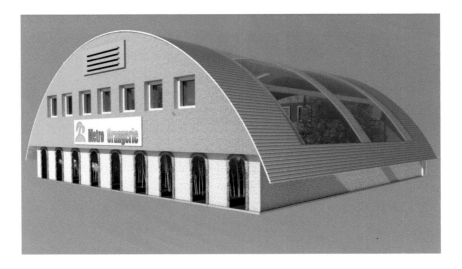

FIGURE 7.1   The orangerie.

KEYFRAMING

Figure 7.2 shows the setup for animating the camera. Notice that the upper right is the view through the created camera, camera1. (This was set by going to Panels → Perspective.) The other three views are the default orthographic views, which are seen through the default camera; this is why we can see camera1 (it is green because it has been selected). The idea is that we use the three orthographic views to guide us as we animate the camera in three dimensions, using the Move and the Rotate tool, all the while viewing the movement of camera1 by seeing what it sees in the upper-right view. The first thing we do is set the number of frames for the duration of time that we want; in Figure 7.3, the number is 1440, which, at 24 frames per second (the default frame rate in Maya) covers one minute of animation.

Why 24 frames per second? You may have seen old-time 2D, hand-drawn animation from the 1940s and 50s. Sometimes, there were so few frames per second that one could see the image flickering. When it comes to frame rate, the only difference between hand-drawn techniques and digital techniques is that our images are created by the renderer, not by

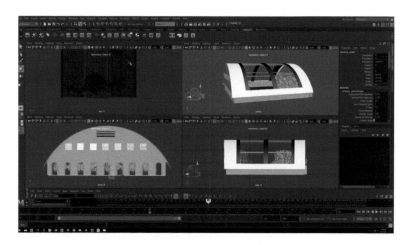

FIGURE 7.2   Placing the camera in the scene.

FIGURE 7.3   Setting the number of frames.

the hand of a Disney artist. It turns out that somewhere around 20 frames per second, our brains perceive continuous motion. This is true for two reasons: first, the frames go by so quickly that the chemical reaction in our eyes from seeing frame x hasn't fully dissipated before frame x + 1 appears, and second, we evolved as creatures to see continuous motion in real life, so our brains in a sense *want* to be tricked. Modern video is usually 30 frames per second or more, but in Maya, the default has been 24 for quite some time, so that is what we will use in this book.

We first left-click on a frame in the timeline, set the camera where we want it in the scene (while using the three orthographic views to judge where we are placing the camera in 3-space and looking at the upper-right quadrant to see what the camera is seeing), hit the character "s" to create a key frame, then move the cursor to a new frame, move the camera in the scene, and hit "s" again. At each step, we move the camera by using Move and/or Rotate. Later, when the simulation is run, Maya will interpolate linearly between the keyframes so that the camera rotates and translates gracefully. We can, of course, move and rotate at the same time if we want. We keyframe the camera as it enters through one of the arches, moves to the back of the orangerie, turns around, and then exits. Then, we left-click on the first frame in the timeline and run the simulation. As the frames go by, we can see what will eventually be rendered by watching the upper-right quadrant. The keyframing process is seen in Figures 7.4 and 7.5.

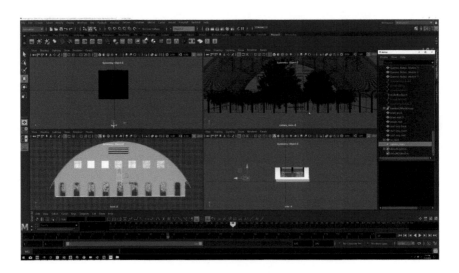

FIGURE 7.4   The four views for camera animation.

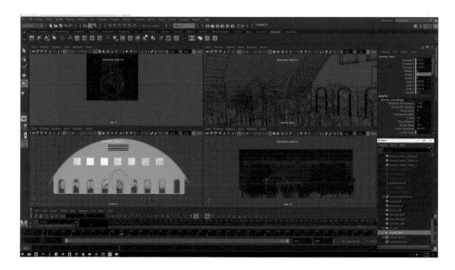

FIGURE 7.5   **Keyframing complete.**

BLEND SHAPE

In a broad sense, there are two ways to animate in Maya or a similar application: by changing the location of an object or the components of an object over time (e.g., keyframing an object over a series of frames, as above) or changing its shape over time—or both, of course. Now, we look at the second technique—morphing an object over time. One of the most flexible ways of doing this in Maya is with the Blend Shape tool. It allows us to create multiple versions (two or more) of an object and then use these as morphing targets. In Figure 7.6, we have a simple humanoid mouth.

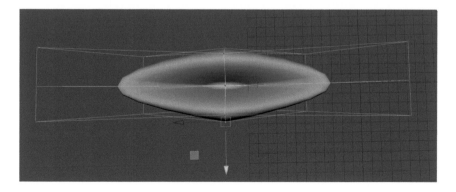

FIGURE 7.6   The mouth and a lattice deformer.

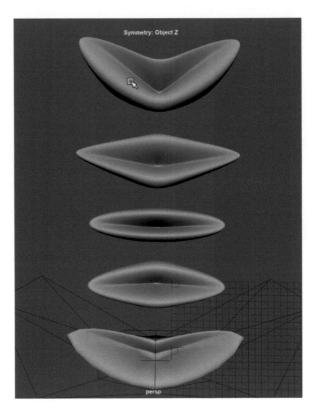

FIGURE 7.7 The series of deformed mouths.

In Figure 7.7, the Main Menu Selector is set to Modeling. We have three versions of the mouth that have been shaped with a lattice deformer; they are on top, and the fourth one is the original mouth. (The bottom shape is only in the figure to illustrate the lattice deformer that has been used to create the three alternative versions; it is not used in this example.) What we do next is shift-select the three copies and then the original, and then, as in Figure 7.8, we choose the Blend Shape tool. Now, we can use the top three deformed versions of the mouth as base versions to create new versions of the original mouth; these new versions created from the base versions are then assigned to frames on the timeline in order to animate the original mouth. When the simulation is run, Maya will transition the mouth through the series of new versions we have created and keyframed.

Next, in Figure 7.9, we pull up the window that will be used to animate the original by creating and keyframing the new versions that are crafted

FIGURE 7.8   Creating the blend shape.

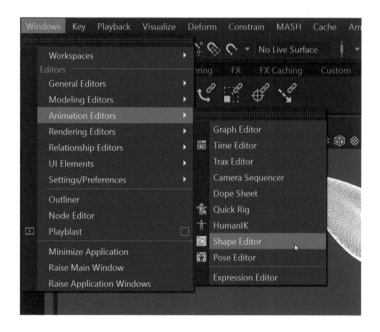

FIGURE 7.9   Opening the blend shape window.

FIGURE 7.10 The blend shape sliders.

by mixing the three deformed base versions in different ways. In Figure 7.10, there are three sliders (labeled Sphere 6, 5, and 3 because the mouth was created from a sphere), one for each of the base versions. They are used to create modified versions of the original, with each slider using its base version of the mouth as a basis for crafting a new version. Before doing this, though, we make sure that all four red dots to the right are clicked on. Then, we move the three levers; this uses the base versions (that were created with the lattice deformer) of the mouth to create a new version of the mouth; each lever in essence controls how much of the newly created version is affected by that lever's version. See Figure 7.11; the green mouth, which is the original, has been reshaped according to the levers. In this case, the green mouth has been influenced by the top two base versions more than it has been influenced by the third base version, as its lever is moved only halfway over. Once we have a new green version that we like, we middle mouse button–drag the top red dot down to a frame on the timeline in order to assign that frame number as a keyframe associated with the version of the mouth that we have just created. We can set as many keyframes as we want; each time, we move the three bottom levers until we like the shape we have made, then we middle mouse button–drag the top red dot down to the timeline to create a new keyframe. When we are

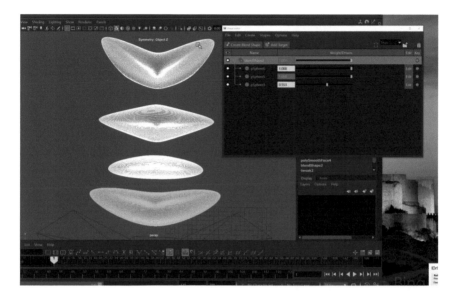

FIGURE 7.11   **Animating** with a blend shape.

done, we run the simulation, and the mouth smoothly morphs between the keyframed versions we have assigned to the timeline.

AN INTRODUCTION TO SKELETONS

Skeletons can be used both to move a character model and to morph that model over a series of frames. This is because a skeleton moves various components of a character with respect to each other, and in doing so, it changes the shape of the character by shifting the appearance of a character's body near the joints that are in motion.

While skeletons are most closely associated with animating character models, they can also be used to do many other things, such as animating the movable, driving components of a locomotive or animating the movement of a flower in the wind. In this chapter, we will look at using skeletons to animate characters and creatures. To get started, we first set the Main Menu Selector to Rigging, as in Figure 7.12.

FIGURE 7.12   The Rigging Main Menu Selector.

FIGURE 7.13 **Creating bones and joints.**

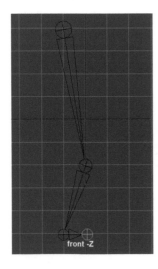

FIGURE 7.14 **A leg skeleton.**

Next, we look at a tool that can be used to create a series of bones connected by joints. In Figure 7.13, we select this tool. In Figure 7.14, we have (1) clicked at the top of this image, creating the top circle, (2) clicked about three-quarters of the way down and a bit to the right, creating the second circle and the bone connecting it with the top circle, (3) clicked at the bottom after moving back to the left, and (4) moved the mouse a bit to the right and clicked again. We end up with a continuous sequence of joints and bones. We have used the tool in an orthographic view; we do this because the leg moves essentially in a single plane, and this makes it easier to lay the joints and bones out in an orderly fashion. We built the leg with the knee flexed to make it a bit easier to perform the next step.

Now that we have created the leg and foot, we will "rig" it, that is, program it to move the way a leg should move. To understand this process, we need to consider two somewhat opposing concepts. The first is called "forward kinematics" or FK. FK refers to a skeleton (in our case, a leg) that is not programmed to move naturally. Forward kinematics causes a series of joints and bones to behave in a fashion very similar to a set of objects that have been placed in a hierarchy in the Outliner. Consider the leg we just made. If we were to click on the top circle in Figure 7.14 with the Move tool engaged, the entire leg below it would move along with the top of the leg. In general, if you move any joint with the Move tool or Rotate tool, everything below it (i.e., further down the chain of joints and bones) will move accordingly. This is an example of forward kinematics, that is, the control of the movement of the leg moves in a forward fashion down the leg.

As it turns out, FK does not model the movement of natural skeletons. I don't move my legs by sending my hips forward knowing that my two legs will follow, and that my feet will then move along with my legs. In truth, control moves in the opposite direction. I move my foot, which then moves my knee and then my hip. That is called "inverse kinematics," or IK. Control passes in an inverted fashion, that is, up the joint and bone chain, rather than down. To rig a skeleton to move in this more natural fashion, we create objects that are called IK "handles."

In Figure 7.15, we select the tool that will let us create IK handles. The handle is something that we will move with the Move tool, and it will in turn cause the skeleton to move in a fashion that follows

FIGURE 7.15 **Rigging the leg skeleton.**

inverse kinematics. The idea is to create an IK handle that connects a joint higher up in the series with a joint further down or with the tail end of a series of joints and bones. If you connect a joint up in the chain with a joint further down or with the end of the chain, that means you want that upper part of the chain to respond to movement lower down. So, we first click on the hip joint, then click on the final (green) circle in the image, which happens to be at the end of the chain. We then hit Enter to terminate the tool. This creates a single IK handle that tells Maya to rotate the hip if the foot is moved. Because it is in between the hip and the foot, the knee will move and/or rotate, as well. This is how an IK handle works: we move the bottom of the IK handle, and all joints up the chain and ending with the root of the IK handle will respond to this movement. Next, we click on the hip and then click on the ankle to create a second IK handle. Now, if we move the ankle, the hip and the knee will respond.

The final "rigged" leg has two IK handles, one connecting the top of the leg chain to the toes and one connecting the top to the ankle. See Figure 7.16. In Figure 7.17, we have selected the end of the joint and bone series

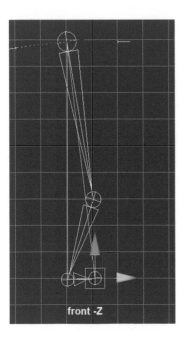

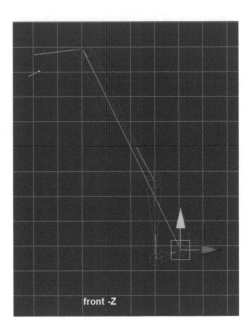

FIGURE 7.16 **Flexing the knee with an IK handle.**

FIGURE 7.17 **Using an IK handle to move the leg outward.**

with the Move tool and pulled to the right; the hip rotates and the knee bends. Compare this to what happens with a skeleton that is not rigged with IK handles and therefore follows forward kinematics (FK). In Figure 7.18, the rigged leg is on the right. We lift the toe up and the knee bends.

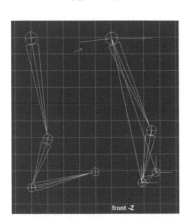

FIGURE 7.18 **FK vs. IK.**

On the left is an unrigged leg; when we pull on the toe, the bottom bone simply grows longer and the foot lengthens! The issue is that with the leg on the left, there is really only one true control point, and that is the hip. If we move it, the entire rest of the leg moves along with it. If we move any other part of the leg, something unnatural is likely to happen; that is, the bone immediately above the joint we move stretches, and everything down below moves along with the joint that has been moved. So, again, we say that the leg on the left follows forward (or down-the-chain) kinematics and the leg on the right follows inverse (or up-the-chain) kinematics.

A FULL SKELETON

Now, we will build a minimal skeleton for a fish and rig it. In Figure 7.19, we have created a skeleton that has three series of bones emanating from a single point at the middle of the fish, halfway between the front fins. First, we left-click with the joint tool at that middle point; then, we click about halfway down the body of the fish (moving upward in the top part of the figure), then we click a little further along, and then we click at the tail. We hit Enter to terminate the tool. We have created a middle joint about halfway from the middle of the fish to the tail, along with two more joints going down the body of the fish. These will be used to create a wave motion of the fish's body as it swims. Then, using the Joint tool, we go back to the middle of the fish, click in the same place we clicked to create the first series of bones, click halfway to the end of the right fin, and then click at the end of the right fin, and hit Enter again to terminate the tool. We go back to the middle of the fish again, click with the Joint tool, click halfway to the end of the left fin, and then click at the end of that fin. These last two sequences of bones and

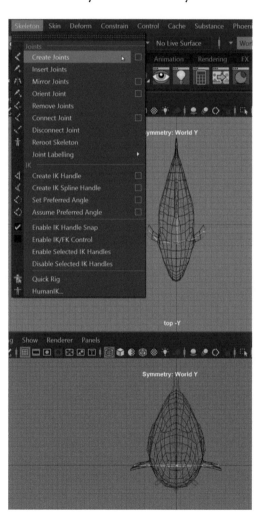

FIGURE 7.19 The fish skeleton.

joints will be used to flap the fish's fins. Note that the skeleton is in a tree formation, with a single root and three series of bones/joints going outward from that point.

To rig the fish, we create three IK handles. One connects the root of the bone/joint tree with the tail of the fish, one connects the root to the tip of the right fin, and one connects the root to the tip of the left fin. See Figure 7.20. There are middle joints between each of the three IK handles. When one of the three handles is moved, the bones and joints up the tree will respond. For the fully rigged fish, look at Figure 7.21.

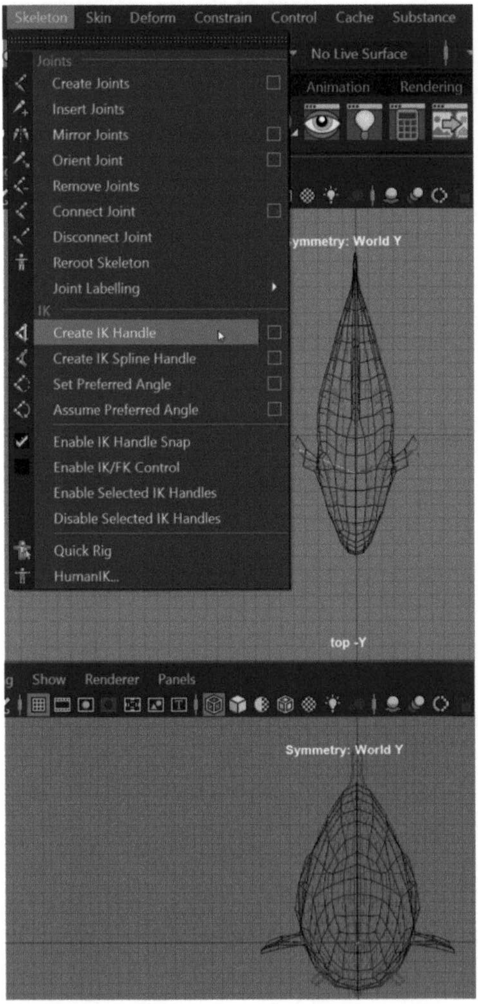

Now, in Figures 7.22 through 7.24, we animate our fish. We create keyframes by first selecting a frame in the timeline with a left-click, adjusting the shape of the fish by moving the fins and/ or the tail of the fish, and then hitting S. We call this position 1. We select another frame further down the timeline, adjust the three handles again, and then hit S. We call this position 2. Then we go further down the timeline, adjust the handles again, and hit S. This we will call position 3. Now, when we run the simulation, Maya will cleanly interpolate the movement of joints between the three positions, each of which is assigned to a keyframe.

Suppose we wanted our fish to flap its fins and wiggle its body for a very long period of time. We don't want to

FIGURE 7.20   Rigging the fish skeleton.

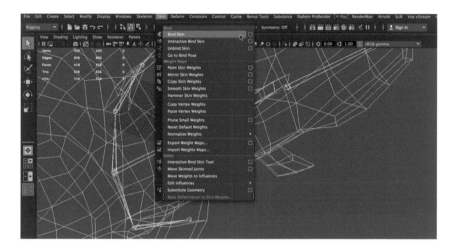

FIGURE 7.21   Binding the fish skin to the fish skeleton.

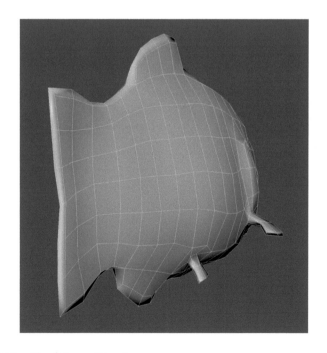

FIGURE 7.22   The fish, position 1.

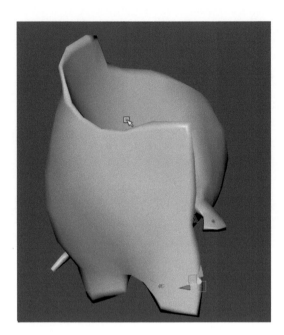

FIGURE 7.23   The fish, position 2.

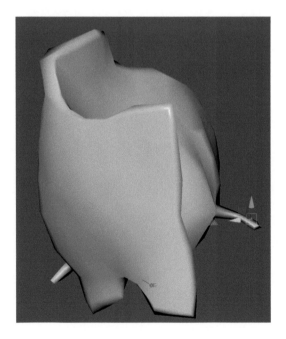

FIGURE 7.24   The fish, position 3.

keyframe it forever. So, we might want to create a "motion cycle." We do this by creating a fourth keyframe, one where the fish ends up back in position 1. We could then repeat this cycle over and over.

There are two more things to mention. First, we will also need to move the fish through the water simultaneously with the repetition of the fins-and-tail motion cycle. We can use the Graph Editor (which we will look at briefly later in this chapter) to repeat the four-position keyframing of the fins and tail. Thus, we could keyframe the fish moving through the water or have the fish move along a motion path (we will also look at this later in this chapter), while repeating the motion cycle that animates the fins and the body of the fish. (We do not show this here.)

Creating a motion cycle is a very common way of making the body of a creature move while it is progressing through a scene. We might build a "walk cycle" where a character takes a full step with both legs; then we loop through this motion cycle as the character is keyframed to progress along the ground. As a detail, we note that we would want to end the walk cycle a bit before the complete two-leg step finishes, so that the character doesn't pause for an instant with both feet rigidly in place at the end of each cycle. By creating this walk cycle, where we use IK handles to move the legs, we can easily have our character walk through a desert or across a park simply by keyframing the body of the character as a whole to move forward.

The second thing we need to mention is that there is actually one more step to animating our fish. Before moving the tail and fins of the fish by using the Move and/or Rotate tool on the IK handles, we had to "bind" the fish body to the skeleton; this was done in Figure 7.21 by shift-selecting first the skeleton and then the fish body, then choosing Skin → Bind Skin. If we had not done this, the skeleton would have moved inside the fish, but the fish itself would have remained rigid. We will look at attaching a body to a skeleton more closely in the next (more complex) example.

CREATING A FULL SKELETON, RIGGING IT WITH IK HANDLES, AND BINDING THE SKIN TO THE SKELETON

We will now look at the process of creating a skeleton, rigging it for inverse kinematics movement, and binding the "skin" of the character to the rigged skeleton. Maya features a utility for creating humanoid skeletons. In Figure 7.25, we engage the Human IK tool. The set of menus and buttons that then pops up can be seen in Figure 7.26. In Figure 7.27, we have opened up the Create dropdown. We click on Create Skeleton.

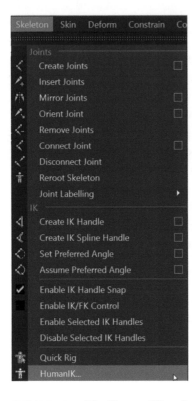

FIGURE 7.25   The Human IK tool.

FIGURE 7.26   The Human IK control panel.

Now we have an opportunity to specify a number of variables concerning the structure of the skeleton, including the number of bones in the back and the number of fingers and toes; see Figure 7.28. Interestingly, we almost never put as many bones in the spine of a human as we have in real life. Putting in more bones might indeed make the character move slightly more naturally, but there is a tradeoff: if we create a very long joint/bone sequence, we are likely to want to create a number of IK handles; this will in turn cause the keyframing process to be more tedious.

Next, in Figure 7.29, we rig the skeleton by letting Maya generate a complete set of IK handles for the skeleton. (The Human IK toolset is built to generate IK handles that mimic the movement of a human.) The ends of these handles are more easily visible than the ones that were created with

FIGURE 7.27 **Creating the biped skeleton.**

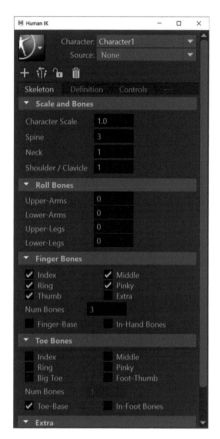

FIGURE 7.28 **Configuring the skeleton.**

the Joint tool we used earlier. The connections between the joints and the handles are not visible, however. There are a few important things to note in Figure 7.30. The root of the humanoid skeleton is at the bottom of the spine, just above the hips. The skeleton branches off in three directions, up toward the head and down toward each of the two legs. And, there is one bone that enters the head of the character, creating a three-way branch-out between the shoulders. Consider Figure 7.31. We can lock the feet of a skeleton to the ground plane. We have done this in the figure, so when we grab the root of the skeleton and pull downward with the Move tool, the character squats.

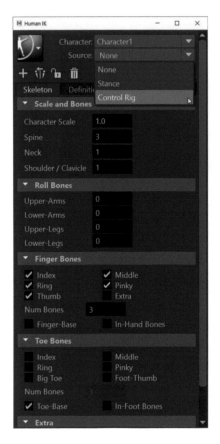

FIGURE 7.29 Rigging the biped skeleton.

Now we will create the body of our character—called the "skin"—and "bind" it to the skeleton. The skin of a character typically consists of actual skin and/or clothing. Sometimes, in order to make a character more reusable for future projects, we cover it completely with human skin, and then later, when we use the character in a scene, we put appropriate clothing over the skin. In this case, it is the human skin that is "skinned" to the skeleton. The clothing is made with polygon surfaces that are turned into nCloth and then constrained to the body in much the same way we constrained the curtain to the rod earlier in this book. In this way, the clothing can respond to the motion of the skeleton and to fields in a natural way. One other detail is that we have to turn the body of the character (which consists of human skin) into a collider so that the clothing doesn't pass through the body; we look at creating colliders later in this chapter.

In our example, however, we will skin the clothing of the character directly to the skeleton. In this case, the clothing will not be made out of cloth and will simply be a polygon mesh. In Figure 7.32, we see the Content Browser window. We will use a couple of pieces of clothing to create a partial skin. We will want to move our skeleton by moving IK handles in a fashion similar to Figure 7.33, but with the clothing (which is the skin of the character) flexing accordingly. Consider Figure 7.34. If we were to take the left arm and move it so that it is horizontal, like the right arm, then the skeleton would be in what is typically called a neutral "bind pose," that is, with both arms straight out, the head up straight, and the legs just a bit apart. The reason the legs are apart is that when we bind the skin (which consists of clothing), we don't want the left pant

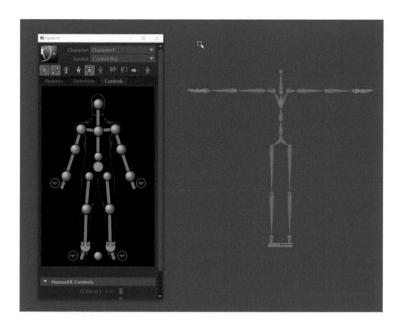

FIGURE 7.30   **Rigging the skeleton.**

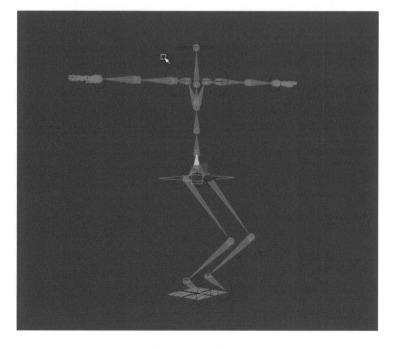

FIGURE 7.31   Using an IK handle to make the skeleton squat.

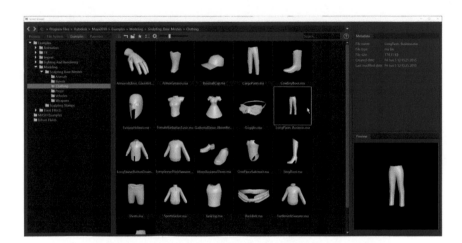

FIGURE 7.32   Human components in the Content Browser.

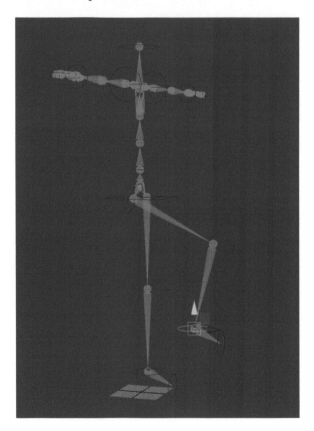

FIGURE 7.33   Using an IK handle to lift a leg.

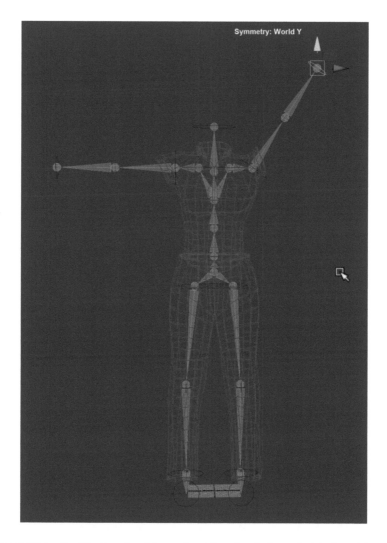

FIGURE 7.34 Positioning the skin and putting the skeleton in bind position.

leg to bind itself to the right leg bones or vice versa. With the skeleton in the bind pose, we have selected the skeleton, then the two pieces of clothing, and then bound the skin (just like we did with the fish). Then we moved the left arm. In Figure 7.35, we see that the left sleeve has moved accordingly. In Figure 7.35, we lift the left foot by moving the IK handle that terminates there—and the pant leg flexes naturally, as well. The binding process makes the skin (in this case, clothing) flex with the skeleton.

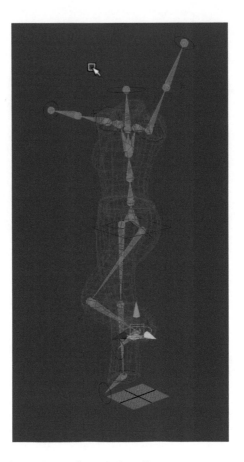

FIGURE 7.35   Bending a leg with an IK handle.

The binding process is actually much more complex than simply choosing the skeleton and the skin and hitting the Bind tool. We want to program each joint to influence the flexing of the skin as we move in both directions away from that joint. This influence diminishes as we move away from the joint. In Figure 7.36, we adjust parameters that control this, among other things.

There is an even more tedious issue that generally pops up. Consider Figure 7.37. We have lifted the foot, causing the knee to flex (because there is an IK handle connecting the left hip to the foot). The pant leg has flexed, as well, because it is bound to the skeleton. But look at how unnaturally the left pant leg flexes. It folds almost like paper. This is because the bones and joints have no geometry; that is, there isn't actually

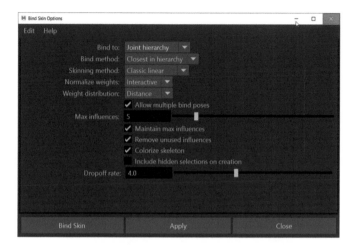

FIGURE 7.36 **Binding the skin to the skeleton.**

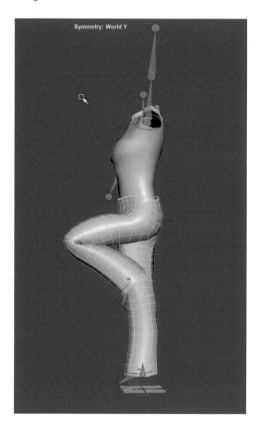

FIGURE 7.37 **A problem with the flexed leg.**

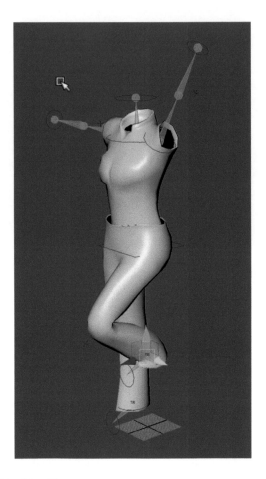

FIGURE 7.38 The flexed leg.

anything inside the pant leg. There is a sophisticated mechanism in Maya that allows the animator to carefully fine-tune the skinning of a character. We can make joints stick out (like knees or elbows) when the skin over them is stretched. We can make collar bones stick out. We can make muscles flex. We don't go into this mechanism in this book. But there is a much simpler tool that can be used to get the job done, albeit not as elegantly as we may like.

Consider the flexed knee in Figure 7.38. What we would like is for the knee joint to appear to have some mass to it as we continue to close the knee joint and bring the foot up toward the hip. In Figure 7.39, we have

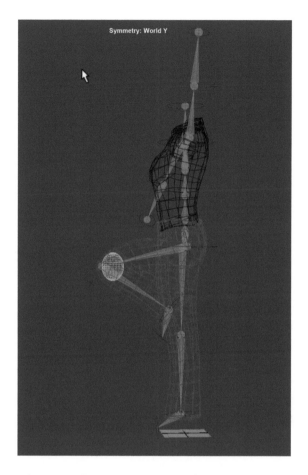

FIGURE 7.39   Placing a sphere to serve as an influencer.

taken a polygon sphere, stretched it out a bit top to bottom, and placed it just inside the pant leg. We shift-select the pants, then the sphere, and in Figure 7.40, we turn the sphere into an "influencer." Now, compare Figure 7.37 to Figure 7.41. The influencer makes the knee appear to have mass, so the pant leg flexes much more naturally.

PARTICLE DYNAMICS

Another way to introduce motion into a scene is to use the Maya dynamics engine, nDynamics. It is accessed by setting the Main Menu Selector to

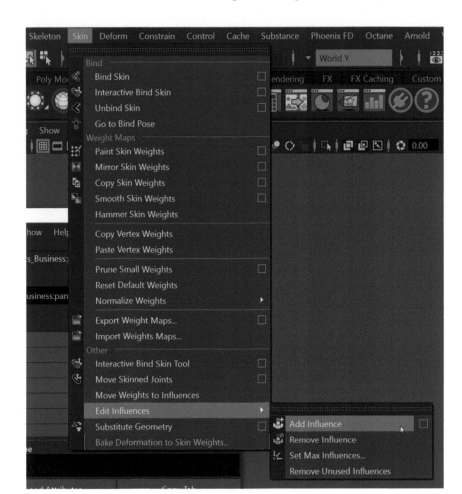

FIGURE 7.40 **Creating the influencer.**

FX. There are two kinds of dynamics in Maya: particle and body. First, we look at particle dynamics. We begin by quickly reviewing the process of making a container via a revolved NURBS curve. In Figure 7.42, we engage the CV Curve tool. In Figure 7.43, we have laid down six CVs. It makes the curve in Figure 7.44.

Now, we're going to use the CV Curve tool to create a container that will hold particles. In Figure 7.45, we have created a series of curves that begins at the Y axis, proceeds upward and outward, and then doubles back to the axis. The final set of curves is in Figure 7.46. In Figure 7.47,

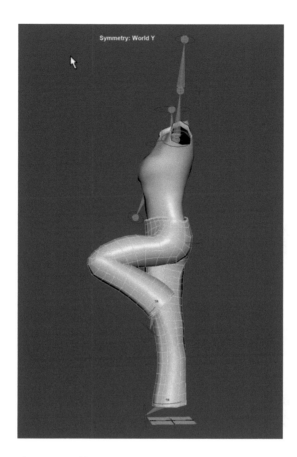

FIGURE 7.41 The repaired leg.

we use the Revolve tool, which creates the bowl in Figure 7.48. This is NURBS geometry, so, in Figure 7.49, we convert it to polygon geometry. Now, in Figure 7.50, we turn it into a Passive Collider by selecting this tool while the bowl is selected in the Viewport. What we are doing is setting the bowl up as an object that will not move but will prevent other objects from moving through it. (We do not use Bullet → Passive Rigid Body, as this is part of the other dynamics system, which we will cover later in this chapter.)

We will use Maya's particle system, called nParticles, to create objects that will hit the bowl. We create an "emitter," then, over a series of frames, particles are emitted from this emitter. The particles are controlled by some field, in this case, gravity; they fall downward and contact the

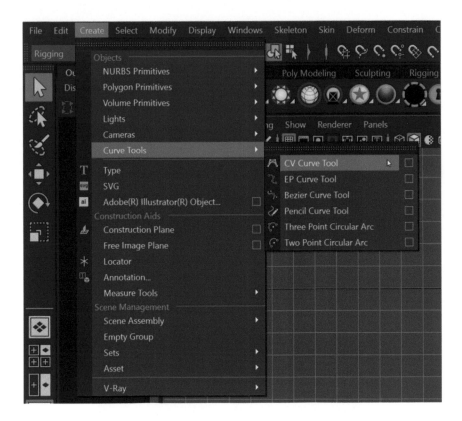

FIGURE 7.42   A curve for the bowl.

bowl. Maya does an amazingly good job of simulating the physics of this entire process. Before we create the emitter, we first choose the kind of particles we want to emit; see Figure 7.51. "Balls"—our choice for particle

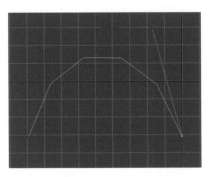

FIGURE 7.43   The control vertices.

type—are actually polygon spheres, but if we had chosen Point, we would have created particles that have no geometry associated with them. Their appearance would have been determined at render time.

In Figure 7.52, we create the Emitter, which will emit balls. The emitter has attributes and the balls have their own separate attributes. In Figure 7.53, we adjust the radius

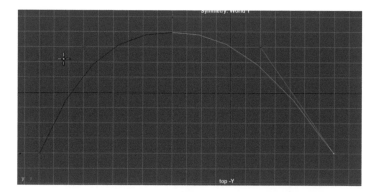

FIGURE 7.44 **The curve.**

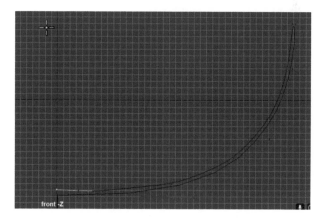

FIGURE 7.45 **Doubling back on the curve.**

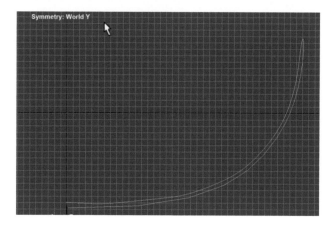

FIGURE 7.46 **The completed curve.**

FIGURE 7.47   Revolving the curve.

of each generated ball. Before we run the simulation, we choose the number of frames over which we want to generate balls from the emitter; see Figure 7.54. Now, we hit the play button on the lower right of the Maya interface in order to run the simulation. The balls are emitted from the emitter. One of the attributes of the emitter that we can adjust is how quickly the balls are emitted. Since the bowl is a Passive Collider, the balls hit it, bounce and roll around, and then come to a rest. The balls will also impact each other and respond accordingly. If we were to fill the bowl by continuing to run the simulation, the bowl would overflow, and the balls would fall downward and disappear from the scene. The filling bowl can be seen in Figure 7.55.

The way the nDynamics system calculates the interaction between particles and between particles and objects is by using what the Maya developers call a Nucleus Solver, which manages all the forces that affect the objects in a given interacting system. There are essentially two kinds of

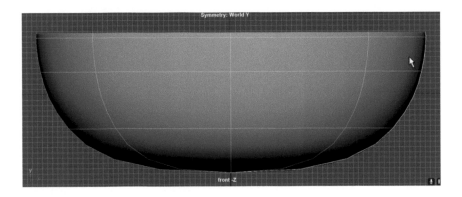

FIGURE 7.48   The NURBS bowl.

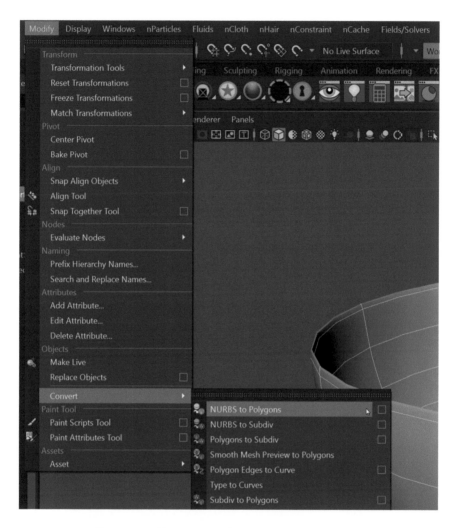

FIGURE 7.49   Converting NURBS to polygon geometry.

forces in such a system: field forces, which are generated by fields like gravity, and nucleus forces, which are internal to the objects in a system. Nucleus forces affect particles, hair, and cloth, as well as passive objects. Another way of looking at it is this: a combination of external and internal forces decides what happens when, for example, a piece of cloth falls through the air and hits an object. The nucleus is an object, and it can be seen in the Outliner shown in Figure 7.56. The node called nRigid1 was created when the bowl was turned into a passive collider.

In Figure 7.57, we have created another emitter. There is an attribute that controls the way particles are emitted from an emitter. The first one we created was an Omni emitter, meaning that particles are emitted from a single point, going out in all directions. In the first particle simulation, the balls all fell downward because there is a default gravity that affects all particles. In Figure 7.57, we see the attributes of a Surface emitter. There is a plane in Figure 7.58; it has been placed at the top of the scene, parallel to the x/z grid. To create the emitter, we first selected the plane, then chose nParticles → Emit from Object. Now the particles will

FIGURE 7.50 **Making the bowl a passive collider.**

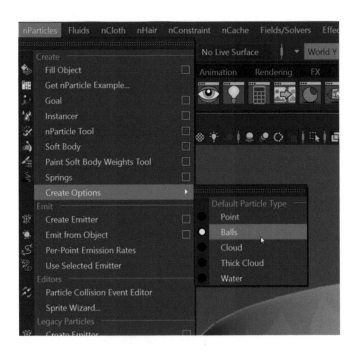

FIGURE 7.51 **Using geometric particles.**

be emitted from the surface of this plane and will fall downward under the control of the default gravity. In Figure 7.59, we see that there is a second way to control the form of particles that are emitted. This mechanism is more fine grained than the one shown in Figure 7.51. Here, there are multiple kinds of geometryless particles; we choose Streak. Only on rendering will they appear to be streaks.

One more thing—we want the particles to hit the

FIGURE 7.52 Creating an emitter.

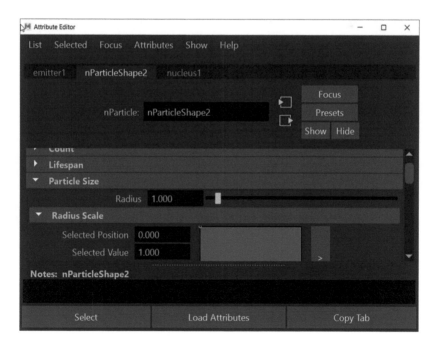

FIGURE 7.53 Scaling the particles.

FIGURE 7.54 Setting the frame number.

ground and bounce. So, we create another polygon plane, which we place at the bottom of the scene. Then we run the simulation and let some particles be emitted from the plane that is at the top of the scene. We shift-select first the particles, then the plane, and choose nCloth → Create Passive Collider. This will cause the Collide box in Figure 7.60 to be checked. Now, the particles will collide with the plane at the bottom of the scene. We have also given the plane a nonzero Bounce value. We left-click at the beginning of the timeline and rerun the simulation; the particles fall, collide with the ground plane, and bounce a bit. We have created rain—as rendered in Figure 7.61. We have rendered this with the Maya Hardware 2.0 renderer chosen in the Render window. The streaks will not render properly with

FIGURE 7.55 Emitting particles.

FIGURE 7.56   An emitter in the Outliner.

the Arnold renderer. This makes sense, as the appearance of geometryless particles is going to have to be determined by the renderer, and Arnold significantly postdates the existence of geometryless particles in Maya. In other words, Arnold wasn't built to work with the particle engine in Maya. But when mental ray was part of Maya, it was generally used to render

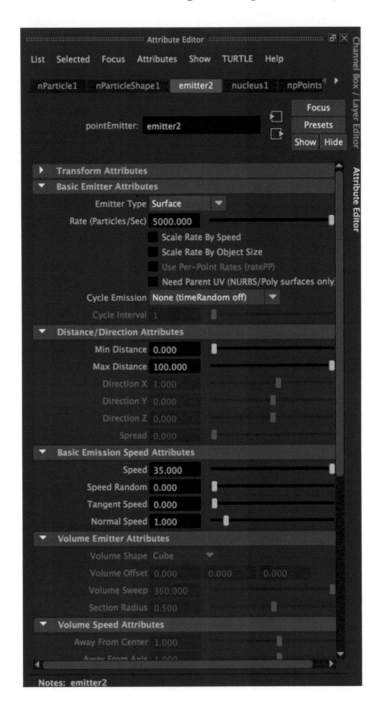

FIGURE 7.57 Setting emitter attributes.

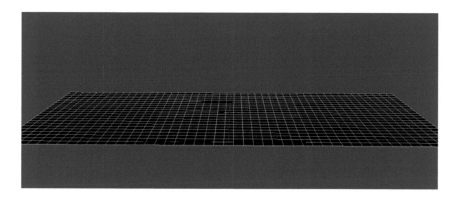

FIGURE 7.58 The surface for creating particles.

streaks; mental ray had been deeply embedded in Maya over a period of years and had been tailored to work with geometryless particles.

There is a very nice option in Maya that allows us to replace particles with arbitrary meshes created by the modeler. In the nParticles dropdown, there is an Instancer tool. One can create an emitter, run the simulation, and then shift-select a target object followed by the particles. Then, the Instancer tool is selected. Now, when the simulation is rerun, the target object shapes, instead of the particles, are emitted. This allows us, for instance, to produce a cloud of butterflies.

USING A SCRIPT TO ANIMATE AN OBJECT

Now we turn to the other form of dynamics—where two or more rigid bodies come into contact with each other. We will use Maya's "bullet" physics engine. As a reminder, since it does not load with the Maya interface by default, we must go to the Plug-in Manager and check off the Bullet bundle. But before we use the bullet physics engine, we will show how to animate an object with a script.

We will use a car that will collide with a wall in our next example. In Figure 7.62, we see a fragment of the Outliner. The four wheels of the car are children under the body of the car in the Outliner; this is so that the wheels may rotate independently as the car moves through the scene and so that the wheels will also inherit the forward motion of the car. This is a key reason we carefully put objects into a hierarchy by middle mouse button–dragging them in the Outliner: if object 1 is a child of object 2, object 1 will inherit the motion of object 2, but object 1 will also be able

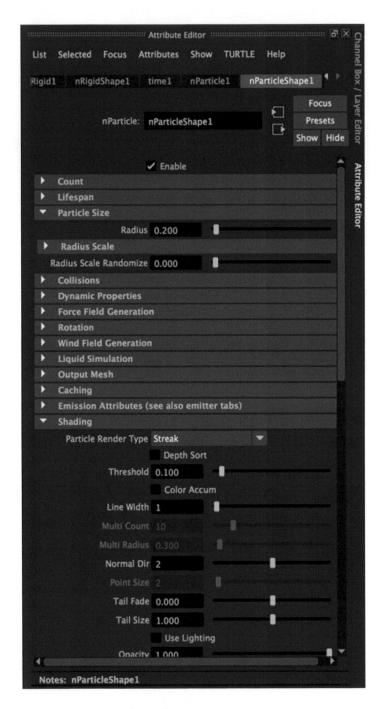

FIGURE 7.59 Setting particle attributes.

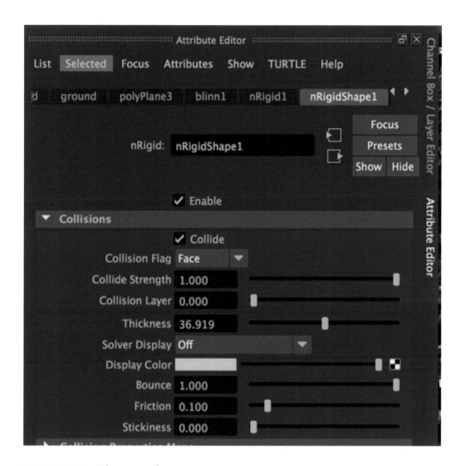

FIGURE 7.60 The ground.

to move independently within the limits of object 2's motion. We would also parent the doors to the body of the car so that the doors can open and close independently and will move forward with the car. Thus, there are two reasons to put objects in proper hierarchies in the Outliner: first, to make it easier to put materials on an object that is a component of another object (e.g., a wheel of a car is made out of different materials than the car), and second, so that an object can inherit the animation of its parent while still having its own animation properties. The inheritance of motion is a transitive relationship that cascades all the way up to a root in the Outliner; more precisely, in calculating the total movement of an object, Maya must begin with that object and then calculate the transitive closure of the "parent-of" relationship in the Outliner.

FIGURE 7.61   The rain.

In Figure 7.63, we have selected one of the wheels and then chosen Windows → Animation Editors → Expression Editor. We remember that every object in Maya comes premade with nine attributes to translate, scale, and rotate it in each of the three dimensions. In the Expression Editor in Figure 7.63, we have written a MEL script to rotate the wheel as the frames proceed during the running of the simulation in the timeline. The system variable time refers to frames, as it is frames that we use to simulate the passage of time. Now, our car's wheels can rotate as the car moves through the scene.

As mentioned in Chapter 1, MEL is the native Maya scripting language. There is a newer Maya scripting language called PyMEL, which is a

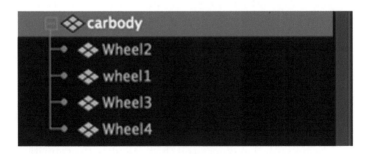

FIGURE 7.62   The parenting of the car wheels.

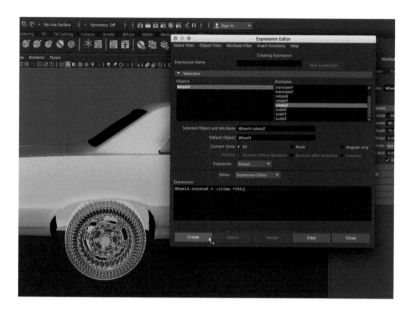

FIGURE 7.63   Rotating the wheels with a script.

translation of Maya commands into Python functions. You can use either language when writing scripts for Maya.

RIGID BODY COLLISIONS

In Figure 7.64, we have shift-selected the car (by selecting the car body, which is the root node for the car in the Outliner) and then the wall, then used the Bullet physics engine to turn them into passive rigid bodies. However, the Maya interface is a bit confusing on this point. Although the dropdown offers two kinds of rigid bodies, there are actually three possibilities, and one of these three can be chosen after the rigid body is created as being either dynamic or static. There are dynamic rigid bodies, which are the most programmable under the bullet system. Then there are static rigid bodies, which remain in place and never move, and therefore do not have to be maintained by the bullet physics engine (and are thus computationally very simple). And finally, there are kinetic rigid bodies, which can move during the simulation, but are not programmable as dynamic rigid bodies (and thus are more computationally complex than static rigid bodies, but less computationally complex than dynamic rigid bodies).

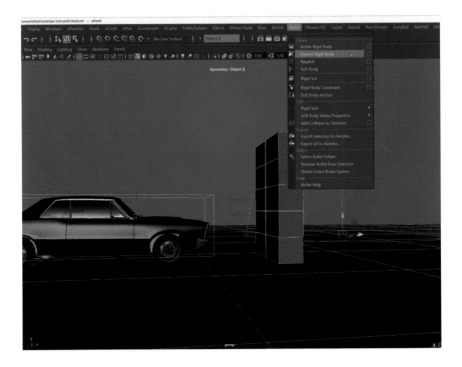

FIGURE 7.64 Making the car and the blocks rigid colliders.

So, what we have done in Figure 7.64 is turn both the wall and the car into passive rigid bodies, but in Figure 7.65, the car and the brick wall are both turned into dynamic rigid bodies. (At the same time, we could have turned either of them into kinetic rigid bodies.) We see in Figure 7.65 that the car is given an "impulse" that moves it along the x axis, which brings it into contact with the wall—which actually consists of a number of separate blocks that are stacked on top of each other. (When the wall and the car were turned into rigid bodies in Figure 7.64, the 10 blocks that make up the wall, along with the car, were all turned into rigid bodies.) The simulation is run—and the result is in Figures 7.66 and 7.67. The car moves and collides with the pieces of the wall—and the blocks react by flying apart. If the wall had been turned into either a static or a kinetic rigid body, the car would have hit it, and then the wall would have simply stopped the car from moving any further. Note that in Figure 7.65, the motion of these objects is being modeled as if the objects were boxes (see Collider Shape Type under Forces/Impulses); other choices are sphere, capsule, and hull. (Remember our discussion above on containing objects and how they are

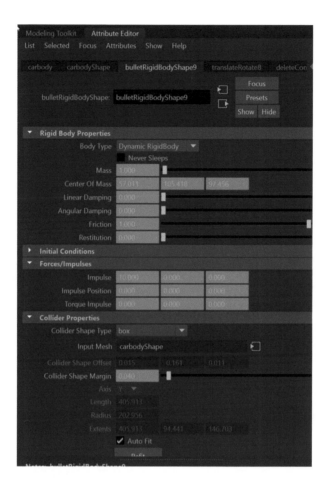

FIGURE 7.65   **Setting rigid body attributes.**

used to estimate the way two or more objects will collide.) For static bodies, there is another important choice, and this is to use the mesh of the object itself in calculating the impact of a collision.

As a quick note, in Figure 7.68, we delete the history. This is a tool that deletes the results of certain computations. If a tool in Maya seems to misbehave, often the problem can be corrected by deleting the history and giving Maya a clean start.

We are not focusing on character animation or on complex animation involving, perhaps, the interaction of several moving models in one scene. But there is a technique that can be very important for the animator, and that is something called "storyboarding." This is the process of drawing out,

FIGURE 7.66   The car in motion.

FIGURE 7.67   Collision between rigid colliders.

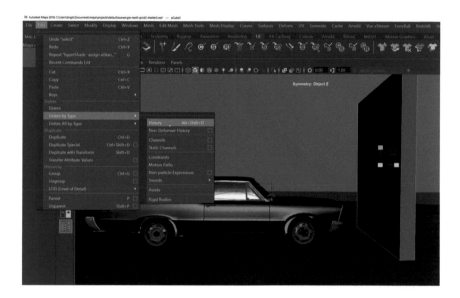

FIGURE 7.68   Deleting history.

by hand, the movement in a scene before setting up any of the animation of the scene. You might hand-draw (or use a drawing program to produce) a series of images that rough out the movement in the scene. Often, there will be a series of images for every camera in the scene, with an image drawn for every significant change in position or shape of the objects being animated. This can save a lot of time by minimizing the amount of work done painstakingly reanimating models within Maya.

USING THE SHATTER TOOL TO ANIMATE A SCENE

Now, we look at breaking the wall apart in a different way. We leave the car and the wall as dynamic rigid bodies, but the wall starts out by being a single solid object—not a stack of separate blocks. We then select the wall and apply the Shatter tool to it, which breaks it up into angular fragments. Once the wall is broken into fragments, they are selected as a group, and under the Bullet engine, they are turned into something called a Rigid Set. This sequence can be seen in Figures 7.69 through 7.73. The Shatter tool can be tailored to fragment an object in varying ways. In this example, we are using it to prebreak the wall into pieces that will fly apart on impact.

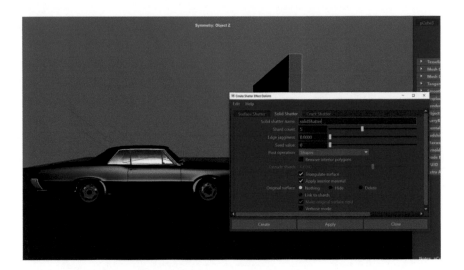

FIGURE 7.69   The Shatter tool.

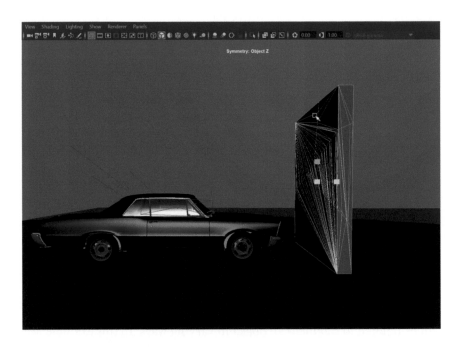

FIGURE 7.70   The shattered wall.

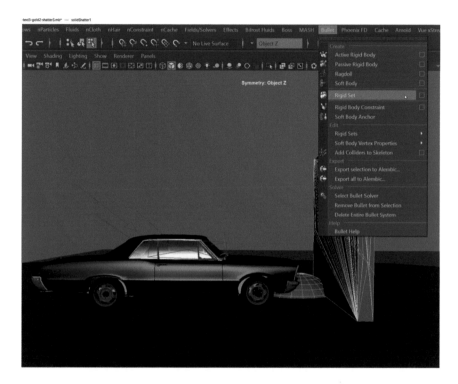

FIGURE 7.71   Making the shattered pieces rigid.

FIGURE 7.72   The car in motion.

FIGURE 7.73   The collision between rigid bodies.

MOTION BLUR

We are rendering this with Arnold. Many renderers, including Arnold, have a "motion blur" option. In Figure 7.74, we turn this option on by checking the box labeled "Enable" under "Motion Blur." This creates a blurred effect for every object that is in motion at render time. The result can be seen in Figure 7.75.

ANIMATING VIA ROTATION

In Figures 7.76 through 7.78, we animate a door opening and closing. We do this by first using the Move tool in combination with holding down the D key to move the center of rotation of the door. We did this in Chapter 6 with the mailbox lid. See the altered yellow square icon in Figure 7.77; the circular marker in the center of the box tells us that the D key is being held down and that we are moving the center of rotation, not the object itself. Then, we keyframe the door while rotating it.

ADDING SOUND TO A SCENE

In Figure 7.79, we import a WAV sound file into Maya. As pointed out earlier, Maya is not an audio editor. We import sound only to use it to time the motion in a scene. We then later import the sound file again, but this time into the video editor, so that the sequence of frames can be rendered along with the sound in order to export out of the video editor a container that includes both video and sound. Also, Maya can import only WAV files (a Microsoft standard) and AIF files (an Apple standard). While most video editors can process MP3 files, Maya cannot.

In Figure 7.80, we click on a small human-shaped icon in the lower right of the Maya interface. This opens up a window that allows us to adjust a number of settings that relate to animation; see Figure 7.81. We can change the frame rate. We can also open up the area above the timeline so that we can better see an imported sound file. We have chosen the largest setting, 4x. Now, we can keyframe the closing of the door to coincide with the click of the strike plate being hit and then with the larger sound wave of the door shutting all the way. Although Maya will play the sound when we run the simulation, we don't have to listen to the sound to know where to set the key frames—we can see the bumps in the sound curve. Also, if we import more than one sound

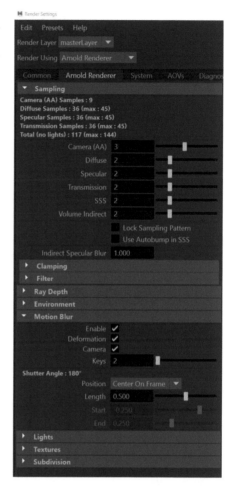

FIGURE 7.74 Enabling motion blur.

file, we can right-click in the sound wave area to choose the sound file we want to use; see Figure 7.82.

THE GRAPH EDITOR

We will give only a brief introduction to the Graph Editor in this book. It can be used to hone the animation in a scene. The Graph Editor displays the animation of any object that is selected in the Viewport when the simulation is run. In Figure 7.83, we see that there is a rotate, translate, and scale curve for each of the three dimensions of the object selected. In

FIGURE 7.75 The blurred render.

this image, we are looking at the curves for the camera we animated earlier in this chapter as it moved through the orangerie. We see that it only moves along one axis (it never moves along the X or Y axes), and it only rotates across one plane. Also, it is never scaled in size, as it is not a physical object. It follows that a camera cannot be animated by scaling it. All of this is borne out by the curves in Figures 7.84 through 7.88.

In Figures 7.89 and 7.90, we perform a modest adjustment. The camera translates along the Z axis, and it rotates along the Y axis. We select each of these curves in turn and then choose the Spline tool. This takes those two curves—which can be seen in their original forms in Figure 7.88—and smooths them a bit so that the camera does not rotate or move in a jerky fashion. The smoothed-out motion is seen in the graphs in Figure 7.90.

A CLOSER LOOK AT TRANSLATING, SCALING, AND ROTATING POLYGON OBJECTS

In Figure 7.91, we take a closer look at translating, rotating, and scaling polygon objects. As a reminder, in Chapter 2, we noted that a polygon object can be specified with only the following information: a set of points in 3-space that are connected by straight lines, that is, $\{(x_{i1}, y_{i1}, z_{i1}), (x_{i2}, y_{i2}, z_{i2})\}$. To translate, rotate, and scale in 3-space, we need to do a bit of matrix

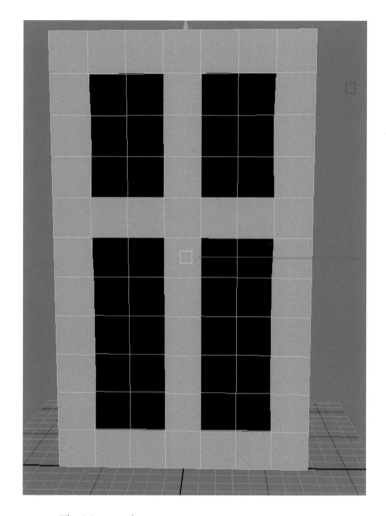

FIGURE 7.76   The Move tool.

mathematics. To simplify the discussion, we will look at the problem in 2-space. We are concerned with taking a vector object in 2-space, that is, an object made out of straight lines, and scaling it, rotating it, and translating it in 2-space.

The notation is simpler for 2-space. All we need to do in order to represent the translation, rotation, or scaling of a 2D object is to know where each point has started and where it will end up. The lines that connect the points don't change. Let's consider a single vertex in a 2D image to be (x, y). Let's consider the translated position to be (x_t, y_t), the

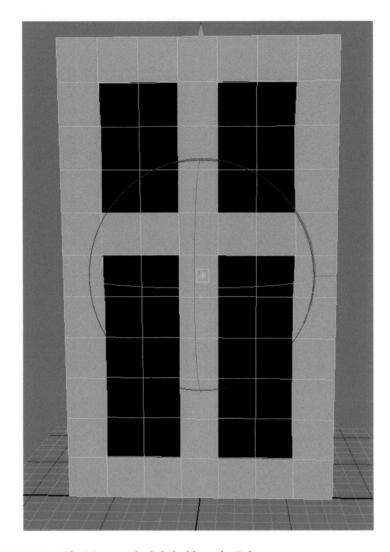

FIGURE 7.77 The Move tool while holding the D key.

rotated position to be (x_r, y_r), and the scaled position to be (x_s, y_s). Here is all we need to compute in order to define the operations of translating, rotating, and scaling:

Translate: $(x_t, y_t) = (x + a, y + b)$

Rotate: $(x_r, y_r) = (x\cos(\theta) - y\sin(\theta), x(\sin(\theta) + y\cos(\theta))$

Scale: $(x_s, y_s) = (ax, by)$

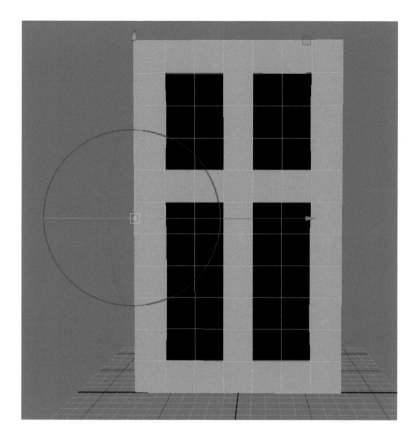

FIGURE 7.78   The moved center pivot.

In these equations, a and b are constants, and θ is the angle of rotation. We have not calculated the cos and sin values, but the cos and sin calculations are very simple. See Figure 7.91. We see that if we draw a circle around the angle of rotation, where we rotate from the end of one black line to the other black line, all we need to do is draw a couple of triangles to get the values we need for the fractions that make up the sin and cos values.

Again, for 3-space, we need a little matrix mathematics, which is just a bit more complicated, but it is still quite simple. The main point is that it is a very quick operation to take a polygon object and translate (move), rotate, and/or scale it in 3-space. This is of great help in real-time graphics, such as in gaming. The simplicity of representing the geometry of a polygon object and of calculating its translation, rotation, and scaling in 3-space is one of the major benefits of polygon modeling. Add to that

FIGURE 7.79 Importing a file.

FIGURE 7.80 Opening up the timeline options.

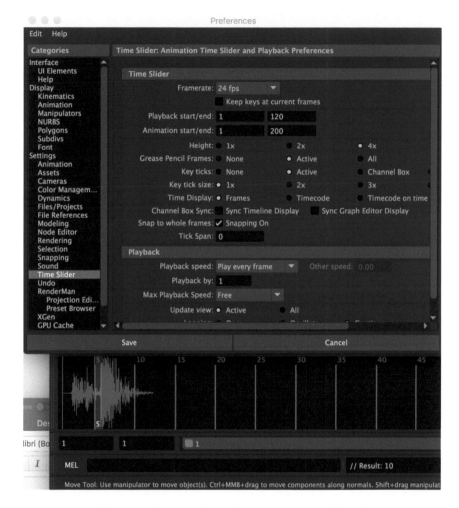

FIGURE 7.81   The opened-up timeline, the sound wave, and the door keyframes.

its conceptual simplicity for the modeler, and we find ourselves with a technology that has remained on top of the 3D modeling world for a very long time. There is yet another benefit: graphics cards (or graphics processing unit, GPUs), as we will see in Chapter 8, are often engineered to process triangles. It is very simple for an application like Maya to turn quads into triangles (just add a diagonal), so the translation of a polygon mesh into something that a graphics card can process is very straightforward.

FIGURE 7.82   Choosing a sound file.

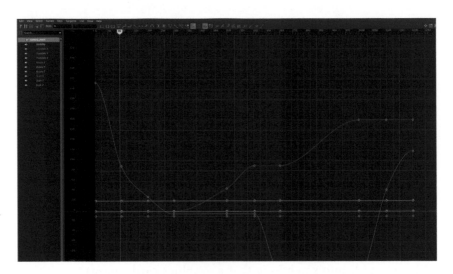

FIGURE 7.83   The camera's movement through the orangerie.

FIGURE 7.84   Translation in x axis.

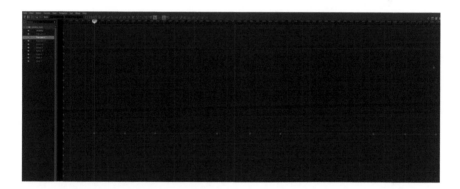

FIGURE 7.85   Translation in y axis.

FIGURE 7.86   Translation in z axis.

FIGURE 7.87   Rotation in y axis.

FIGURE 7.88   Translation in z axis and rotation in y axis.

ANIMATING WITH A MOTION PATH

One of the easiest ways to animate the movement of an object through a scene is by having it move along a curve as the simulation is run. While we do this, we can manipulate the angle of the object; this allows us, for example, to bank a plane as it moves in a loop. Such "motion paths" are very easy to set up. First, draw a loop (or even a series of connected curves that don't form a closed loop), as shown in Figure 7.92; set the timeline for the

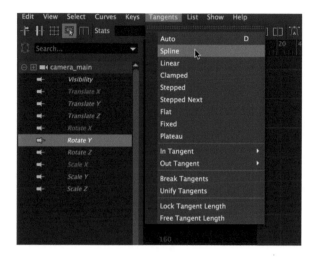

FIGURE 7.89   The Spline tool.

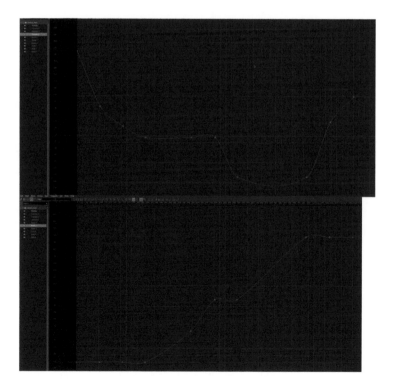

FIGURE 7.90   Splining the translation and rotation curves.

$$\cos(\Theta) = f_d \,/\, h$$
$$\sin(\Theta) = g_d \,/\, h$$

black lines = hypotenuse = h

red = g_1, yellow = g_2, green = f_1, green | brown = f_2

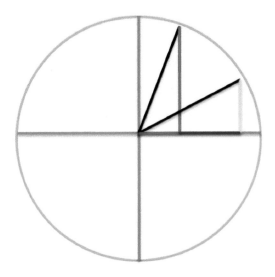

FIGURE 7.91   Calculating sin and cos.

number of frames you want to have go by during a single traverse around the loop; then shift-select the object, then the loop, and then select the tool shown in Figure 7.93. This turns the curve into a motion path and binds the object to that path. Note that, as in Figure 7.92, you often want to create the loop in an orthographic view so that the loop is all in one plane. Figure 7.94 shows what happens after the car, then the loop, is shift-selected. Maya tells us that the car is now bound to the path by having it jump onto the path. Then we run the simulation. A perspective view of the scene is in Figure 7.95. A rendered frame is in Figure 7.96.

VUE

So, how did we get the ground, the sky, the sun, and the trees used in our motion path example immediately above? There are many free and commercial plug-ins for Maya. One rather expensive one is called Vue

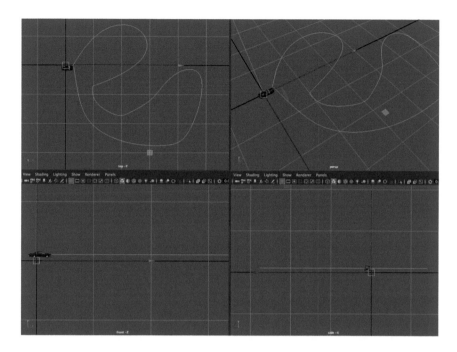

FIGURE 7.92   A NURBS loop.

(e-onsoftware.com). It runs as a standalone app, as well as a plug-in to Maya. When the plug-in is installed, a dropdown menu is created in the Main Menu. In Figure 7.97, we create a Vue scene within Maya. Vue, which installs in one of about three different versions—and Vue XStream is the version that I use with Maya—can be used to create very realistic

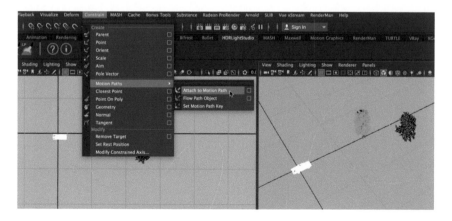

FIGURE 7.93   Turning the curve into a motion path.

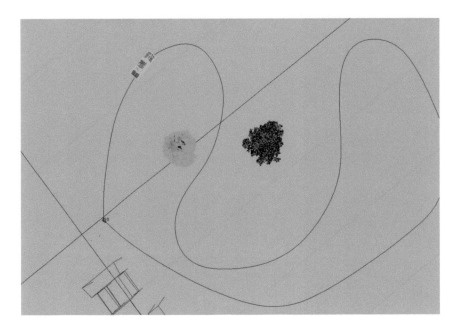

FIGURE 7.94 The car attaching to the path.

natural environments. It tends to create scenes with very large numbers of polygon faces that therefore are very time consuming to render. Vue has its own native renderer that it can use when it is run standalone. But when Vue is run within Maya, it uses V Ray—an expensive renderer that we will look at briefly in the next chapter of this book. The first thing one does

FIGURE 7.95 The car and path.

FIGURE 7.96   The rendered car on motion path.

after creating a Vue scene within Maya is choose a sky environment; this can be seen in Figure 7.98. Vue gives the user very fine-grained control over the sorts of environments one can build, but we only look at simple defaults here.

In Figure 7.99, we use the Vue Create menu to add to our scene. We are keeping it very simple and adding a couple of trees to the scene. We will

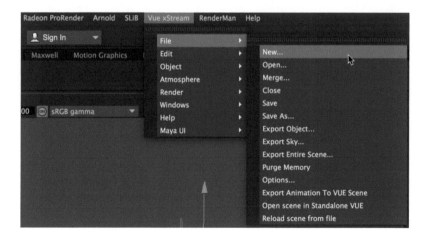

FIGURE 7.97   Inserting a Vue scene into Maya.

FIGURE 7.98   Choosing a Vue sky.

FIGURE 7.99   Choosing a plant.

FIGURE 7.100   The tree and plant choices.

leave the ground in its initial state, with no interesting topography. In Figure 7.100, we see the prefab trees that one can choose from. There is a companion program called PlantFactory (e-onsoftware.com), which can be used to carefully craft plant life, which can then be fed into Vue, and then through Vue into Maya. Natural terrains and plant life are very easy to create with Vue and PlantFactory, so having these applications can radically simplify the process of placing Maya models in outdoor environments. You can also create bodies of water, as well as rain and snow, with Vue. The render in Figure 7.96 was done with VRay, which is available as a plug-in to Maya.

MAYA HAIR

Earlier we looked at VRay hair (fur); we did this as a modeling example. Here, we take a very quick look at Maya hair; we cover it in this chapter because Maya hair will respond to fields and is thus a way to add motion to a scene. The hair mechanism gives you precise control over the hair you create, and it is good for creating animal fur, as well. (We looked at the native fur capability in Maya in Chapter 6, but Maya fur is very difficult to animate, and Autodesk has deprecated it. It is unclear when it will be removed from Maya.) Rather than building our own, in Figure 7.101, we pull down a menu in order to choose from a very small number of complete hair examples; see Figure 7.102. We will choose one of the dreadlock examples.

FIGURE 7.101 The nHair toolset.

The way one typically creates a hair style is by attaching it to a skull cap that can then be placed on a character's head and reshaped to fit precisely. In Figure 7.103, we have quickly fitted the skull cap with the dreadlocks on it to our Moai head. Note that the hair does not preview very well in the Viewport; it must be rendered to see what it will look like. In Figure 7.104, we see the Outliner and note that the hair system creates a subtree within the Outliner. The rendered dreadlocks are in Figure 7.105. In Figure 7.106, we adjust fields that are supplied with the hair facility; there is no need to go to the Fields/Solvers menu and create them independently. In Figure 7.107, we have run the simulation and rendered a frame with Arnold.

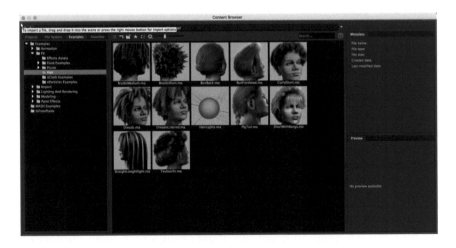

FIGURE 7.102 The example hair sets.

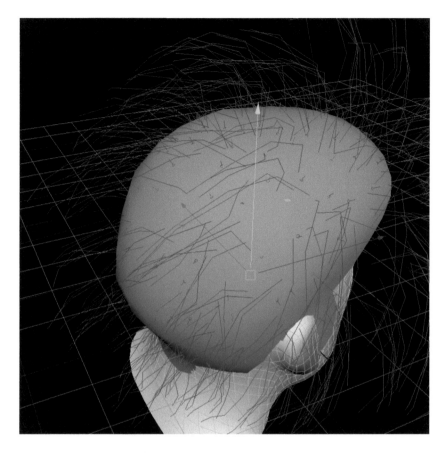

FIGURE 7.103   **Placing the skull cap.**

CINEMA 4D

There are, of course, other 3D applications that compete with Autodesk Maya. Maxon of Germany sells a product called Cinema 4D (maxon.net), which has a very large and loyal user base. It is in many ways comparable to Maya. In my personal opinion, Maya has a better 3D modeler, but with respect to animation, Cinema 4D does have some advantages. In particular, it is often used to create basic "motion graphics." The opening visual effects of news and other TV shows, title and credit effects in movies, rotational and quick particle effects for TV commercials—these could loosely be called motion graphics. (Below, we will create some simple motion graphics with Cinema 4D.)

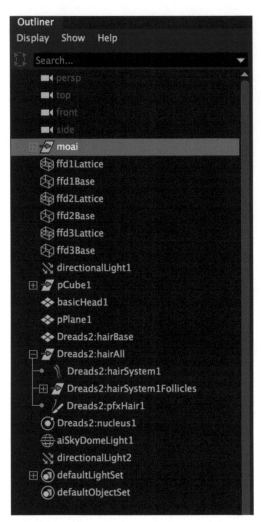

FIGURE 7.104   The Outliner with hair system.

The interface of Cinema 4D is easier to learn than interfaces to some other 3D apps. (Some consider it easier to learn and use than Maya.) Its native renderer is very good and reasonably fast. It supports a 3D painting engine, soft and rigid body dynamics, particle dynamics, and, of course, a complete 3D polygon modeling system. It also has a hair system and it comes with a distributed rendering tool. There is a general-purpose version, as well as specialized versions for motion graphics and architectural design.

Cinema 4D is available as a free student version, but it does not allow plug-ins that need serial numbers. For a few hundred dollars, a student can buy a version that does support licensed plug-ins. Cinema 4D comes bundled with Prorender, the free renderer from AMD (the GPU manufacturer), which we will use in the next chapter.

In our example, we will make a chair bomb, that is, a bomb made out of chairs—something that has obvious practical value. In Figure 7.108, we see the Cinema 4D interface with a single chair in the scene. In Figure 7.109, we create a Cloner object so we can make many chairs. In Figure 7.110, we see the two objects in the scene, the chair and the cloner, and in Figure 7.111, we embed the chair under the cloner by using the left-button mouse to drag the chair up to the cloner. In Figure 7.112, we

FIGURE 7.105 A render of the hair.

create a grid, 15 by 15 by 15, of chairs. We also put them into the form of a sphere. We see this sphere by scrolling outward; see Figure 7.113. In Figure 7.114, with the cloner selected, we give it a Simulation Tag that is a Rigid Body; then, in the right portion of the interface, as in Figure 7.115, we select Collision and have the children inherit this tag. Now, in Figure 7.116, we have the sphere of chairs selected (the cloner) and put them under the control of a particle simulation with an "attractor." Then, on the right side of the interface, we select Falloff and give the simulation a spherical shape; see Figure 7.117. In Figure 7.118, we give the attractor a strong negative value. In Figure 7.119, we see the resulting system. In Figure 7.120, we run the simulation by using the green control at the bottom of the interface. In Figure 7.121, we see the result of the

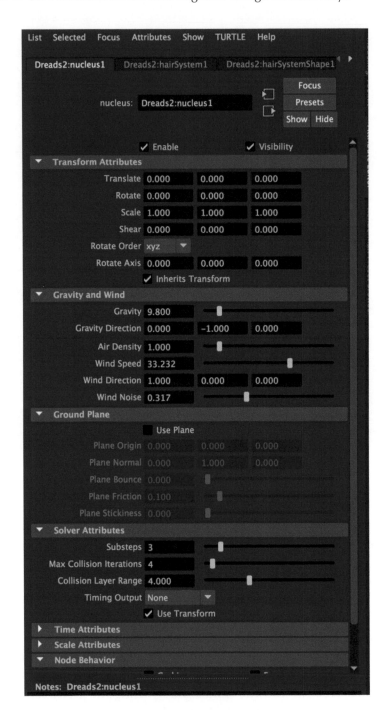

FIGURE 7.106 The nucleus attributes.

FIGURE 7.107   The hair after running the simulation.

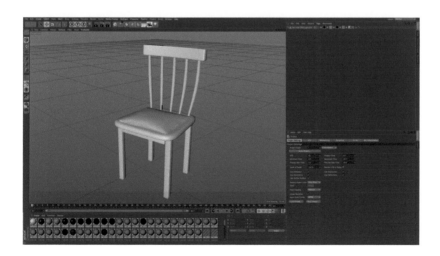

FIGURE 7.108   The Cinema 4D interface.

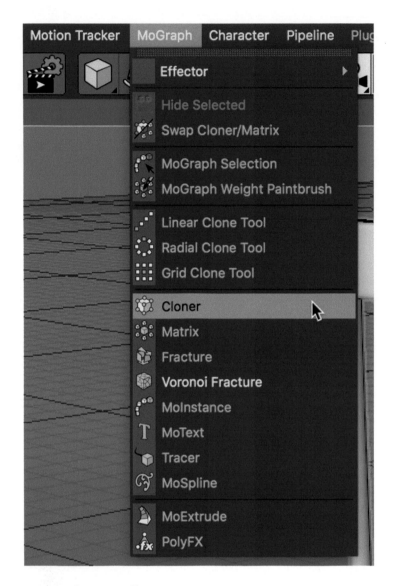

FIGURE 7.109   Creating a Cloner.

simulation. And in Figure 7.122, we see the result with the Cinema 4D default renderer.

(Finally, the author notes that there is significant concern, at the time of this writing, that the CIA will prevent the chair bomb example from being published...)

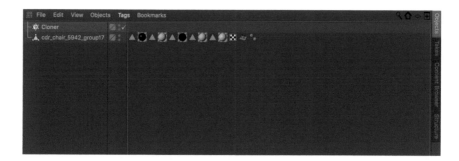

FIGURE 7.110   The Cloner and the chair.

FIGURE 7.111   The chair under the Cloner.

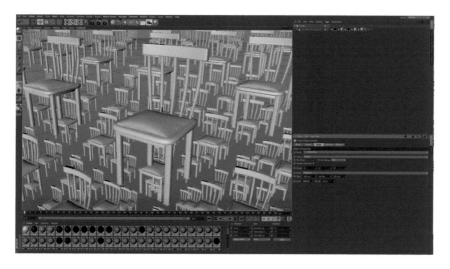

FIGURE 7.112   The 15 by 15 by 15 cluster of chairs in a spherical shape.

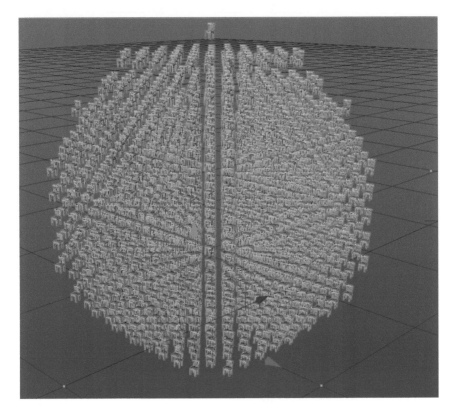

FIGURE 7.113   The sphere of chairs.

HOUDINI

Next, we look at another very popular 3D modeling, animation, and rendering application: SideFX's Houdini (sidefx.com). It is used heavily for its dynamics effects. I believe that, like Cinema 4D, it is not as good a modeler as Maya, but its dynamics capabilities are truly impressive. In particular, it comes with a number of powerful water effects simulation tools that make it relatively easy (given the inherent complexity of water effects) to create ocean and other moving water effects. It also comes with some very nice tools for creating fire and smoke effects. I personally find Houdini harder to learn and to use than Maya or Cinema 4D. One of the reasons for its high level of complexity, however, is that it has as a central focus the ability to create a system for generating some effects in a way that allows the designer to tweak them for use in a different project while reusing most of what was previously built. In this way, Houdini is

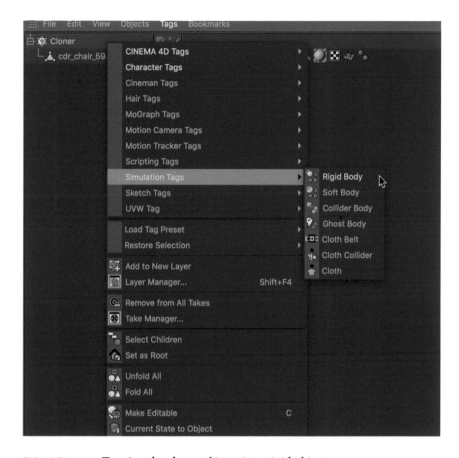

FIGURE 7.114 Turning the cloner objects into rigid objects.

FIGURE 7.115 Setting up the cloner to collide and the children inheriting this property.

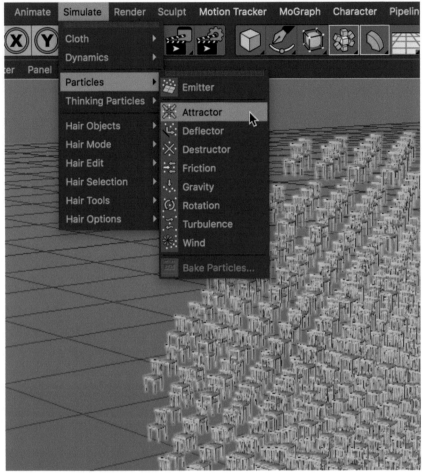

FIGURE 7.116   Putting the ball of chairs under a particle system that will attract.

a bit of a of "meta" tool, and it uses an approach the SideFX people call "proceduralism." It uses a node-based architecture, as most 3D applications do, but with Houdini, this is a dominant aspect of the system. Houdini has a reputation for easily scaling; that is, systems with very large amounts of data run smoothly, provided the hardware is appropriately powerful. I found the native Houdini renderer to be particularly good at modeling the interaction of light and water effects. It is also a fairly fast renderer.

We will take a quick look at a couple of the tool sets for doing fire and water effects. In Figure 7.123, we see the Houdini interface. It is much

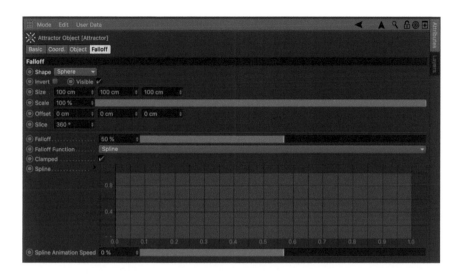

FIGURE 7.117   Creating a spherical shape to the attractor system.

FIGURE 7.118   Giving the attractor a strong negative strength.

like the Maya and the Cinema 4D interfaces, with a large working area for the designer, key tools along the left, controls to run simulations and animations at the bottom, and important menus at the top. There is also something very similar to Maya's Attribute Editor at the top right. There is a window for displaying graphs at the lower right. In Figure 7.124, we select a tool that will allow us to create a compact water effect. In Figures 7.125 and 7.126, we create an instance of a water tank. In Figure 7.127, we see the resulting particle effect. In Figure 7.128, we have created a camera and are now creating an environmental light. In Figures 7.129 through 7.131, we are using a canned Houdini texture and applying it to the light. It will create a natural daytime lighting effect. (We will look at a way to do something very similar in Maya in the next chapter.) In Figure 7.132, we have selected the camera in the graph window in the lower right, and we choose the

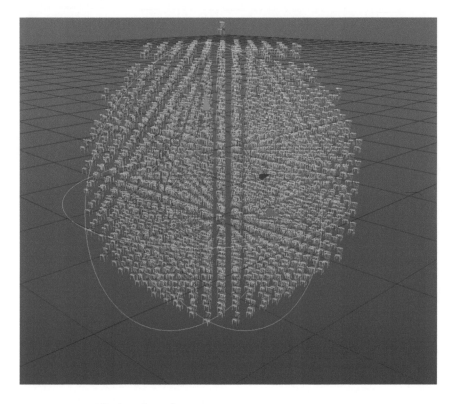

FIGURE 7.119 The bomb ready to go.

FIGURE 7.120 Running the simulation.

rotate tool. In Figure 7.133, we rotate the camera to change the angle at which we are viewing the scene. In Figure 7.134, we see a rendering of the water effect.

In Figure 7.135, we create a sphere, and with the sphere selected, assign a fire primitive to it in Figure 7.136. In Figure 7.137, we see that the fire has been applied to the sphere shape. Figure 7.138 shows the main window after the simulation has been run for a handful of frames. A close-up of the resulting render is in Figure 7.139.

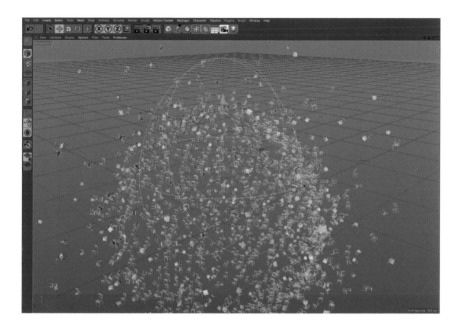

FIGURE 7.121   The explosion.

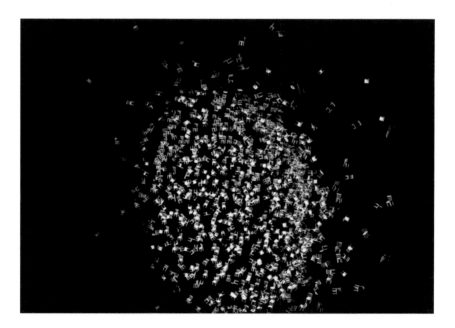

FIGURE 7.122   The render of the explosion.

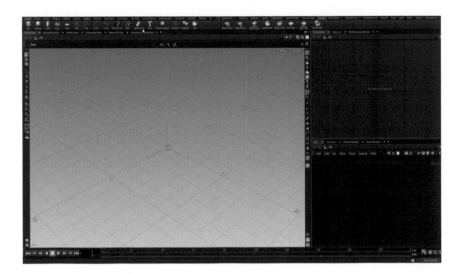

FIGURE 7.123 The Houdini interface.

FIGURE 7.124 The water tank tool.

FIGURE 7.125 Editing the water tank tool.

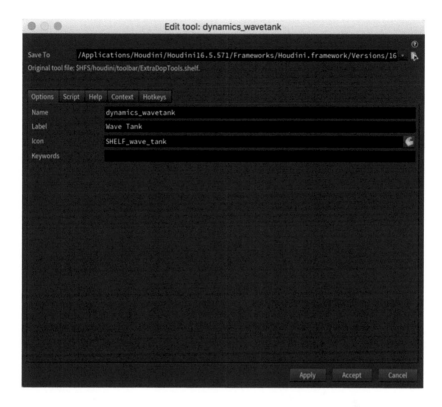

FIGURE 7.126   The water tank tool.

FIGURE 7.127   The particle effect.

FIGURE 7.128   Creating an environmental light (and a camera).

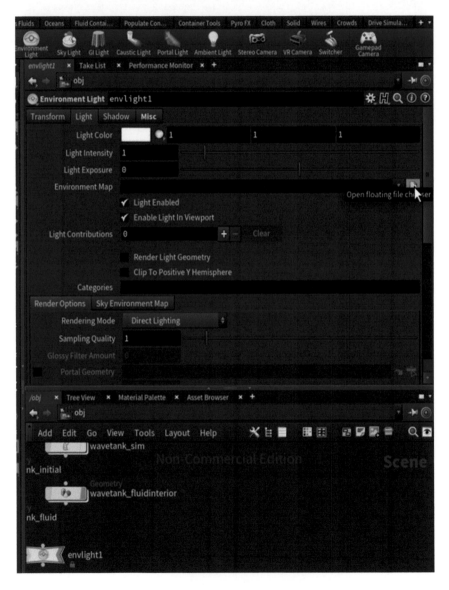

FIGURE 7.129   Selecting an image for the environmental light.

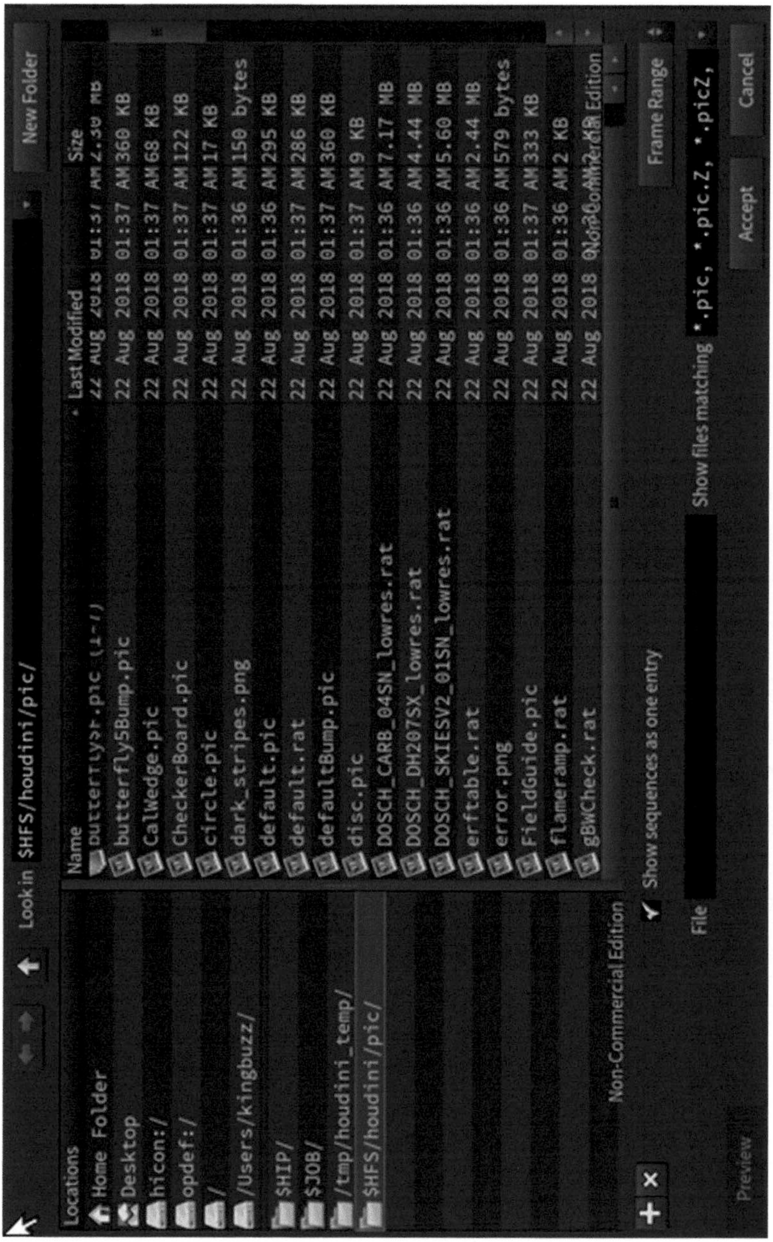

FIGURE 7.130   The sky (and other) Houdini built-in textures.

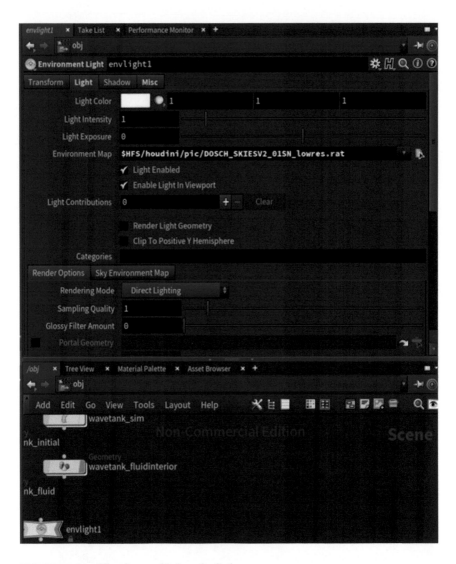

FIGURE 7.131 The sky applied to the light.

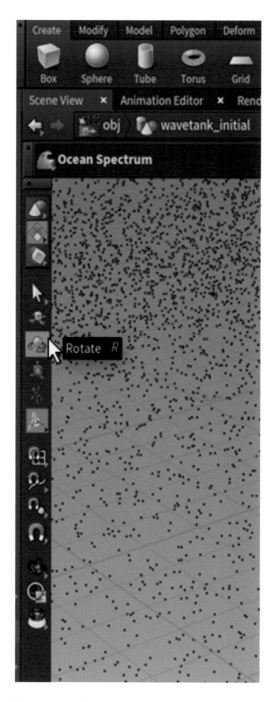

FIGURE 7.132 The Rotate tool.

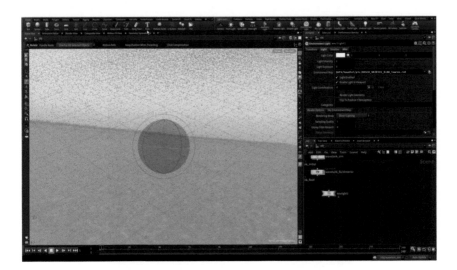

FIGURE 7.133   **Rotating the camera.**

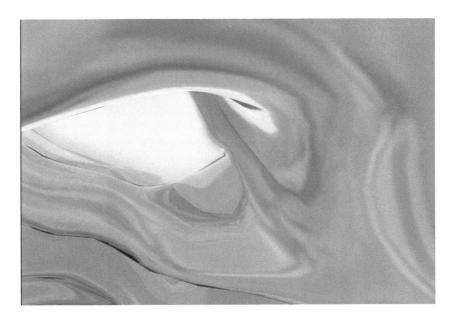

FIGURE 7.134   The water effect rendered.

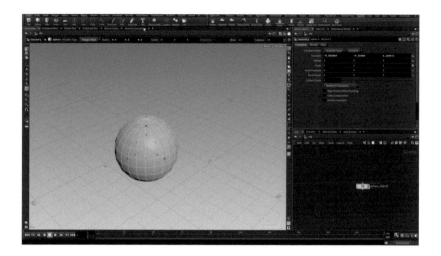

FIGURE 7.135 A sphere to apply fire to.

FIGURE 7.136 The fire tool.

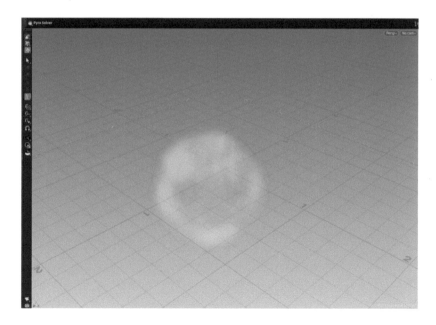

FIGURE 7.137 The sphere turned to fire.

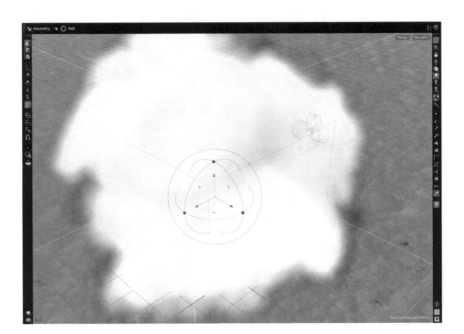

FIGURE 7.138   After running the simulation.

FIGURE 7.139   The edge of the fireball.

CHAPTER 8

Rendering and Lights

With examples: *Rendering a balcony close-up, rendering a glass table, a "tooned" cow and flamingo, lighting up a moving car, a camera aim pointing at a car which is hitting a wall, adjusting camera settings, fixing the shadow under a glass table, the Vray toon shader, a dome light which is providing a 360-degree environment, and putting toon materials on the sun face and the painted face.*

THERE IS A REASON that the vast majority of rendering plug-ins for Maya supply their own materials and lighting systems: lighting, materials, and rendering are tightly interdependent. In this chapter, we look at a number of renderers that can be used with Maya. We consider the basic underpinnings of most photorealistic renderers, as well as some specialized rendering techniques.

RASTERIZATION AND RAY TRACING

A popular trend in recent years has been moving much of the logic of rendering from software running in the main CPU of the computer to the graphics card, or GPU, of the computer. (To be precise, a graphics card holds one or more GPUs.) The goal: faster, more photorealistic renders, with a focus on the faster part. The dominant algorithmic technique used in photorealistic rendering is called "ray tracing." To see what ray tracing is all about, let's consider something called "rasterization."

In short, rasterization is a faster, but less effective, technique (with respect to photorealism) than ray tracing. The goal of either technique is to take a bunch of 3D wireframe objects in 3-space, each with its own material properties, and create a 2D pixel-based image. In rasterization, a polygon mesh is first turned into a mesh of triangles. (Quads are split into triangles and hopefully the modeler is using good modeling practices and not creating five- or more-sided polygons.) If the model is NURBS-based, it must first be turned into polygon geometry. Next, when determining the color of any given pixel that represents part of the surface of some object, the renderer only considers the material properties of that object when light first hits it; the way reflections off and refractions through other objects might affect the color of that pixel are not considered in calculating its color. And, usually, the term rasterization refers to an algorithm that does not compute such things as shadows and reflections. Historically, rasterization was used heavily in game engines, as rendering had to be done in real time. With the advancement of GPUs and rendering software, gaming engines now often do much more than just raw rasterization. Rasterization can be made more realistic by using shader software that simulates the way a surface may appear if light does not bounce off sharply (causing diffuse light) or if an object is partially in shadow.

Ray tracing, on the other hand, simulates the movement of light rays as they come into contact with an initial object, then refract or reflect, and then hit other objects. In a basic ray-tracing algorithm, for every pixel to be rendered, the path of a single ray is simulated. Another way of looking at it is that ray-tracing techniques allow the hardware/software to calculate how other objects might affect the coloring and shading of a given object. Ray tracing can not only detect the presence of one object casting a shadow on another (thus preventing it from being seen), it can look at the properties of a material and, given the lighting situation, determine how sharply light rays reflect or refract, or whether one ray is broken up into a number of smaller rays, creating a diffuse appearance on the surface of an object. Both rasterization and ray-tracing algorithms can detect hidden objects so that no time is spent calculating their appearance. But if an object is hidden by shadow, not by an actual object, a raw rasterization technique typically will not realize that it is hidden.

There are major, ongoing advances in GPU technology that are affecting the efficiency of ray-tracing algorithms. This is allowing gaming software to use ray-tracing algorithms and thus provide a much more photorealistic effect. GPU vendors like NVIDIA are supporting ray-tracing algorithms directly in the GPU in a combined hardware/software fashion. In general, the goal is to allow hardware to pick up the tasks of calculating reflections, refractions, and shadows.

Finally, we note that a ray-tracing engine needs information about the materials that lie on the surfaces of objects and about the location and properties of light sources. For this reason, there is a strong interrelationship between materials, lighting, and ray-tracing software/hardware.

A PIECE OF ADVICE

A beginner animator is most likely doing work on a personal computer that has limited capabilities. Maya can be used on almost any computer for modeling, applying materials, working with lights and cameras, and doing single-frame renders. There are two critical issues to consider, though. First, if there are too many polygon faces in a scene (a very rough guide is that you do not want hundreds of thousands of polygons in a scene) or if the texture images used in the scene are of an extremely high resolution (and thus very big in terms of the number of bits needed to store them), a scene might overwhelm the memory of a machine. And second, batch or sequence rendering of a scene can be extremely time consuming. Thus, it is very important for beginners to have several key issues in mind from the moment they conceive of a project. Factors controlling render time are: (1) the resolution of the rendered images, (2) the storage size of file textures used to make materials in the scene, (3) the number of polygon faces in the scene (the renderer must calculate the effects of light hitting all of those faces), (4) the number of lights (each of them generates light that the renderer must track as it moves through the scene), (5) the density of particle simulations (particularly costly simulations are ones that are highly dense, like water effects), and (6) the ray-tracing settings of the renderer. Even with proper planning, it is not uncommon for a relatively low-definition frame to take over a minute to render on a typical personal computer.

In this book, we use the default Arnold ray-tracing settings; these settings can be found in the Ray Depth dropdown in the Arnold Renderer tab of the Render Settings. The settings for ray tracing control how far the renderer calculates the movement of light as it reflects and refracts through the scene. (Remember that the renderer cannot do what nature does, and that is follow the movement of light for effectively an infinite number of reflections and refractions. The renderer must terminate its calculations at some point.) Lowering the Ray Depth numbers can speed up the rendering of a scene, but the rendered images might be of lower quality.

As we will discuss later, another decision that will affect render time when using Arnold is choosing the Camera Sampling in the Render Settings and the Samples setting for each light. Raising the first one in particular will increase render time, but this will also tend to remove a common problem with Arnold—spotting in the rendered image. Similarly, low light Samples settings can also cause spotting.

THE BUNDLED NATURE OF RENDERERS, LIGHTS, AND MATERIALS

If you install a renderer plug-in into an app like Maya, the renderer typically installs with its own materials and lighting systems. With respect to materials, keep in mind that materials are simply mathematical properties assigned to an object's surface, so the renderer must be written to interpret the way these values are represented and stored. In fact, if you try to use the materials of one renderer with a different renderer, your model might not render at all—as if there was nothing in your scene—because the renderer cannot process material properties that are in a format that it was not built to understand. (Or it could be that the material on your model will look radically different than you anticipated.) You are likely to get similarly bad results by trying to use a different renderer's lighting system. The reason for this extreme level of interdependence is simple: a renderer calculates the effect of bouncing light off the materials on an object in order to render it. And, like the materials on that object, the light isn't real—it's a software simulation. In sum, the renderer isn't measuring some real-world phenomena; it is highly dependent on the kinds of materials and lights supported by the renderer and on the internal representation of those materials and lights. Another complication is that some 3D applications like Maya often ship with a handful of native lights, materials, and procedural textures. When a given renderer is ported to a new 3D application (usually by creating a plug-in), software developers must often retrofit their renderer to work with the lights, materials, and procedural textures that come with the 3D application.

CENTRAL PROCESSING UNIT VS. GRAPHICS PROCESSING UNIT RENDERING

An off-the-shelf consumer-grade computer will usually come with one of three kinds of graphics: the native graphics built into the motherboard, the motherboard graphics in combination with a standalone Nvidia graphics card, or the motherboard graphics in combination with a standalone AMD graphics card. (More powerful computers might have multiple graphics cards or graphics cards with multiple GPUs on them.) For modeling purposes, an application like Maya will actually run just fine on most recently made computers that only have the native (usually Intel) graphics on the motherboard; the problem arises when it comes time to render— often, renders are painfully slow on such machines. Since renderers are extremely computationally intense, they need very substantive processing power. There are two ways of doing this: put a lot of cores and memory in the computer and build the renderer to make optimal use of these resources, or build the renderer to rely on a standalone graphics card. More and more, renderers are written to make use of both kinds of resources, but there are renderers that require specific standalone graphics cards.

In fact, renderers that are built to fully leverage the native capabilities of Nvidia cards often will only run on Nvidia cards. Why is this? It has to do with the nature of a graphics card, which has on it one or more GPUs. A GPU is a computational device with its own processor and memory— but GPUs have different instruction sets than CPUs. Nvidia cards have a software layer, which is called CUDA; it sits on top of the native instruction set of the graphics card. Importantly, CUDA is proprietary, meaning that only Nvidia cards can legally run it. CUDA is, in a sense, a general-purpose programming environment that is executed inside Nvidia GPUs using the GPU's native processor, instruction sets, and memory. The CUDA layer is thin, meaning that it gives direct programming access to the hardware environment inside the GPU. A handful of renderers are written largely in CUDA, run only on Nvidia cards (and sometimes only on Nvidia cards that are in Windows machines), and have a reputation for being very fast. We will discuss some of these renderers later in this chapter.

There are also renderers that are written to run in a software layer called OpenCL, which is to some extent a competitor of CUDA. Since it is not proprietary, GPUs from other manufacturers, in particular Radeon AMD, can use it. Like CUDA, general-purpose programs can be written to run on OpenCL, so renderers can be written to run on OpenCL-compliant GPUs. We will look at one particular OpenCL renderer that has been developed by AMD.

Finally, as GPUs have become more powerful, there is a trend to move computations from the CPU to the GPU. Most renderers that run almost solely in the motherboard's CPU and memory are at this point being adapted to take at least minimal advantage of CUDA and/or OpenCL capabilities that are available directly inside GPUs.

A QUICK SURVEY OF SOME MAYA-COMPATIBLE RENDERERS

Since Maya is arguably the most popular general-purpose 3D modeling and animation application, a large number of renderers are available as plug-ins for Maya. All of the ones we will discuss here are of professional quality and produce extremely good renders. They vary in how materials are created and managed and in how they engineer lights. But perhaps their most significant difference, from a pragmatic perspective, is how many premade materials are available for them. This is something that changes over time, of course, as the vendors of renderers increase their libraries of materials and as third-party vendors produce materials for sale. To be precise, most (but not all) renderers come with a handful of presets for their materials, but these tend to be homogeneous materials, like glass and reflective metals. Where they differ significantly is on how many other nonhomogenous premade materials (like tile, wood, and brick) are available. A renderer that comes with a large library of premade materials can allow for a radically shortened process of putting materials on models.

We will look at a series of renders that consist of close-ups of the indoor courtyard area that we examined earlier. Figure 8.1 was rendered with

FIGURE 8.1   Arnold render.

FIGURE 8.2   Maxwell render.

Arnold; Arnold comes with a modest number of premade materials that are available as presets for the Arnold standard material. These materials are homogeneous in nature, such as metals, glass, and plastic. I have found that for materials that have texture patterns in them, like wood, brick, and tile, I have had to make them myself or find ones for sale by third parties.

Figure 8.2 is a Maxwell (nextlimit.com) render. Maxwell comes with a sophisticated standalone materials editor that is integrated into the plug-in; it provides a very wide variety of premade materials—and is thus very convenient. Maxwell was, however, the slowest of the renderers used in the writing of this book; on both a Windows machine with an Nvidia card and an Apple iMac Pro with an AMD card, the renders took substantially longer than renders made with other renderer plug-ins for Maya.

Figure 8.3 was made with Renderman (pixar.com), Pixar's renderer that anyone can use for free as long as they are not using it for commercial purposes. It comes with a very nice library of premade materials, some of them grunged, and they are very easy to work with.

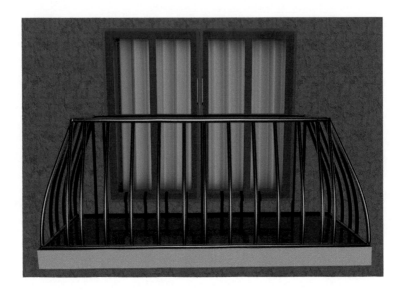

FIGURE 8.3 Renderman render.

Vray (chaosgroup.com) was used to make the render in Figure 8.4. Vray has a particularly rich materials system that makes it easy to create a very wide variety of materials. But to get premade, ready-to-go materials, one must scrounge around online or buy them. Since Vray makes plug-ins for a

FIGURE 8.4 Vray render.

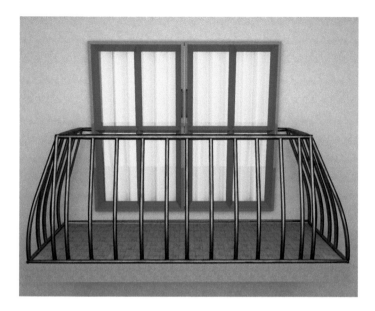

FIGURE 8.5   Vray and Substance render.

number of popular 3D applications, there are a lot of materials for Vray that were not specifically made for use with Maya, but the Vray plug-in comes with a facility to ease the task of importing generic, premade materials. Figure 8.5 is also a Vray render, but the materials were made with Substance by Allegorithmic (allegorithmic.com), a very powerful materials editor that can be used with a number of renderers and a number of 3D applications. It is popular among people who prefer to craft their own highly specialized materials. Substance has a significant, but not overwhelming, learning curve. And, for a (large) monthly cost, Allegorithmic has a library of premade materials that can be downloaded.

Substance is a bit unusual in that it is a plug-in for building materials only, and not a renderer. But it is arguably the most sophisticated and flexible materials builder available. Lightmap makes a product called Light Studio that is also unusual, in that it is only a lighting plug-in. Figure 8.6 is a Vray render with Vray materials using Light Studio to set up the lighting. Light Studio is simple to learn and to use. In particular, the Maya Light Studio plug-in greatly simplifies the process of setting up lights for a single-frame render where the goal is to highlight a model, such as a product design.

Figure 8.7 was done with Prorender (radeon.com), which is a free renderer made by Radeon AMD. Radeon GPUs are somewhat less popular

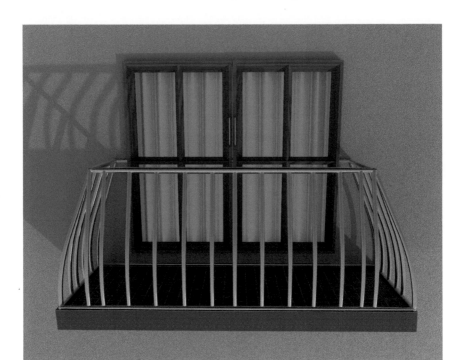

FIGURE 8.6   Vray with Light Studio render.

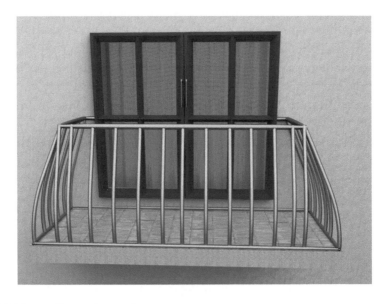

FIGURE 8.7   Prorender render.

than Nvidia GPUs. Prorender is entirely free and comes with a large library of premade materials. It is easy to work with and uses OpenCL. Below, we will look at renderers that run only on Nvidia GPUs and run mostly inside the GPU; running on an iMac with 18 core, Prorender is competitive speedwise with the Nvidia-only renderers.

So far, all the renderers we have looked at install as plug-ins to Maya, along with their own materials and lighting systems. Keyshot (keyshot. com) was used to make the render in Figure 8.8. It is a bit different. There is a plug-in that installs into Maya, but unlike the other renderers, one does not put materials on models and add lighting via the Maya Viewport. Instead, the Maya scene is imported into Keyshot's standalone interface; materials are applied, lights are added, and the render is then done in the Keyshot interface. Essentially, one does the wireframe modeling in Maya and the rest is done in Keyshot. Keyshot comes with a very large library of materials, and the renderer itself is quite fast. Of all the renders in our balcony close-up sequence in Figures 8.1 through 8.8, Keyshot provided the easiest environment for adding materials and lights, and its renderer was the fastest. It is used heavily to create single-frame renders that highlight models, in much the same way that Light Studio is used to provide lighting for highlighting models.

FIGURE 8.8 **Keyshot render.**

A HANDFUL OF NVIDIA-BASED GRAPHICS PROCESSING UNIT RENDERERS

Figures 8.9 through 8.12 were created with renderers that are written largely in CUDA and therefore must run on Nvidia cards. All of the renders in the previous section were done on an iMac Pro; the renders in this section were all created on an Alienware Aurora running Windows 10.

The renderers are:

1. Furry Ball (Figure 8.9). Furry Ball (aaa-studio.eu) does not come with any premade materials, and I found the materials editor difficult to work with. Furry Ball is no longer being sold as a product, and as of the time of this writing, it was available for free.

2. Iray (Figure 8.10). Iray (nvidia.com) is made by Nvidia and works with a large set of premade materials that are available for free from Nvidia. These materials are also very easy to tailor to create variations. Of the four renderers in Figures 8.9 through 8.12, I found its materials editor the easiest to use.

3. Octane by Otoy (Figure 8.11). Otoy (otoy.com) sells plug-ins for a large number of 3D applications. Otoy does, however, release

FIGURE 8.9   **Furry Ball render.**

FIGURE 8.10   Iray render.

FIGURE 8.11   Octane render.

new versions of their plug-ins very slowly. When a new version of Maya is released each year, other renderer vendors tend to release corresponding new versions of their renderers far more quickly than Otoy. But Octane does come with a very large library of materials that can be downloaded and accessed directly through an Octane window within Maya.

FIGURE 8.12   Redshift render.

4. Redshift (Figure 8.12). Redshift (redshift3d.com) was the fastest of these four renderers, although they were all fast, compared to the largely CPU-based renderers used in the sequence of images in Figures 8.1 through 8.8. And given that this was a single-scene, single-frame, very informal experiment, it's only fair to say that the Nvidia-only renderers were all roughly equal in speed. Redshift does not come with a library of premade materials, but the materials editor was far easier to work with than Furry Ball's.

A COUPLE OF IMPORTANT MAYA RENDERING SETTINGS

If you are using Maya on a consumer-grade machine and also creating renders that will be shown on consumer-grade displays, you will discover that batch renders (true batch renders, not sequence renders, as discussed in Chapter 1) tend to look darker than single-frame renders that are created in the Render View window. To correct this—to make the batch renders look like the single-frame renders—you might want to follow the instructions in Figures 8.13 through 8.15. First, pull up the Preferences and set the Color Management to 2.2 gamma. Then, go to Metadata in the Common tab of the render settings and set the Color Space to Use View Transform.

FIGURE 8.13 **Maya preferences.**

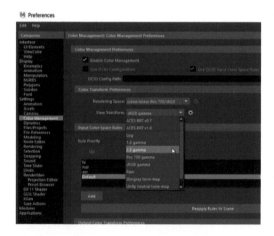

FIGURE 8.14 **The Color setting.**

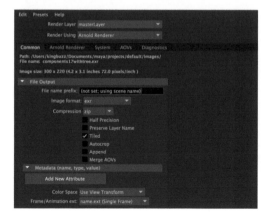

FIGURE 8.15 **The View Transform setting.**

A SPECIAL TOON SHADER IN MAYA

Maya is now in a transitionary phase, as mental ray is no longer distributed with Maya and, in fact, is no longer even sold (by Nvidia). As a result, there are some things in Maya that were specifically engineered to work with mental ray and do not work well with Arnold. One of them is particles with no geometry (as we have seen), and another is the Toon shader. The Toon shader does not render with Arnold, at least not as of Maya 2018. This might well change, as Arnold is incrementally embedded more deeply into Maya. The Toon shader does, however, render with the Maya software renderer, which is not used much professionally and generally does not produce high-quality renders. As our eyes move away from where the light hits directly on a model and toward a partially shaded area on the surface of the model, a photorealistic material will gradually become darker. What the Toon shader does is take a 3D model and give it two- or three-color materials with sharp divisions between the colors. (You can typically add black lines around the perimeter of models as well with a Toon shader.) Figures 8.16 and 8.17 have Toon shaders on them. The first was rendered with mental ray, the second with the Maya software renderer. Note that these are full 3D renders, not vector renders. (We do not discuss vector renderers in this book.)

FIGURE 8.16 The Mad Cow Dairy toon cow.

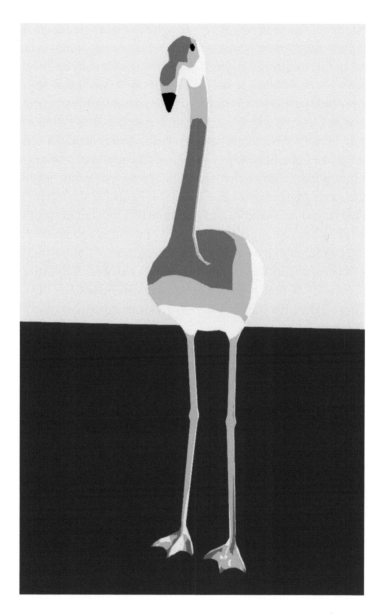

FIGURE 8.17   A tooned flamingo.

LIGHTS

Maya, combined with the Arnold plug-in, comes with two sets of lights. There are native Arnold lights. There are also native Maya lights—most, but not all, of which work with Arnold. In this section, we will quickly overview native Maya and native Arnold lights; we won't be comprehensive, and will point out the overall natures of these lights and some of the useful attributes of these lights. In Figure 8.18, we see the six native Arnold lights. In Figure 8.21, we see the native Maya lights. First, we look at the Arnold lights. Area lights are emitted from a surface and are perpendicular to that surface, which can be a quad, a disc, or a cylinder. The cylinder has no top and no bottom. Area lights have an attribute to control the softness of the edges of the light. The Mesh light allows the user to turn any polygon surface into a light, and in that sense, is like an extremely flexible Area light. Area and Mesh lights have a slider (Shadow Color) that controls the darkness of their shadows. A Photometric light is used to simulate a finite set of real-world lights manufactured by various companies. A Sky Dome light simulates an infinitely wide hemisphere of light, with the light shining inward, not outward, as with a cylindrical Mesh light; later in this section, we will see that a 360-degree image can be used as the color of one of these lights. Photometric and Sky Dome lights also have Shadow Color sliders.

Figure 8.19 shows some of the attributes of the lights. Arnold lights can have both intensity settings and exposure settings. Exposure is a powerful setting, which, when incremented by 1, multiplies the current intensity by a power of two. A Samples attribute controls noise in shadows and reduces noise caused by specular highlights; this can be an important attribute, as a small value for a Samples attribute can cause a scene to render with a

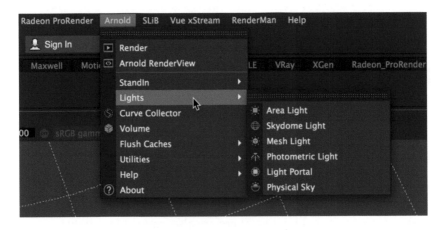

FIGURE 8.18 Native Arnold Lights.

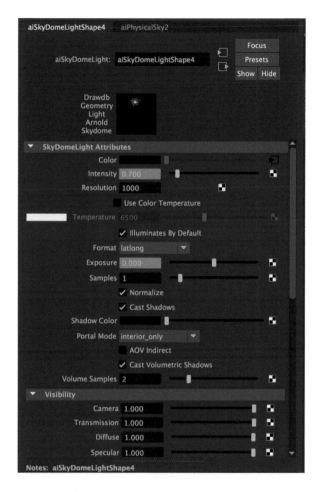

FIGURE 8.19 **Settings for Sky light.**

very high level of spotty noise. Figure 8.20 has only one light source, a Sky Dome. The color of the sky can be changed.

A Physical Sky is a shader, not a light, and can be used as the color of a Sky Dome light. It is used to simulate certain forms of solar radiance. A Light Portal is also not a light; it is used in conjunction with Sky Dome lights to reduce noise.

Figure 8.21 shows the native Maya lights. Arnold Area lights are best used rather than Maya Area lights, although Maya Area lights do work with Arnold. Ambient lights do not work with Arnold, and with renderers where they do work, Ambient lights tend to wash out shadows, as they deliver light evenly everywhere—so they are dangerous to use, anyway.

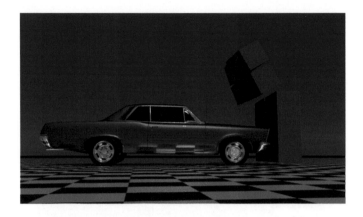

FIGURE 8.20   Render with Sky Dome light.

FIGURE 8.21   Native Maya lights.

Directional light is emitted in parallel rays from an infinitely large plane; all that matters is the angle of the light in 3-space, not its position in a scene. Directional lights are meant to simulate sunlight, as the light from the sun comes from so far away that its rays are effectively parallel. A Point light generates light that goes out in all directions from a point with no geometry. A Spot light simulates a physical spotlight and has a cone angle, which allows one to control the width of the cone of light it emits. When a Spot light hits an object, it creates a circle of light; the Penumbra Angle controls the softness of the edges. Maya Point, Spot, and Area lights have a Decay Rate setting. Like Arnold Area and Mesh lights, Maya lights have a Shadow Color slider. Volume lights do not work with Arnold.

Figure 8.22 shows the settings for a Directional light. Note that Maya lights have only an intensity, not an exposure. Figure 8.23 shows our car illuminated only by a Directional light; the arrows icon shows how the light is oriented in 3-space. As with any object in 3-space, it's best to look at it simultaneously from the three orthographic views when reorienting it. In this scene, the light is pointing a bit downward and a bit to the left. Figure 8.24 shows the car with both a Directional light and a Sky Dome. The Sky Dome gives us a natural open sky environment, while the Directional light gives us highlights and shadows.

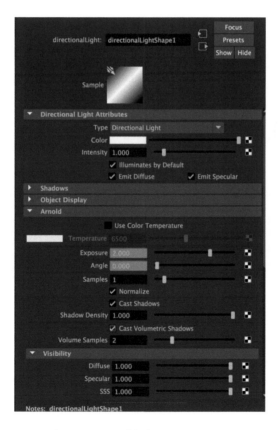

FIGURE 8.22   Settings for Directional light.

FIGURE 8.23 Positioning of Directional light.

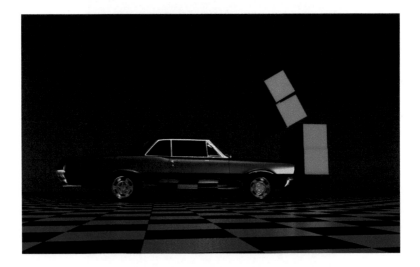

FIGURE 8.24 Rendering with Sky light and Directional light.

CAMERAS

The three components of rendering that usually come with a renderer plug-in are materials, lights, and the settings of the renderer itself. But there is actually a fourth component that is used in Maya's live footage metaphor and is critical to rendering: Maya, and not the renderer, supplies cameras. The modeler/animator creates cameras and then sets the renderer to view the scene through one of those cameras. Remember that we also view scenes in the Viewport through the perspective of a camera; Maya supports a default camera that can be used for creating models, but it is typically not used for final renders.

In Figure 8.25, we see a special kind of camera being created, one that has an "aim." (We are viewing the scene through the default camera, so we can see the new camera.) In Figure 8.26, we see that the aim has been placed on the front right wheel by moving it with the Move tool. The aim forces the camera to remain pointing at the right front wheel as the car moves. Now, in Figure 8.27, we change the view to look through the camera with the aim. Figure 8.28 shows us what the camera sees. In Figure 8.29, we are again looking through the default camera, and the right front wheel has been selected. The wheel is rotating, and the car is moving forward. In Figure 8.30, we see the positioning of the aim after the car has hit the blocks: the aim stays on the rim of the wheel. Figure 8.31 shows us the view of the camera with the aim after the blocks have been hit.

FIGURE 8.25 **Creating a camera with an aim.**

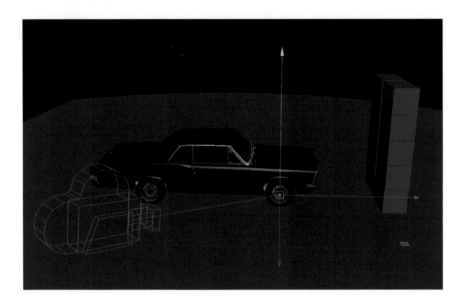

FIGURE 8.26   Perspective view of camera and aim.

FIGURE 8.27   Changing to the view of camera1.

Figure 8.32 shows us the attributes of the camera. The Focal Length is 35. In Figure 8.33, the Focal Length has been increased by 50. Thus, the Focal Length attribute acts as a sort of zoom. Notice also the Near and Far Clipping Planes attributes. They control the area that will be rendered; that area lies between two planes that are perpendicular to the ground, where the far plane covers a bigger area. The two clipping planes, in effect, form a rectangular funnel shape going outward from the camera. The tip of the funnel—which can be viewed as being on the lens of the camera—is cut off

FIGURE 8.28   The view through camera1.

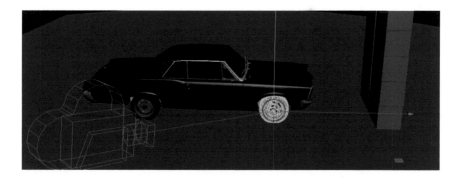

FIGURE 8.29   The view through the perspective camera.

to create the front plane. In Figure 8.34, the far clipping plane is 10,000. In Figure 8.35, the far clipping plane is 550; if you look at the area between the front of the car and the brick blocks, you can see that the far clipping plane, since it is now much closer to the camera lens, does not allow for the rendering of the back of the scene. Compare this to Figure 8.35. In Figure 8.36, the Scale attribute has been changed from 1 to 2, which, in effect, pulls the camera back from the scene.

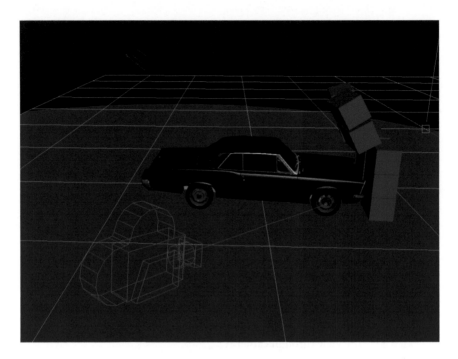

FIGURE 8.30   Perspective view after the car has moved.

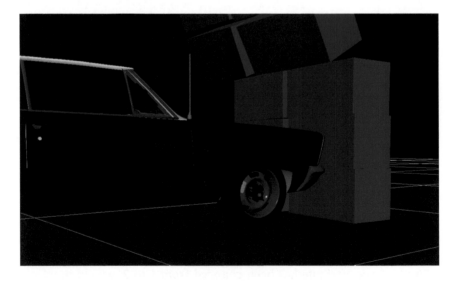

FIGURE 8.31   The view through camera1 after the car has moved.

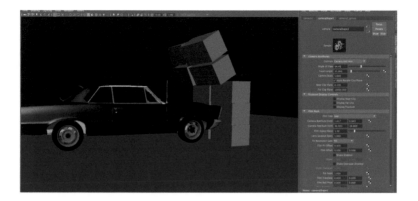

FIGURE 8.32   Camera1 with focal length 35.

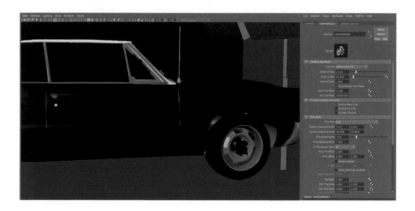

FIGURE 8.33   Camera1 with focal length 85.

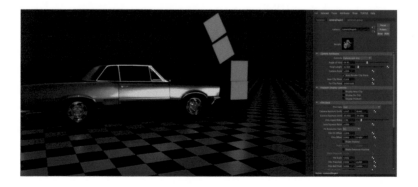

FIGURE 8.34   Camera1 with far clipping plane 10,000.

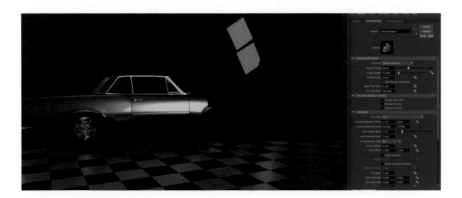

FIGURE 8.35 Camera1 with far clipping plane 550.

FIGURE 8.36 Camera1 with camera Scale 2.

A LIGHTING EXAMPLE

In Figure 8.37, we see the settings for an Arnold Area light. It is the only light in the scene in Figure 8.38. The table top is glass. Note an embarrassing problem: the glass disc is casting a solid shadow. This makes no sense, but some renderers, like Arnold, will treat all materials as opaque unless settings are changed. In Figure 8.39, we have gone to the settings of the glass object (not its material), and we have unchecked "Casts Shadows." In Figure 8.40, we have changed the shadow color to be gray and not black. We also add a soft Dome Light, as in Figure 8.41, in order to enhance the shadow cast by the rim alone. The resulting soft shadows from the table frame can be seen in Figure 8.42.

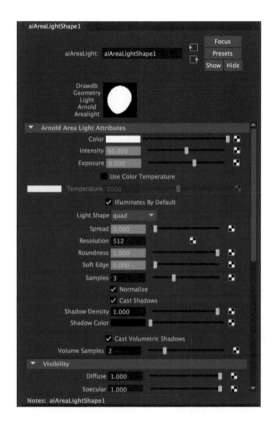

FIGURE 8.37   A light to illuminate a glass table.

FIGURE 8.38   An opaque rendering of glass.

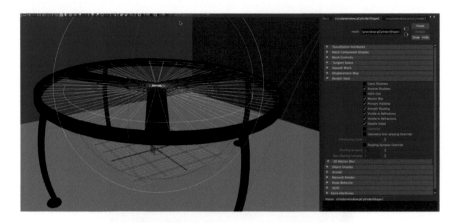

FIGURE 8.39   Keeping the glass from casting a shadow.

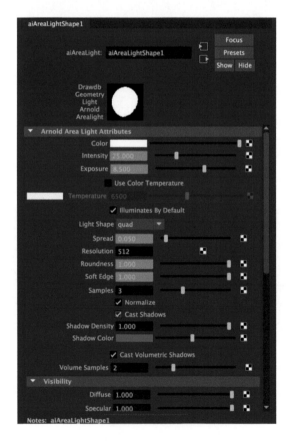

FIGURE 8.40   Adjusting the light.

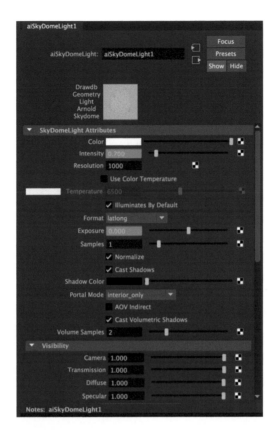

FIGURE 8.41   **Adding a soft Dome light.**

FIGURE 8.42   **An improved render.**

A BETTER TOON SHADER: VRAY

Figure 8.43 is a render that shows the use of a Toon shader that has recently been added to Vray. It is far more sophisticated and tailorable than the native Maya Toon shader—and it produces beautiful results. Our toon bird stands on a photorealistic deck; the flamingo has a flat look to it, but the flamingo blends into the scene by casting a shadow on the wall. As with the Maya Toon shader, Vray applies the colors according to how close a portion of the model is to the light source; in this case, I have made the parts of the animal that extend toward the light a bright pink. On the right-hand side of the figure is the Toon shader, as seen in the Hypershade. By clicking on the tiny circles above the three rectangles with the three colors, one can choose the three colors used by the shader, one by one. You can also add and delete colors if, for example, you want your model to have only two colors (for a flatter look) or several colors (to start approaching a photorealistic render). The Vray shader is a very sophisticated shader with many attributes.

FIGURE 8.43 The new native Vray toon shader.

AN ENVIRONMENT LIGHT

In Figure 8.44, we see the settings for an Arnold Sky Dome. The color has been set to an image, which happens to be a 360-degree image of a body of water and surrounding territory. Figure 8.45 shows the Hypershade graph for the light. A rendered image using this light is in Figure 8.46. The only

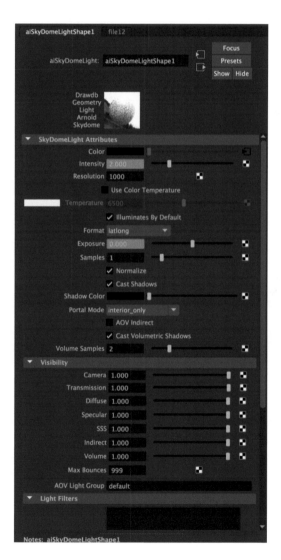

FIGURE 8.44   The Arnold environment light.

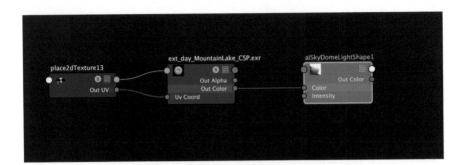

FIGURE 8.45　The environment light in the Hypershade.

FIGURE 8.46　The flamingo on his dock.

object in the scene is the bird; the rest is just the image being cast in a spherical shape by the Sky Dome. The Arnold renderer does not have a Toon shader as of Maya 2018, so the tooned bird was created manually by putting flat-colored materials (using the special Arnold Flat shader available in the Hypershade) on the bird.

CAMERA SAMPLES

We noted earlier that to get clear renders, it is often necessary to crank up the number of samples of the renderer itself, as a low camera sampling will typically create a scene that is badly spotted. The setting of 3 in Figure 8.47

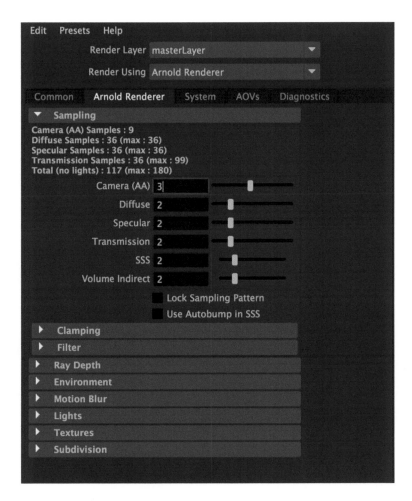

FIGURE 8.47   The camera samples setting.

will often result in a terrible render. Raising the Camera Sampling setting—a value of 5 is often needed—can significantly increase render time. (We also noted that raising the sampling of a light will increase render time, but usually to a lesser degree.) This is perhaps the most frustrating aspect of the Arnold renderer: to get excellent results, you need a high sampling level on the camera (Render View → Options → Render Settings → Arnold Renderer tab), but it can make Arnold noncompetitive in terms of speed when compared to Vray, Prorender, or Renderman. (But I find it still faster than Maxwell, even with a high Sampling setting in the Render Settings.)

FIGURE 8.48   The sun face tooned.

A TOONED SUN FACE

We return to the sun face that was modeled earlier in this book. In Figure 8.48, we see that the moon and outer ring of the face have Vray Toon shaders on them; the first in two shades of blue and the second in three colors: red/orange/yellow. A couple of stars have been added; these do not have Toon shaders, and neither does the background. The Toon shaders bring out the outlines of the moon's face and accentuate the outward spikes of the outer ring in a striking fashion.

A STAMPED, TOONED FACE

Here is one last example of the Vray Toon shader. Figure 8.49 shows the Toon shader used on the stamped face model created with the Imprint tool in the Sculpting toolset. (See the end of Chapter 4.) The blue color ended

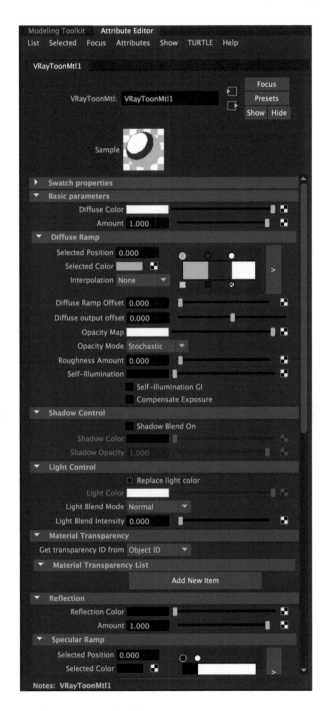

FIGURE 8.49   The Vray toon shader.

up on the crests of the sculpting indentations, the purple settled into the lower areas of the sculpting, and the white landed on the flat, unsculpted part of the cube. The final Vray render is in Figure 8.50.

FIGURE 8.50 The tooned face.

Index